Leadership and Teams

Leadership and Teams

The Missing Piece of the Educational Reform Puzzle

Lyle Kirtman

PEARSON

Boston   Columbus   Indianapolis   New York   San Francisco   Upper Saddle River
Amsterdam   Cape Town   Dubai   London   Madrid   Milan   Munich   Paris   Montreal   Toronto
Delhi   Mexico City   São Paulo   Sydney   Hong Kong   Seoul   Singapore   Taipei   Tokyo

Vice President and Editorial Director: Jeffery W. Johnston
Senior Acquisitions Editor: Meredith Fossel
Editorial Assistant: Krista Slavicek
Vice President, Director of Marketing: Margaret Waples
Senior Marketing Manager: Christine Gatchell
Senior Managing Editor: Pamela D. Bennett
Production Project Manager: Carrie Mollette
Senior Operations Supervisor: Matt Ottenweller
Text Designer: Electronic Publishing Services Inc.

Senior Art Director: Diane Lorenzo
Cover Designer: Jennifer Hart
Cover Image: © Shirley / Fotolia
Full Service Project Management: Electronic Publishing Services Inc.
Composition: Jouve
Printer/Binder: R.R. Donnelley/Harrisonburg
Cover Printer: R.R. Donnelley/Harrisonburg
Text Font: Adobe Garamond Pro

Credits and acknowledgments for material borrowed from other sources and reproduced, with permission, in this textbook appear on the appropriate page within the text.

Every effort has been made to provide accurate and current Internet information in this book. However, the Internet and information posted on it are constantly changing, so it is inevitable that some of the Internet addresses listed in this textbook will change.

Library of Congress Cataloging-in-Publication Data
Kirtman, Lyle.
  Leadership and teams: the missing piece of the educational reform puzzle / Lyle Kirtman.—First edition.
    pages cm
  Includes bibliographical references and index.
  ISBN-13: 978-0-13-277895-4
  ISBN-10: 0-13-277895-5
  1. Educational leadership—United States. 2. Educational change—United States. 3. School management
    and organization—United States. I. Title.
  LB2805.K523 2014
  371.2—dc23

                                                    2012036834

10 9 8 7 6 5 4 3 2 1

ISBN 10:   0-13-277895-5
ISBN 13: 978-0-13-277895-4

Lyle Kirtman, CEO of Future Management Systems Inc., has been a leadership development consultant for 30 years. Future Management Systems specializes in conflict management, coaching, executive searches, and strategic planning. Examples of the varied clients that Future Management Systems has served beyond education include Environmental Protection Agency (EPA), Massachusetts General Hospital, Harvard University, Channel 5 TV in Boston, Farm Aid, Cisco Systems, and the Association of Latino Administrators and Superintendents (ALAS).

Lyle has also served as the chairman of the Governor's Task Force on Innovation in Massachusetts. He has been an executive coach to leaders in education, industry, government, non-profits, and health care. To the educational reform debate that exists in this country, Lyle brings a unique perspective on leadership, which is now being embraced by many of our best leaders. He draws on his experience in the public and private sectors, along with his education in counseling psychology and his business experience, to advance the change and improvement efforts of school districts. Lyle and his firm are known for a direct and honest approach with leaders that has resulted in significant behavioral change and major results for their organizations. He has consulted with over 300 school districts nationally and has held a central administrator position for the Boston Public Schools.

FOREWORD

Leadership and Teams: The Missing Piece of the Educational Reform Puzzle provides a previously unaddressed perspective on how schools can and should run. This "breath of fresh air" is a direct consequence of Lyle Kirtman's background in business and human resource consulting. He connects this expanded view of leadership to school improvement in a way that focuses on positive outcomes for students, teachers, and principals.

At the core of this book are Kirtman's Seven Competencies. When faithfully executed, they can build leaders who have the skills to create sustainable change. When reading this book, I found that the emphasis Kirtman places on challenging the status quo, establishing trust through clear communication, creating a concrete plan for success, facilitating strong teams, fostering a strong sense of urgency for positive results, growing personally, and building strong networks and partnerships within and around the school community align well with current research on successful leadership in schools. Specifically, I believe they match up nicely with the 21 school administrator responsibilities reported in the book *School Leadership That Works* (Marzano, Waters, & McNulty, 2005). For example, Lyle's competency of "challenging the status quo" aligns closely to the principal's responsibility to be a change agent who is willing to challenge how things are done and seek better solutions.

Kirtman is particularly eloquent and insightful on the dangers of rigid approaches to reform. Specifically, he warns that implementing "quick fixes" through highly directive leadership may produce short-term results but is not a recipe for ensuring long-term change and student success. He rightfully guides principals and district administrators to focus on building strong leadership teams that can implement, lead, and sustain effective, research-based ideas and initiatives in their schools.

No doubt to the delight of administrators who read this book, Kirtman accurately describes the complex challenges facing leaders today as they are called on to fill an increasingly numerous and diverse collection of roles: instructional leader, networker, change agent, planner, communicator, team leader, team builder, resource provider, fiscal manager, mentor, and coach. Along with the expanded roles expected of administrators, Kirtman speaks to the ever-increasing list of "customers" administrators must serve. He notes that, in addition to those traditionally seen as clients of a school (students and their parents), administrators must now answer to the members of their community, municipal leaders, and elected officials at the state and federal levels. Although managing these outside forces can be overwhelming, Kirtman offers practical strategies for each role and each situation.

Of particular interest to educational administrators might be the linkages Kirtman makes between the education field and other sectors. While acknowledging that each sphere has its own unique challenges, Lyle asks thought-provoking questions and raises interesting issues that emanate from these comparisons. In addition, he highlights specific strategies that might be transferred to educational settings.

The Workplace Personality Inventory, although not the main focus of the book, provides a diagnostic perspective that is unique from other similar instruments. Kirtman reviews his research and provides case studies and examples that highlight common situations facing school administrators today and describes how they might use the seven leadership competencies to facilitate organizational growth and change in education.

Finally, Kirtman encourages leaders to question existing processes and practices to identify those actions that have the greatest impact on student achievement. Although he points out that some compliance is necessary to maintain a guaranteed and reliable curriculum across schools and districts, Kirtman strongly asserts that effective school leaders should identify and eliminate those compliance tasks that are nonessential to their role and that may not contribute to a school's overall success.

In short, Lyle Kirtman's *Leadership and Teams: The Missing Piece of the Educational Reform Puzzle*, is a needed and welcome addition to the many previous books on leadership in modern-day education. Readers will find it informative, insightful, and most important, immediately useful.

Robert J. Marzano
CEO, Marzano Research Laboratory

Education is a unique sector that is both heralded for its importance for our future and criticized for its continual underperformance. I have spent 30 years working with educators; at the same time, I worked with leaders in industry, government, health care, and the nonprofit arenas. I have been dedicated to the field of education and to working with educational leaders because I do believe their work is critical for the United States to maintain its position as a global leader.

Are educational leaders so different from leaders in other sectors? The answer is *yes* and *no*. I find the commitment of educators to the lives of young people to be inspirational. They dedicate their lives to the future and revel in the moments of learning and success for kids that they experience regularly, which is not as prevalent in any other field. They are singular in their commitment, focus, and hope for every child. They need and deserve the public's admiration for their steadfast commitment.

The differences lie in their isolation from integration with other sectors. Education is rather insular and difficult to break into from outside fields. Certification requirements and the internal culture of schools make it difficult for outside expertise to be readily accessed by schools and school systems. Educational direction and policies are usually made in isolation of the influence of outside perspectives. Educators seem reluctant to look for expertise from outside the educational environment.

Perhaps it is the nature of an industry that is so often criticized to circle the wagons and protect its interests. This protectionism culture exists in other sectors but seems more prevalent in education. I lead CEO groups for leaders, and it is hard to find educational leaders who want to be involved in a learning experience on leadership with people from industry or the nonprofit world.

I have been in a unique position to have worked with so many educators and to be accepted by most as a colleague when I did not come from their ranks. They know that I have the utmost respect for what they do every day. They have honored me with the respect to allow me to be critical of their work, and they are open to my perspective, which has been influenced by my varied background, education, and experience. They seem to know and accept that my criticisms are grounded in a complete commitment and desire to help them succeed.

I often sit in rooms with educators who are watching a video of a teacher speaking to a child or a student performing and presenting his or her ideas to a group of adults. Although I am impressed with the childrens' abilities, the look of delight in a principal's eyes is unique and heartfelt in a way I can only relate to as a parent with my child.

I wanted to contribute my observations, experiences, and learnings to a field that is constantly under fire but is often misunderstood. The opportunity to share significant data and research on effective leadership allowed me to build on my own experiences and observations. I believe that every educator wants to see students achieve. Unfortunately, the field of education has floundered so much over such a long period of time and it has been inundated with so many silver bullets for change that were touted as the panacea for the continual ailments in education. This constant state of flux has created a field that has lost many high performers to other sectors, burnt out many people to the point that they are so cynical and closed to change, and has resulted in many fine educational leaders counting their days until retirement. These negative conditions have opened up education to even more criticism and the proposal of more new initiatives for change.

I believe it is important to simplify the rhetoric and make an attempt to stop the solutions de jour from continuing. It is clear that effective leaders succeed in a variety of difficult and even dire situations. Leadership is not another silver bullet or new initiative. It is a tried-and-true focus for success for all organizations to be successful in meeting their mission for countless years. Great leaders know what to do and are open to change and improvement. Highly effective leaders can be successful in the southern, eastern, northern, and western parts of our country. They know how to learn about new cultures, adjust their behaviors, and build leadership capacity for sustained improvement.

Great leaders inspire people around them to reach extraordinary levels of performance. They attract the best people to their organizations. They develop new leaders for their school systems and for their field. They form leadership teams and develop a culture of innovation that evolves as the conditions change.

Education will always be of critical importance and be under constant attack. There will always be new initiatives that will be heralded as the answer. Politicians will always campaign about how they know what it takes to make education work and why kids are our future. None of this matters to our great leaders!

The best leaders know how to stay focused on what matters and on their values and beliefs. They know themselves very well and how they affect the behaviors of all constituents. They are remarkably similar in who they are and what they do. They are not stressed by the constant changing landscape or burned out by one more unfunded mandate.

We must change our approach nationally to one of motivation and respect for educators. Hopefully, this book provides some perspective as to what it takes to be an effective leader that is motivational and inspirational. If we want educators to inspire our children, we must inspire them.

The current mode of accountability is being overemphasized. Accountability, evaluation, and the removal of poor performers will always be necessary and important functions in education, as they are in all sectors. However, we must stop the rhetoric that accountability will be the approach to creating an excellent education system across the country.

Accountability and evaluation are management tools, not strategic approaches for leadership to reach our goals for students. No organization has ever been known for its excellence based on its approach and focus on accountability.

It is my hope that this book will encourage educational leaders to reflect on their own leadership competencies and qualities and broaden their perspectives on the resources available to support them in their work. There is a great deal that I have learned from working with over 700 organizations (including 300 school systems) and my years as a central administrator in the Boston Public Schools. I hope that my perspective will allow more people like me into the inner circle of educational policy and practice.

This text will demonstrate what the role of leadership is in creating sustainable change. As the reader, you will learn that the work starts with you learning about yourself as a leader, with all your strengths and areas for improvement being openly discussed by your team. This text will explore what it takes to genuinely work on your craft as a leader and how to build a team of people that can support and challenge you.

The chapters ahead will be filled with real-life examples of leaders who have struggled and, in many cases, succeeded. However, there are also examples of problems that have occurred and that confront leaders every day. You will be able to self-assess your leadership style and, as you read this text, determine how you might handle the problems and challenges that have faced other leaders.

Finally, you will be able to create a leadership development plan (LDP) for guidance on your journey of leading schools and school systems in today's educational arena. The message of this text is one of hope that you can figure out the best course of action for success without the need to be told from an outside source how you should lead. You must be open to all input from government, colleagues, and leaders in other sectors and universities. However, you and your team can chart your own course for success.

This text will attempt to use leadership assessments in a manner that would be commonplace in other fields. The information and trends gathered and presented in this text are intended to help the reader look more in depth at the discipline of leadership in a personal and professional manner. The opportunity to analyze one's own leadership style, behavior, and values is a key premise in this text to help leaders enhance leadership capabilities in an effort to improve student achievement.

HOW TO USE THIS TEXT FOR YOUR LEADERSHIP IMPROVEMENT

Caution for all readers! This text may contain new concepts and points of view that are counter to accepted practice in education today. While this caution is meant to be tongue in cheek, it is the hope of the author that you will explore methods that will help you grow as a leader and that you will learn from the practical examples found here. The data in this text were the catalyst for the Kirtman Seven Competencies for highly effective leaders in education and follow a different paradigm for school leaders that will be new to many people. It is the hope that each reader will objectively review and understand the information provided and realize that the personal journey of leadership development is important for all leaders. Leadership development will make a difference in student achievement and have an impact in the education field. There will be reflective questions after each case study to help readers assess their own profiles, which will allow them to fully use the concepts and practices outlined in each chapter.

It is important for leaders to work every day on improving their craft. Creating a vision for what effectiveness means to you as principal, central administrator, or superintendent is important as you develop a plan for improvement. This text provides you with a range of approaches to create your vision to be an effective leader. Reading the case studies, answering the reflective questions, and using the tools for assessing your leadership will all help you increase your effectiveness.

It is important to note that the language regarding leadership roles may be different for leaders in certain parts of our country. Some areas use the term *school board,* while others use *school committee.* Certain leaders are elected, whereas others are selected. Unions play a key role in some areas and are not much of a factor in others. High-performing leaders realize that the principles of effective leadership can and will always be applicable across all cultures and segments of our country. While reading, determine how you would apply the learning in your situation, despite the different conditions that may exist.

To begin your journey, complete an exercise that is in the Appendix. This exercise will allow you to rate yourself on the seven competencies and to receive initial feedback on what you need to work on to improve your leadership. These ratings will allow you to work on your own improvement as the chapters unfold.

It is not necessary to complete the competencies exercise to use the chapters as a resource for your development. There will be reflective questions at the end of each case study to help you reflect on the competencies and the key points in each chapter. Explore your own leadership skills and learn how to build effective teams to meet and exceed the goals of your school and school system.

As you read, think about your strengths and areas for improvement on the seven competencies. The data from the inventories, the author's observations, and the myriad of examples of real-life work of today's school leaders will help you determine your path for improving your leadership skills and building a high-performance team that supports your goals for students.

The final chapter will allow the reader to begin to develop his or her own leadership development plan. Although there are data, research, and information from a variety of sources, the work of leadership improvement is personal and relies on your commitment to being vulnerable as you hear new ideas about who you are and how you can improve your practice.

MOTIVATING, NOT EVALUATING

I will end this Preface with brief stories about two teachers whom I encountered in urban districts. Both of these teachers consistently received negative evaluations, and the districts were trying to move them out for their unwillingness to change and learn today's new concepts. They are the reason why we are so focused on teacher evaluation as a solution to our educational problems.

Teacher 1 refused to work on a new curriculum for math and was unwilling to attend any professional development workshops. I was told she was a very poor teacher who was unwilling to listen to anyone. I asked the teacher why she was in education. She stated that she loved the kids each year and was excited to see them learn. I asked why she would not participate in this new math curriculum and attend the workshops. She said she was a veteran teacher who struggled with so many changes every year. The fact that she was told that this new program meant that she had to move the desks in the classroom was very disruptive to her. I asked if she did not have to move the desks would she participate. She said *yes* and did attend the workshops and implement the new math curriculum.

Teacher 2 was seen as a teacher stuck in the past and not willing to learn new ideas about improving his teaching. Everyone saw him as negative and a poor teacher. The evaluation process was being used to try to push him out of teaching. I asked if I could talk to him. I asked this veteran teacher whether he could remember when he was last excited about teaching. He said it was 20 years ago. I asked him what happened to him that made him lose his excitement for his profession. He responded that each year a new idea would emerge that was similar in many ways to concepts of the past. Each year, everyone would act like this new idea was totally unique and the veteran teachers needed to let go of the past. He became jaded by a profession that had so little respect for past practices and always gets so excited by the shiny new toy. I asked him to try something for fun: find a document about a new teaching practice from 30 years ago that he could revise and put a new title on with a current date and then send it to the superintendent with a note about his exciting new idea for change. He agreed and said it would be fun.

I received a call that Sunday from the superintendent. She asked, "What did you do to him?" She said he sent her a great new idea for improving teaching practices. I told the superintendent what I did to this teacher. The superintendent learned something that day, and the teacher finished his career with respect and dignity.

Please think about these stories as you read this book, and remember that we need to reach out to each person to motivate first and evaluate second. That is what high-performing leaders do every day!

DO YOU SHARE THE PATTERN OF SUCCESSFUL PRINCIPALS? TAKE A FREE SELF-RATING AND FIND OUT

The difference between a good and great principal is often personal style and leadership. But what are the traits that matter most? The Workplace Personality Inventory (WPI) from Pearson TalentLens assesses 16 work styles, or work-related personality traits, shown to be important to job success in a wide range of occupations. To see how you compare on six work styles that the U.S. Department of Labor has identified as being important for principals, take 2 minutes and rate yourself at http://us.talentlens.com/principals. The complete Workplace Personality Inventory (WPI) is available as part of Principal Compass, a comprehensive professional development system that builds the competencies of effective school leadership—connecting what happens in the principal's office to success in the classroom. To learn more about Principal Compass, visit www.principalcompass.com.

ACKNOWLEDGMENTS

This book is about leadership styles and openness about one's strengths and weaknesses and building a team around you to meet your goals, so I must begin by admitting my personal challenges. My leadership style does not match the typical focused and disciplined authors who write the many educational books that are part of the field today. My lack of discipline and focus (ENFP in the Myers Briggs) presented a major challenge for me to complete this book and meet the deadlines required. Therefore, I needed a team around me to support me at home and at work.

The understanding and commitment of many people allowed me to reach the finish line. I will begin by thanking my mother for teaching me the values of self-confidence, continuous improvement, integrity, and customer service. Now in her late 80s, she is still my number one leadership coach. Thank you for your love and support.

My wife, Kathy, a highly skilled and respected psychotherapist, models the discipline and commitment that I wish I had. Her understanding of the long hours and time away to write this book cannot be put into words. I love you for supporting me, especially when it separated me from our family and from my focus, which should have been more on your goals and dreams.

My son, Sean, is about to graduate from business school in marketing at the University of Texas at Austin and is the real writer in the family. I have and will always respect his skills and viewpoint as a colleague. His editing skills are remarkable, and his direct critical feedback on my writing was incredibly valuable.

My sister, Gail, has played a major role in my understanding and learning about education. As a former special education teacher, she has always grounded me in the realities of teaching as I studied the concepts and practices of leadership and educational policy.

The support of many people at Pearson has been very important to me. Stefan Kohler is one person who provided me the opportunity to write this work. He believed in my work and me and has been a constant support and mentor to me throughout the process.

I must also thank so many educational leaders that I have worked with over the years. I have learned so much from all of you. I would like to especially thank Bobbie D'Alessandro, a former superintendent, and David Driscoll, a former commissioner, for their unconditional support and belief in me.

Special thanks to Mike Odom, a former executive at Digital Equipment Corporation, for his willingness to support my transition to education.

I owe my gratitude to Beth Saunders, my assistant and bookkeeper, for her editing help and support, and to Bill Garr, a senior consultant at Future Management Systems, for his input and expertise on leadership, which contributed to many of the concepts presented in the book. You kept the business going when I was not always available.

My final thanks are for the special arrangement that I made with a new principal and former colleague on leadership development at the state level. Terry Nugent and I made a bartering arrangement from the beginning of the writing of this book. She agreed to coach me on how to write this book in the same way someone else helped her with her dissertation. In exchange, I coached her on her new role as a principal of a school. Thank you, Terry, for the gift you gave me. Your ability to use my leadership profile as a resource to helping me compensate for my weaknesses and build on my strengths kept me focused throughout this process. I hope that I was helpful to you as a new principal.

One can only achieve his goals with a team of talented people in his corner.

I would also like to express my appreciation for those individuals who reviewed the manuscript throughout its development: Thomas G. Bean, Loyola University Chicago; Margarete Couture, South Seneca Elementary School; Bobbie D'Alessandro, Educational Consultant; David P. Driscoll, Commissioner of Education; James L. Finley, West De Pere School District; Sean A. Haley, President of Haley Responsive Education Corporation; Sandra C. Harrison, Mosley High School; James R. Kahrs, Haymon-Morris Middle School; Elizabeth Madison, Robert Gray Middle School; Carol Alford Rine, Mosley High School; Jason P. Sherlock, Bayard Rustin High School; Karen Ward, Centennial Middle School; Mark D. Wilson, Morgan County High School; and Traci Wodlinger, Director of Professional Development at Eagle County Schools.

BRIEF CONTENTS

CONTENTS

6 HIRING THE RIGHT LEADERS WHO WILL GET RESULTS   123
Stop the Insanity: Now It Is Time for a New Hiring Process

7 BUILDING YOUR LEADERSHIP DEVELOPMENT PLAN   147
Customized Action Plans That Allow You to Take Charge Now!

1

Educational Change for a World of Urgency and Accountability

Why Our Best Leaders Succeed Now!

I s the wolf at the door or are there termites in the basement (Schultze, 1989)? Is there a crisis in education that needs immediate action (the wolf), or is the education system deteriorating slowly so we do not even realize what it takes to improve it (the termites)? The debate about the state of education in America continues every day. In election years, the rhetoric escalates about whether the education system is broken and whether we are falling behind other countries in preparing students for the 21st century. Currently, the Global Imperative brings together 20 countries annually to focus on how they can improve education to prepare students for the present and future needs of industry. The three areas of focus are training and developing quality teachers, developing school leaders, and delivering 21st century skills. With each election, we hear new terminology and new approaches that will supposedly make the difference and solve the problems in education. Leaders must understand new initiatives to determine what will be valuable to their success.

This text will not try to settle the education debate. It will not just react to the wolf by providing one more approach to straightening out the education system. Instead, this text will position the importance of leadership as a factor in improving school performance. Whether we are discussing a turnaround situation in a rural or urban school or district or just raising the bar on performance in a more affluent suburban district, leadership needs to be elevated in importance in order to see sustainable change and improvement.

WHY IS LEADERSHIP IMPORTANT?

Leadership is core to success in other sectors, such as health care, the military, nonprofits, and industry. Books are written on great leaders, such as the recent biography of Steve Jobs, who was a leader in industry. We do not see the same types of books on great educational leaders. Why is this? It seems there is a greater interest in prescribing what schools and school districts need to do in great detail; the government, politicians, the media, and others in the educational policy arena do not believe that educators know what to do to be successful.

If we find leaders with competencies to succeed and support them in their heroic efforts to improve achievement for all students, education can and will improve. In fact, there are success stories every day. We seem to want to tell everyone what he or she should do, rather than bring in the body of work used in leadership for other sectors and integrate it with our most successful examples of high-performing leaders.

Too much effort is put into short-term change instead of sustainable change. Although a sense of urgency is important for short-term results, new leadership competencies are needed to create sustainable change. In order to prevent the wolf from being at the door again in the future, it is critical that the leader expand his or her focus to a cadre of people in every school and district who will have the same sense of urgency for sustainable improvement as the leader. The ability to develop high-performance teams (HPT) will build the capacity for sustaining change in our schools. A high-performance team is a group of people in a school or district that work interdependently to meet or exceed the established goals. Team members hold each other accountable for results and are able to act independently, but they are aligned with the leader.

Too often, superintendents are brought in to straighten out our lowest performing districts. The cases of cities such as Philadelphia, Washington, D.C., and Atlanta are cited as examples where leaders needed to come in and create a sense of urgency and accountability for change. Although there may have been some success in these districts, the approach of top-down accountability is not sustainable. The assumption that the wolf at the door must be responded to with a top-down immediate change approach is dangerous in that it directs improvement rather than creating a culture for improvement.

Why do we choose this top-down approach of accountability for change? In countries that are heralded for their educational success, such as Finland, they do not focus on accountability for sustainable change. In the literature on successful companies, such as *Good to Great* (Collins, 2001), the leadership (which he calls level five) was not top-down or accountability-driven. The level five leader builds a team of leaders who focus on sustained improvement. In many cases, the level five leader is just part of the team and not noticeably out in front driving change. There is very little rhetoric about a particular initiative or approach that will make the difference. Instead, it is about getting the right people and working hard to produce sustainable results.

There are many knowledgeable and well-known educational authors who write about models for successful leadership in education. Robert Marzano's book *School Leadership That Works: From Research to Results* (2005) is one of the seminal books on leadership in education today. Marzano presents data on the importance of improving student achievement to increase the longevity of superintendents and developing improvement plans with a broad base of stakeholders to sustain results. Although Marzano and other prestigious authors touch on the importance of leadership outside instruction, their core work is on how to improve the teacher–student relationship, which is critical to improving student achievement. Work in the classroom and the building of school culture to support the learning process are paramount to most instructional leadership books.

This text is intended to add an element about leadership to the body of work in education. This new focus on leadership will help remove the obstacles that prevent the elegant interaction between student and teacher that we all want to create as the foundation for long-term learning.

Most successful stories of sustainable change in both the public and private sector document leaders who are not charismatic, top-down accountability leaders. In fact, the examples of success note the vulnerability of the leaders and their team orientation. Even the military, noted for a high sense of urgency and accountability, places high emphasis on team development. Though the military leader has to promote discipline and accountability, the building of teams is critical to the success of a soldier. The automatic support and back-up of others save lives.

WHAT IS A SUCCESSFUL LEADER IN EDUCATION?

Education has defined success for leadership in terms of instructional leadership and the increase in student achievement in a school or school district. The simplistic way to measure leadership success is the quantitative increase in student achievement. This is similar to medicine defining *successful leadership* as *medical leadership* and the number of lives saved or how fast people are cured from their illnesses. In education, the focus on instructional leadership and the quantitative improvement in student achievement is relatively new (The Wallace Foundation, 2010). As the Center for Creative Leadership has noted (2010), in medicine, medical expertise has been the model for leadership for many years. Medicine has shifted to a broader definition of successful leadership as the complications of operating medical facilities and networks of care have required a broader set of skills and competencies. Education needs to realize that the same shift that has been happening in medicine is relevant to education. The best medical doctor is not necessarily the best medical leader. Likewise, the best teacher is not necessarily the best educational leader.

The definition of leadership in education is elusive, with each book or policymaker defining the roles differently. The simple definition that is guiding the contents of this text is that high-performing leaders build leadership capacity that results in meeting and exceeding the goals of the school system based on the needs of the local, state, and global communities. Our most successful leaders in education are results oriented and need to produce improvements in student achievement. However, the simple measurement of increase in student achievement from standardized test scores is too narrow a definition for a successful leader. The successful leader has to demonstrate success in several areas to sustain improvement.

High-performance education leaders have a range of leadership skills, competencies, and personal attributes. Although the core service in education is instruction for students, the leader's role is to ensure that the highest quality of service is provided. The instructional services must be provided in an effective and efficient manner and need to be sustainable and adaptable over time. The services need to be flexible to the changing needs of the students and must prepare them to be successful in a global society.

The "customer" is very important to any leader. In medicine the customer is usually seen as the patient. However, medicine has had to expand its definition to serving families. If the patient in the emergency room survives major trauma but the family is ignored and treated poorly, the family often will move the surviving patient to another hospital for follow-up care. This loss of continuity of care can have a negative effect on quality of care and clearly results in negative financial results for the hospital.

Similarly, in education the student is the primary customer, but students' families are also essential to ensuring a quality education. School systems are very inconsistent in their focus on families as customers in the educational process. Especially in urban districts, educators may encounter parents (or nontraditional family or guardian structures) who are struggling financially and are so overwhelmed by their personal circumstances that they cannot provide the attention that the educator believes is necessary to support the student. The time and effort needed to engage families is difficult for educators to find in their overwhelming schedules. However, the participation of a parent, or a strong support system for education outside of the time in school, is essential to student performance (Smith, Conway, & Houtenville, 2008).

In health care, there are regulators, funders, insurance companies, competitors, and other outside forces that act like customers. The medical leader must have skills and competencies to effectively manage these outside forces to ensure that quality care is the focus for the direct care physicians and nurses.

The same issue exists in education. In addition to families, the community, the municipal leaders, and the state and federal governments are all demanding results and acting like core customers. The educational leader must have the skills, competencies, and time to manage the federal and state mandates and the demands of the community and municipal leadership to ensure that quality education is delivered every day in the classroom. Just as a hospital administrator who goes on doctors' rounds would not have time to manage the outside forces that affect medical services, the educational leader cannot spend too much time on instructional rounds and educational content because it will prevent him or her from dealing with the outside forces that affect the educational services.

The superintendent obviously has the broad position of being the "CEO" of the school system. His or her role is to ensure quality education to students and families, to build strategic partnerships and alliances, and to manage outside forces that will affect the short- and long-term educational services. Focusing specifically on the educational content is more important for the principal than for the superintendent.

A successful superintendent realizes that he or she has a significant internal and external role and immediately focuses on forming a high-performance leadership team to increase the leadership capacity of the school system. The external work of building support from the community, parents, and municipal and industry leaders takes time. The ability to run a school system in its day-to-day operations and in the effort to provide a superior education for all students can be overwhelming. The high-performing superintendent understands that there is a need for a strong team of people that can effectively lead the functional internal areas of the school system. These leaders must be able to work in a team and support each other to maximize resources for the system. Once a leader identifies the key functional roles that are critical to success and makes sure that there are the highest quality people in these areas, he or she can mold the group into a team. The ability to hire the best team of leaders is also based on the marketplace. For many key central office leadership positions, it may be difficult to hire the very best people. Therefore, it is important to build a strong human resource team that can help hire and develop "talent," who are integral to the success of a school or school system.

The successful leader must have a set of competencies that is broader than instruction and is measurable based on the comprehensive roles of the leader in other sectors. One can achieve short-term results in student achievement but can be creating an environment that is not conducive to sustainable change and improvement. A superintendent who has a top-down approach and drives an agenda of results on standardized tests can show short-term results. However, this noninclusive and autocratic environment can create dissent from administrators and teachers and does not build and expand the locus of leadership. If a major problem happens or the superintendent leaves, there is no capacity for sustainable change. If an autocratic leader leaves, the people who remain have not developed the skills and competencies to lead change and improvement. The teachers and administrators are so used to waiting for instructions on what they are supposed to do that they are not equipped to act on their own. There are several examples of urban districts that have hired superintendents to clean up poor performing school districts; most of these superintendents have lasted for short periods of time. Several have been fired or asked to resign by the same school boards that hired them to clean up the system.

If we broaden the competencies we use for hiring and developing leaders in education, we will improve our districts in a sustainable manner that will outlast any single hero leader. A leader who can build capacity by training, supporting, and motivating people to do their best for students will succeed over time.

KIRTMAN'S SEVEN COMPETENCIES FOR SCHOOL LEADERSHIP

A *competency* is an observable behavior that demonstrates skills, learning, and experience. Leaders in education need to demonstrate behaviors that show they know what it takes to be effective in their role as a leader in a school or district. It is the author's belief that his data on leadership and the observations of numerous educational leaders indicate a set of observable behaviors that are common for the highest-performing leaders.

Leaders can improve their effectiveness by understanding these competencies and being willing and able to honestly assess their current level of competency to begin to develop a plan for improvement. One never masters any particular competency. Because the challenges and conditions are constantly changing in education, leaders need to adjust and adapt their plans for improvement for the needs of their position.

The competencies for today's educational leaders are based on the author's work with over 300 school districts and more than 1,000 educational leaders. The seven competencies discussed here represent observations of effective leaders and the results of data analysis of over 600 educational leaders on a series of highly validated and reliable leadership inventories. In addition, they integrate leadership competencies from other sectors, including health care, business, government, nonprofit organizations, and the military. These competencies are derived from research-based data that have been an outgrowth of vast field experience and that have been field tested with over 700 organizations over 30 years.

The inventories used in this text are designed to help leaders assess their style, behaviors, and values. These well-validated and reliable tools are self-assessments and are highly predictive of how a leader will perform their role. These inventories are frequently used for coaching, team building, conflict management, and hiring. They provide common language for conversations and the opportunity to use objective data for honest discussions of difficult problems. The use of objective data tends to decrease people's defensiveness and reactive behavior when others make critical comments. Understanding one's own leadership profile and how it affects other people can avert major problems. True self-awareness means understanding yourself not only through your own eyes but also through the eyes of others.

The data on the Myers Briggs Type Indicator, the DISC inventory, the Workplace Motivators or Values Inventory, and the Workplace Personality Inventory (WPI) show the following characteristics of highly effective educational leaders:

- Lower focus on following rules and compliance
- Lower focus on being detail oriented
- Ability to communicate their message clearly to others
- Ability to influence others to act
- High sense of urgency for results
- Ability to handle stress and critical feedback
- Ability to think systemically
- High orientation to planning
- Commitment to developing teams to enhance results
- Strong ability to develop and follow a plan for success
- High visibility with stakeholders
- Ability to think and act quickly
- Comfort with change and flexibility
- Ability to coach others to improved performance
- High energy and enthusiasm

Based on the preceding and the author's experience and knowledge of high-performance leaders, the following competencies are needed for today's and tomorrow's challenges. It should also be noted that a leader can generally focus only on sustainable change and improvement for a maximum of seven competencies. Books that promote a list of more than seven leadership competencies create an unrealistic expectation for change and improvement. It takes a significant amount of time and effort to improve on each competency. If the list is too long, a person cannot put enough time and effort into genuine sustained improvement. The following are the seven competencies for high-performing leaders in education, with accompanying subsets that can help leaders focus their professional development.

1. Challenges the Status Quo

- Delegates compliance tasks to others
- Challenges common practices and traditions if they are blocking improvements
- Is willing to take risks
- Looks for innovations to get results
- Does not let rules and regulations block results and slow down action

This competency relates to high performers characteristically having less focus on rule following and compliance. This does not mean that high-performing leaders break rules. It does mean that they start with a focus on their vision for success and the results they want to achieve. They focus more on motivating people toward goals than making sure they follow rules. They tend to challenge current practices if they are not directed to the goals of improving student achievement. They are willing to take risks to achieve results. They are often courageous leaders pursuing the best for all students.

2. Builds Trust through Clear Communications and Expectations

- Is direct and honest about performance expectations
- Follows through with actions and on all commitments
- Ensures a clear understanding of written and verbal communications
- Is comfortable dealing with conflict

This competency focuses on a leader's ability to influence and motivate others through clear communications and expectations. The trust piece is very important to these leaders because they tend to build teams in their schools and develop trust and confidence with their staff to achieve results. They tend to use trust and motivation instead of discipline, rules, and punitive approaches to get results. Trust is earned by a leader who you can count on and who is consistent with his or her actions to achieve results.

The leader who demonstrates strength in this competency is clear about performance expectations for all staff and partners. High performers are usually comfortable dealing with conflict and are able to build trust with people who do not always agree with their ideas.

3. Creates a Commonly Owned Plan for Success

- Creates written plans with input of stakeholders
- Ensures that people buy into the plan
- Monitors implementation of the plan
- Adjusts the plan based on new data and clearly communicates changes
- Develops clear measurements for each goal in the plan

This competency is consistent in highly effective leaders. They tend to focus on a written plan for success. The plan is strongly led with a systemic focus for the school and the school system without a lot of process in its development. The high-performing leader wants input in a stream-lined manner to make sure that he or she can more quickly move ahead with execution. Although the leaders involve stakeholders in the planning, they do not need to have everyone's approval to move ahead. High-performing leaders place more focus on teams and buying into the imple-mentation effort.

High performers are able to develop clear measurements for success and monitor and report on progress to all constituents. They are also flexible enough to change plans to ensure results and clearly articulate the reasons for change to all groups.

4. Focuses on Team over Self

- Hires the best people for the team
- Commits to the ongoing development of a high-performance leadership team
- Builds a team environment
- Seeks critical feedback
- Empowers staff to make decisions and get results
- Supports the professional development of staff

High-performing leaders know that they cannot get results by themselves. A leader is only as good as the strengths of the people around him or her. Leaders tend to give credit to their staff, the par-ents, and the community over relishing in the accolades they receive for their performance. They know they have to build a team rather than just assume that they can direct change. They also know that they do not own all of the best ideas. They want strong people around them that can be high-performing leaders and strong members of the leadership team in the school.

High performers are able to put their egos aside for the sake of their team's development and the results that are essential for students. These leaders hire the best and never settle for less.

5. Has a High Sense of Urgency for Change and Sustainable Results in Improving Student Achievement

- Is able to quickly move initiatives ahead
- Can be very decisive
- Uses instructional data to support needed change
- Builds systemic strategies to ensure sustainability of change
- Sets a clear direction for the organization
- Is able to effectively deal with and manage change

The common issue among the high-performing leaders is they have a high sense of urgency for results. They want action and fast movement on key issues and tend to quickly solve problems. They work toward coaching and building leadership in the schools and building a sense of urgency among all staff. They build and support teams. However, they are not reticent to make tough decisions to help students rather than get caught up in too much process that would delay action. They make change sustainable by hiring the best people and building leadership at all levels in the school. The top-down leaders that are hired to drive change do not create sustainable change and improvements. The suc-cessful leaders use instructional data in the change process and create the sense of urgency for all constituents.

6. Commits to Continuous Improvement for Self

- Has a high sense of curiosity for new ways to get results
- Possesses a willingness to change current practices for themselves and others
- Listens to all team members to change practices to obtain results
- Takes responsibility for their own actions—no excuses
- Has strong self-management and self-reflection skills

The high-performing leaders are always trying to improve and are curious about new ideas and practices. They are looking to learn from colleagues and any resource, whether in education or other sectors. They are never satisfied with their own leadership ability, and they know they can always learn and improve. The high-performing leader is open to criticism and looks for honest feedback on how they can improve.

High performers are focused on improvement and results and do not waste time telling people why they were not successful.

7. Builds External Networks and Partnerships

- Sees his or her role as a leader in a broad-based manner outside the work environment and community walls
- Understands his or her role as being a part of a variety of external networks for change and improvement
- Has a strong ability to engage people inside and outside in two-way partnerships
- Uses technology to expand and manage a network of resource people

The strongest high-performing leaders tend to be extroverted and comfortable networking with a range of people in their school, community, and state, as well as nationally. They are constantly building networks of contacts and resources that can help them in their roles as leaders in their school systems and communities. This competency is critical in other fields and seems to be losing ground in education. Because the consistent focus is on improving instruction by working internally, the time that leaders have for networking and building partnerships is decreasing. This internal focus is detrimental to strong leadership. The high-performing leaders build teams and delegate work and thereby find time to spend with parents, teachers, students, community members, school system leaders, and other leaders inside and outside of education. These networks produce new ideas, practices, and materials that can be effectively used to improve results in their schools.

These competencies are focused on the role as a leader of a complicated organization that needs to change and focus on results. The competencies are not about instruction, which is not the role of the superintendent, but about leadership. Instructional experience and knowledge are critical for the principal in order to have credibility with teachers and to be able to recognize and reward exemplary practice. However, the roles of the superintendent and the principal need to be balanced between content and organizational leadership. These competencies involve building instructional leadership into the culture of the school and building strong leadership in teachers. The educational leader is the overall leader of instruction, but he or she needs to have time and skills to motivate and build teams and develop leadership capacity in his or her school for change. The educational leader should try not to do too much on his or her own in the instructional arena.

High-performance leaders do not excel in all of these competencies. However, they do exhibit strong skills and practices in almost all of the competencies. All strong leaders understand that they must continually improve, and they realize that they can never master all these competencies.

A high-performance leader often shows results in each competency and has plans to improve as times and conditions change in his or her school district, community, and state, as well as in the country.

The competencies proposed are based on observation and the experience of the author. What makes this text unique is that these observations and experience have been verified by objective research to produce the seven competencies of high-performing leaders for education today and in the future.

The author's observations have been integrated into the trends and patterns from a database of 600 educational leaders nationally who have completed three leadership inventories that are highly validated and reliable and used extensively in other public and private sector organizations for hiring and leadership development. The 600 people in the database were selected by administrators in coaching and team development efforts in schools or systems and from aspiring leaders programs.

LEADERSHIP INVENTORY ASSESSMENTS

The results of assessments in this text are one of the key points in the analysis of what makes someone a high-performance leader. In addition, the data can be helpful for policymakers to review as they reshape educational policy to improve education. Finally, the data and the assessment tools are a vehicle for each educational leader to improve their craft. The information gathered from leadership assessments and other assessment and evaluation data can be used in coaching, team development, hiring, and in the formulation of strategies for sustainable change and improvement. The leadership inventories should not be used as evaluation tools. They are designed for leaders to objectively develop plans for improvement.

The use of leadership inventories is commonplace in most sectors today in both the hiring process and to assist in professional or leadership development efforts. For example, Southwest Airlines uses the Myers Briggs Type Indicator (MBTI) in its training of new employees. The Environmental Protection Agency (EPA), as well as other government agencies, uses similar assessments for its leadership development programs. Colleges and universities are now using inventories such as the DISC and MBTI in their programs for students at both undergraduate and graduate levels in business, education, psychology, and other fields of study. The health care industry uses a range of assessment inventories in both hiring and professional development and training programs. The leadership assessment business is a multi-billion dollar industry designed to ensure that organizations hire the right people for key positions and train and develop them to be as effective as possible in their work.

As we all know, the Internet has become a vehicle to obtain just about everything we want in life. The inventories are no exception. The inventories cited in this text are highly validated and reliable. However, there are websites through which people can take the nonvalidated MBTI and the DISC inventories for free. The author has completed sample inventories on these sites and has confirmed that they are not valid or reliable. Some of the scores were accurate, but one score was completely wrong and another score was significantly lower than the score received from the reliable and validated version of the inventory. This inaccuracy would change the analysis of a leader and would prescribe actions that would not improve results and could even be detrimental to the person's effectiveness. Inventories can be very helpful, but only if the source is valid and reliable and if a professional interprets the inventory.

In education, there is relatively small use of leadership assessments. The strength finder by Gallop is used in some school systems, the MBTI is relatively popular, and other inventories are sporadically used. It is interesting that education, which is so data based with students, pays minimal attention to data on leaders and employees, who are seen as critical in other fields. Perhaps it is because the human resource field is somewhat underdeveloped in education. In some states, the positions are still called *personnel directors,* which is an antiquated term in most other sectors. Some small districts do not even have human resource directors, and personnel-related responsibilities may be handled by several people.

Although there are many leadership assessments that can be used to assess one's leadership profile, this text will focus on three: the MBTI, the DISC, and the Workplace Motivators or Values Inventory (commonly referred to as the Values inventory). In addition, a new inventory that is well validated in industry and health care, the WPI, will be introduced to validate and add to the findings made from the MBTI, the DISC, and the Values inventory. Other assessments, such as emotional intelligence, 360 development assessments, and the WPI, will be reviewed in a cursory manner throughout the text. It is important to note that the more singular focus on the evaluation process, while important, is very limited in helping understand one's leadership profile and to develop a plan for improvement. In education today, the focus is often on triangulating data—using three points of information for analysis of student outcomes. Using the three assessments discussed in this chapter will allow one to triangulate data for leaders.

The information provided in this chapter was developed by administrating one, two, or all three inventories to leaders in a coaching process and to leadership teams who were working on becoming high-performance teams. The WPI data is from a research study that is re-norming a leadership assessment for the role of the principals nationally.

The three inventories will be explained in greater detail in Chapter 2, in order to apply the results to the case studies and examples of leaders who are facing challenges in their districts. The MBTI is the more common assessment. The MBTI is designed to determine one's problem-solving style in work and life. The MBTI is also used for team development in most sectors, including education. The MBTI is not validated for hiring. A team can be more effective if there is representation of all MBTI styles. The MBTI profile of a team can help determine where there are gaps. The profile of the team can also help in developing questions for interviews. These questions will help determine whether the candidate has the style that is needed for the team to have a balanced profile.

The DISC inventory, which is the predominant assessment used in this text, is focused on a person's work environment only. The DISC deals with how you do your work naturally and your adaptation to your work environment. The DISC capability for showing your most comfortable natural work behaviors and how the work culture affects your behaviors is very important for today's educational world. If a person's adaptation to the demands of their position is excessive it can be an indicator of too much stress and could affect performance and even one's health. The new focus on urgency and accountability is showing dramatic effects for educational leaders.

The Values inventory is designed to determine why one acts a certain way, as well as the core values of an individual. This inventory is especially useful in the coaching leaders who are attempting to make significant change.

The Myers Briggs Type Indicator (MBTI)

The MBTI has a long history of being an effective tool for leadership and team development. A school leader can complete the MBTI and receive important data on their leadership style and how they interact with others. Often, conflicts between people can be traced to differences in their MBTI profiles, which allow the leaders to find new and effective ways to rebuild their working relationship.

For example, a commissioner in an eastern state was having difficulty with the chairperson of his board. They were seemingly in conflict over philosophy and the state's direction on education policy. In fact, the press and the whole education community were watching anxiously as these two top leaders were having difficulty working together.

The two leaders completed the MBTI as part of the process of building a positive relationship that was critical for the state's success on education reform. It was immediately clear that their conflicts were more about style and less about content and philosophy. One aspect of their conflict was that the board chairperson was more introverted and expected structured, in-person meetings to discuss key issues before board meetings. The highly extroverted commissioner tended to have phone conversations with the chairperson on key issues. The commissioner assumed that these conversations were adequate to make sure that issues were clear and agreed upon before the meetings. To the board chairperson, they were only discussions that did not count as meetings and nothing was settled. This resulted in the board chairperson raising issues at the board meeting that caught the commissioner off guard. This created conflict that the commissioner felt was potentially sabotaging the work they were doing to reform the state's education policies.

Once the style issues were reviewed, one easy adjustment was made: From now on, the only meetings that counted were those that occurred in person, with an agenda and a clear and agreed-upon outcome. Phone conversations were fine but not for decision-making processes. Due to the resolution of style issues between the two key leaders, they worked so well together that the state became a leader in educational reform and student achievement for the country. Although there were still philosophical differences between these two leaders, they were able to work as a team, trust each other, and improve results for students.

This text features the MBTI scores of many leaders in specific examples and case studies. There are trends about certain profiles that can be more effective in specific situations, such as turnarounds of underperforming schools. The MBTI results indicate two important trends for consideration. The leaders who are most successful, especially in turnaround situations, tend to be the ENTJ profile. The following is a brief explanation of the ENTJ profile, which is reviewed in more detail in Chapter 2.

Extroverted (E): A strong communicator who builds a network of support

Intuitive (N): A strategic thinker who tends to look for root causes for problems

Thinking (T): An objective and analytical thinker

Judging (J): A leader who can develop and execute a plan of action with a focus on results

In the 600-person database examined by the author, the ENTJ is the most frequent style on leadership teams in schools and school systems.

A person with the ENTJ profile (sometimes called the "field marshal") is usually very active and interested in leadership positions. His or her ability to take charge of a situation or a problem does have a benefit in a turnaround situation. Although each profile has positives and areas for improvement, the ENTJ frequently shows results in school systems. However, the ENTJ can be too directive and top-down in its style. If a leader is too direct, the results tend to be short-term and the sustainability of success is questionable.

The second trend is that the combination of the strong, take-charge style of the ENTJ with the DISC high score in the behavior of influence, which fosters high-performance teams and coaches and supports the building of leadership capacity in schools, results in a leader who creates a high sense of urgency for sustainable change.

The influence behavior in the DISC is a critical component to help the ENTJ develop a team of people that can work together on increasing the success for students. Other styles of leadership are important to create a well-balanced team. We need people who can tell us when morale problems are occurring that can affect results. We need people to be analytical about data and present information that can change instructional practices. The combination of a strong, take-charge ENTJ with a well-balanced, high-performance team is very powerful in creating sustainable change and improvement.

As we triangulate data for student achievement, it is important to use the same approach for leaders and teams. Multiple sources of data provide a more robust approach to building effective leaders who get results.

The DISC Inventory

The DISC profile presents the most dramatic findings and trends for leadership in education. The DISC profile measures how leaders would naturally act if they could complete their work at home under ideal conditions that they could control. The DISC also measures how a leader adapts to the culture of his or her school or district. The ability to understand how leaders adapt to their workplace is very important information that is needed to ascertain how culture affects behaviors.

Figure 1.1 shows that the highest scores for leaders in their natural state are in compliance and steadiness. This means that the predominant leadership behavior for educational leaders is to be in a support role, working behind the scenes on activities such as data analysis. In addition, the compliance leaders are people who follow the rules set by others and make sure all regulations are followed. This behavior is usually for people in the finance world or regulation field, not the leadership roles we need in education. Those with high compliance and steadiness profiles are not people who have a high sense of urgency for results. They are more cautious and tend to follow other leaders.

The adapted profile shown in Figure 1.2 indicates that the leaders stay in their steadiness and compliance behaviors as they adapt to the work environment. The dominance does increase, and the influence behavior decreases. This means that the effect of the emphasis on urgency and accountability is increasing the dominance behaviors of some leaders. This text outlines how the dominance increase actually has a negative effect on sustainable change and results. The steadiness

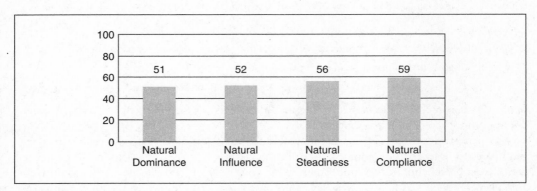

FIGURE 1.1   **DISC Natural Profile (Median) for Current Educational Leaders**

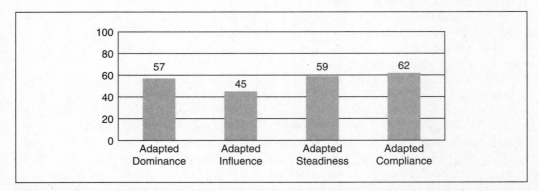

FIGURE 1.2   **DISC Adapted Profile (Median) for Current Educational Leaders**

and compliance are still high. People within these profiles do not change and focus on improvement at a faster rate when top-down urgency and pressure increase. The influence behavior should be increasing in order to develop teams and coach people to change if the goal is faster and sustainable change. In that regard, the decrease in influence behavior will result in slowing down change.

Figure 1.3 shows similar trends on a mix of educational leaders. The median DISC bar chart is based on a sample of 200 principals nationally. The natural behavior of principals is highest in influence and steadiness. The high influence behavior is positive. The steadiness score is a sign of cautiousness, which will result in more focus on process and less focus on faster results. The need for lower steadiness to increase short-term results is clear. The adapted behavior of principals is the concern. Their compliance scores rise significantly, and the steadiness increases. This is another indicator that the culture in education today focuses on data analysis and is resulting in principals being overly cautious, with little action and a minimal sense of urgency. The dominant behavior increases and the influence decreases because the pressure to obtain results forces principals to be more dominant and less influential. Although the dominant increase is positive, it needs to be accompanied by a higher score on the influential behavior to create sustainable change and improvement.

Figure 1.4 shows how a specific group of leaders—Hispanic leaders in an aspiring superintendent program—scored on the DISC. This is only one subset population, so it will be important to look at other subgroups to determine whether we are placing the right leaders for change in schools and districts. These findings help us focus on the professional development and coaching that are needed for leaders to turn around schools.

The Hispanic leaders in a superintendent training program show very interesting results. This very competitive program selected leaders who can be effective based on this data analysis. Although this is only one aspiring leadership program, it does demonstrate that the people in the program

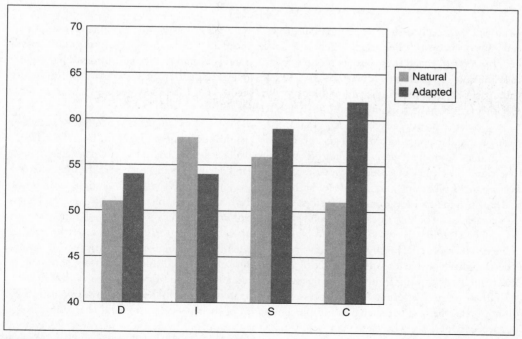

FIGURE 1.3   **DISC Results (Median) for Principals**

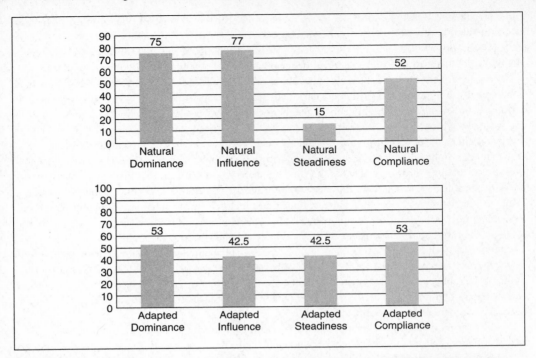

FIGURE 1.4   DISC Results (Median) for Association of Latino Administrators and Superintendents

(who will eventually assume superintendent roles in several U.S. urban districts) have profiles that can be very successful. Because this behavior profile is different from the norm in education, it will be important to coach these leaders on how to create and sustain a change and improvement effort in schools. If these talented leaders do not have the right change strategy, they could have difficulty gaining support for their ideas and methods. If they become too strong for their staff and communities, they can become frustrated and lose their effectiveness.

Leaders who are categorized as ENTJ in the MBTI inventory are often very effective at setting clear goals and expectations for change, as can be seen in this text's case studies. However, if the ENTJ person does not score high in influence behavior, they will tend to be ineffective in sustainable change. There must be change in leadership work in education, and the influencing leaders are the most effective because they build teams and increase leadership capacity. They also involve parents and the community and are open to new ideas from other sectors. The dominance behavior still needs to be the second highest behavior because it is critical to act boldly and make difficult decisions to improve education.

The steadiness behavior needs to be less prominent because this score indicates the pace of change. The most effective leaders are lower in this area and have a high sense of urgency for action. The compliance behavior is the most critical trend from the DISC. All the focus on accountability and regulations coming from policymakers has created a leadership profile in schools that shows a fearfulness to act. The examples and case studies of the most successful leaders are the opposite; they do not break the law, but they put a minimal amount of their personal time and energy into compliance activities. They delegate many of them to their team and determine which ones will benefit their school or school system's efforts to obtain high results for students. They start with goals and outcomes and adjust for the compliance requirements.

The DISC is validated for hiring. It is recommended that it be used for a smaller part of the decision-making process and as one aspect of a package to determine the right hire. There are, however, some companies that use the DISC for all hiring. It is important data because it tells a story about a person's natural inclinations and how he or she is adapting to his or her current environment. The DISC can be administered to candidates for a position before they are hired. The results can be used as part of an overall hiring process to assess how the person's behavior can match the needs of the position. The DISC can show whether the adaptation from the natural to the adapted behavior of the person in their current position is too stressful for a person, which could be important data for hiring. It is recommended that once the DISC is complete, the supervisor uses it to further probe a person's references, based on the results. The DISC is then helpful for when the person is hired. The supervisor can sit down and immediately develop a professional development plan based on the needs of the position and the skills, abilities, and behavior style of the new hire.

Policymakers want a high sense of urgency for change and results in education in order to be competitive worldwide. However, the nature of the approach to prescribe accountability and to emphasize evaluation has the potential of decreasing the success rate of our schools. It is fortunate that our high-performance leaders have already figured out what our policymakers have not: Rules and regulations are important but not as motivators to achieve great results for students and staff.

The Workplace Motivators or Values Inventory

The Values inventory has not shown many specific trends for education. Values are personal and are important for coaching and the change process. If one takes action against your values, your ability to sustain the actions will diminish over time. In fact, if the job is counter to your values, you could lose interest and productivity. The key data point that is most significant from the values or workplace motivators inventory is that most educators score relatively low in the utilitarian value. This low score on the utilitarian value is defined as a low motivation for personal satisfaction derived from financial status. Educators do not tend to enter the education world for personal financial return. In addition, the low priority that educators place on financial factors (as opposed to interpersonal factors, which are typically strong motivators for them) means that educators are generally not motivated to ensure that there is a clear return on investment of educational dollars in relation to results for students. They may not be inclined to use financial information in the same manner that a person who was highly motivated by money would. Educators may not place a focus on how the programs and services provided by the school system result in a return on investment for stakeholders. This data is important for superintendents when presenting to business or financial people in the community or municipal government.

Most educators have similar values based on the results of this inventory. They are very committed to their mission, want to assume leadership roles to make a difference, and are generally data oriented. Although the patterns do not provide direction for leadership hiring and professional development, they do play an important role in the coaching and professional development processes. Too often, mentors tell new leaders what they did that was successful. Instead, the Values inventory indicates that coaching is more effective with attention to the data on what motivates people for sustainable change and improvement.

The Workplace Personality Inventory (WPI)

New research is in process that is substantiating the results and trends used here. The data on the three inventories was a key element in the formation of the Kirtman Seven Competencies. To provide further verification of the conclusions on leadership presented here, the WPI (published in

2007) was used to determine whether the conclusions are similar. The WPI is a reliable tool that has been used and validated in the private sector, health care, and higher education arenas. New norms for the WPI had to be created for principals. Therefore, a study was conducted to create norms for this occupational group and to establish the connections to the leadership competencies. Two hundred principals completed the WPI. Their superintendents and/or supervisors rated each of these principals on the seven leadership competences described earlier. In addition, the evaluators were asked if the principals were in the top 10% of principals, top 20%, top 30%, top 40%, top 50%, top 50–75%, or in the lower 25% in their performance. The researchers then developed a new WPI educational version and a profile of highly effective principals.

The purpose of this research was to test the data and trends from the sample of 600 educators completing the three inventories. Would another well-validated tool indicate similar trends? The results from the research to date follow. The WPI has 16 variables that can be used in hiring and professional development. The inventory is currently in the process of re-design that will include changing terminology to match the educational world. The actual items in the inventory will not be changed to ensure that the validity and reliability data are intact.

The following correlations of the WPI elements were connected to the Kirtman Seven Competencies. Because the WPI is about behavior, it is also sensible to compare the results with the DISC. The high-performing principals show higher scores then lower-performing principals in the following areas:

- Achievement
- Leadership
- Persistence
- Adaptability (very significant)
- Initiative (highest significance)
- Analytical (slight significance)
- Innovation

In addition, high-performing principals tend to:

- Score high on the ability to not let critical feedback negatively affect them. If you can handle critical feedback without stress, you seem to be more effective as a leader.
- Score low on concern for others. If you are overly sensitive to people, it may affect your ability to make tough decisions and can negatively affect your performance.
- Score higher on the ability to control their emotions and display self-control. If you cannot control emotions or anger, it can be a problem for your credibility as a leader.
- Be less detail oriented than lower performers. If you spend too much time on detail and do not delegate and trust your staff, it may cause trust issues.
- Be less inclined to strictly follow rules. The people who tend to follow rules more rigidly are less inclined to be creative and innovative and may not meet their goals.

Areas that do not show any significant differences between low and high performers are cooperation, dependability, independence, and unlikely virtues. The high score areas do seem to have similar characteristics to the DISC influence behavior. The people who have high steadiness and compliance scores seem to match people who score lower in the leadership behaviors on the WPI.

With the WPI it is possible to compare principals to other occupational groups. One interesting trend is related to work style of stress tolerance. The principals in the research sample had lower stress tolerance scores, on average, than several other occupations (nurses, executives, administrative assistants). This suggests that principals, in general, may be somewhat sensitive to stress and criticism.

However, higher-performing principals are not as sensitive to critical feedback. Policymakers need to take a careful look at this data. Because the education world is all about presenting data for critical review of student, teacher, and administrator performance, this finding raises questions about the role of stress tolerance in helping principals successfully perform their jobs. It also raises a philosophical question about the impact the media, with their negative coverage, is having on the development of effective leaders. If principals are to receive objective student data and regular feedback from teachers on performance, they must improve their ability to integrate this data into their practice without stress and defensiveness. This has major implications for school initiatives, such as Professional Learning Communities (PLC), that rely on the principal and teachers to review student data and work on improving practice. If the principal and teachers believe this data will be used to criticize them, they will not be fully focused on the learning process.

2

Successful Leaders Challenge the Status Quo

Conforming Is Less Risky, but Does It Work?

Educational culture has historically focused on educators being the ones with all the answers. Teachers were supposed to be experts, and their focus was on being the best teachers they could be. The world of education is evolving and the teacher is no longer considered the person who has all the answers. Now, as teachers help students learn to use facts to organize their ideas and gain understanding of concepts, administrators also need to shift from the expert mentality to focus on helping their staff develop the problem-solving and judgment skills necessary to meet the needs of a diverse set of stakeholders.

THE CHANGING ROLE OF THE ADMINISTRATOR

The role of the administrator is no longer transactional, but transformational. The *transactional* role involves the day to day interactions between people that require a need for information, data, and materials to do your job. You need information and another person provides what you need. A *transformational* role involves focusing on common goals and aspirations that are needed to make fundamental change and improvement. Today's world of technology has allowed leaders to focus on higher-level learning and transformational change. Accountability and urgency are the central themes of education. School leaders are immersed in a reactive and responsive mode every day of their working lives. To deal effectively with these changes, leaders need to be visionary, insightful, thoughtful, and self-aware.

Today's world of urgency and accountability applies pressure on finding ways to provide the best possible education for students to meet the changing needs of a global society. The leaders that are preparing for this global society are spending their time learning about 21st century skills and determining how to integrate them into their curriculum. They are looking for literature on leadership that teaches them the skills they need to be successful in a global society. They work with their staff on development plans and improvement strategies for students. They are not spending their time on transactional tasks. They are spending time on transformational ideas to alter their approaches to education.

To commit to urgency and accountability, leaders must be willing to look at their own behavior and ensure that they are serving as models for the staff. The spirit of accountability is to ensure that decision making and resource allocation are based on real data pertaining to student performance. Accountability is based on holding educators responsible for their work in educating our children.

Urgency means that we cannot use excuses for another generation of students not getting the opportunities they need to be successful. Urgency is about the skills needed for success in the 21st century. These issues require thought, insight, and input from many people. These are not compliant activities on issues such as how many pages are needed for approval of our school improvement plan. They are high-level conceptual ideas for change that need as many minds as possible to determine a path for success.

THE PERSPECTIVE OF AN EFFECTIVE SCHOOL LEADER

To be successful in these changing times, school leaders must be able to, as Ron Heifetz (2002) states, "Get up in the balcony," meaning they must gain perspective by looking at their work objectively and from a distance. A retired superintendent who was very successful in several districts once stated that, "As a principal and central administrator, I always thought my job was to do the tasks myself. Then finally, I stepped back and understood that now I complete tasks through other people."

Each successful leader who is referenced in this text realizes that his or her job is not about getting tasks done. The leaders' job is to look at themselves as leaders, capitalize on their strengths, and learn how to prevent their weaknesses from becoming barriers to leading others. The job of an administrator is about insights, not tasks. Insight requires stepping back, being proactive, thinking, and not just moving forward and acting. Leaders must ask more questions and give fewer answers. They also need to ask questions that do not have clear answers. A principal might ask the following:

1. If many teachers are feeling overwhelmed, how can we decrease the pressure on them and increase their motivation to succeed?
2. How can we help our students stay focused with all the distractions that interfere with their learning?
3. How can we use the resources of people in the community to help us handle the overwhelming tasks that need to be completed? Could we develop a volunteer program?

A superintendent might ask these questions:

4. How can we help the school board respond to the pressure from the community on accountability and make them understand that they can be supportive of our work?
5. How can I meet the compliance requirements of the state and still motivate staff to be risk takers?

A central administrator might ask the following:

6. How can I build a team culture in my department when there is not a team environment in the district?
7. How can I support the principals when I am required to enforce certain regulations from the federal government?

In answering question one, a leadership team would explore methods to motivate teachers rather than focus on evaluation. Teachers want to teach, not worry about test scores and reports and documentation. Although it is important to document, and test scores are key indicators of success, it is important to show how data can be helpful to teachers' practice and support their efforts. It is worth trying to minimize their work outside the classroom on administrative tasks to allow them to spend more time supporting their students and their families. This is not easy to do and to make sure key administrative work is getting done. However, a genuine effort by administration will go a long way toward motivating and recognizing teachers and will raise their accountability for their students' success.

The second question requires a team to discuss a series of key strategic issues. What are the distractions that interfere with learning at school and at home? How could the school partner with parents, employers, and community leaders to help students stay focused on their learning? What could the guidance department do to better support students in dealing with these distractions? This discussion is very important, and schools often do not take the time to talk about and follow up on these issues.

Question three would involve the superintendent and the school board spending time in either a workshop or an open meeting talking about how to handle the pressure from the community. They must show they are holding people accountable for results while trying to support the leaders to be motivated to get results. Often school boards miss the opening to publically support current successes to show that they are focused on accountability and results. The superintendent needs to realize that it is difficult for elected officials to manage this dilemma. If the board is too supportive, they can be perceived as just being a rubber stamp for the superintendent's agenda. Typically, superintendents and their staff feel a lack of support from school boards that succumb to the pressure of the community, the media, and the policymakers. However, the superintendents and their staff need to understand that just supporting the administration may not demonstrate the sense of urgency for change that is needed for results.

The fourth question involves how the school board can show the community that they are holding the administration accountable to results. The school board members believe they need to be independent of the superintendent and make sure accountability is clear on all goals and operations. Unfortunately, school board members can appear to be negative and critical of administrators and may even micro-manage to check on outcomes, which creates a difficult situation for a superintendent. The board needs to realize that they can stand for accountability and not be overly negative and critical. The superintendent needs to understand that the board can't just support everything the superintendent states.

The fifth question deals directly with the issue of being compliant and taking risks. The data in this text seems to indicate that compliance can overtake the risk taking behavior. If one focuses on meeting goals first and taking risks to ensure that the goals are met, can this mitigate the constraints of the compliance requirements? Once goals and plans are developed, looking at the state and federal requirements as a means—not an ends—can free up a leadership team to take risks and be innovative.

Question six raises the question of how to build a team culture when the system-wide environment is not collaborative. It would be easy to say that a department in a system cannot do this alone. However, if a leader establishes a team environment, can it influence other leaders in the district? If you develop a team, they can work in small groups with other departments in a manner that could change others' behaviors. If your team gets great results, that can get the attention of leaders who can change the culture.

The final question is not that simple for a superintendent. If the superintendent is focused on results, the answer can be clear. The principal who achieves results but struggles with the requirements needs to build a team to provide support on compliance activities. However, the message still needs to be presented by the superintendent that compliance is part of the work of the principal.

These are complex issues and need time for discussion and to develop plans for resolution. If the leaders are spending their time on reacting and complying, these discussions never happen. Responding to symptoms and crises prevents developing real plans to solve problems and create sustainable change.

THE QUALITIES OF AN EFFECTIVE SCHOOL LEADER

Few great leaders in education today are sufficiently prepared to sustain student improvement. The job is difficult, but tremendously rewarding. To achieve it, school leaders need to focus on their school system and the needs of the students they are charged with preparing for the challenges of the 21st century. These leaders must have a vision for education in their communities and a staff of excellent educators. The leaders must understand the needs and abilities of their staff and must motivate the staff to meet the students' needs. The leaders must be open to the resources, input, and ideas from the people in their districts, parents, community members, universities, and the state and federal government.

A proper leadership mentality is key. For example, when a staff member resigns and the leader must take over a program, a strong leader might use the opportunity to evaluate the effectiveness of the program and the staff's abilities. The leader might look at this as an opportunity for building capacity in the organization and return to his or her role as a leader with new knowledge of the effectiveness of a program. The leader will be able to identify key staff with the potential to handle more responsibility and will learn about why high-performing people may be holding back from reaching their potential.

Each day every administrator in education is faced by an endless list of tasks that must be done. Teachers are complaining about lack of supplies. Principals are telling the central office, "let us stay in our schools and reduce the professional development programs that pull us away." School board members are calling because they just heard a parent say that there is a problem with the new bus routes. Another call has come in that the lights are out on the football field and there is a big game tonight. The department of education is on their way to audit the school advisory councils.

The list is endless, and the priorities differ for each person. The weight of the myriad of tasks can be a burden for administrators. Add 100 or more e-mails, texts, and phone calls, and this list becomes a 24-hour responsibility.

Some of these tasks could be effective uses of a leader's time if done with a leadership mindset. For example, visiting schools and classrooms is important from an instructional leadership standpoint. However, if the superintendent or principal spends an excessive amount of time on this task because he or she is being told that strong instructional leaders visit schools every day, the leader may sacrifice the positive effect of this activity. Could the time be used differently to obtain even better results?

A successful superintendent in a suburban community once told me that he took all the letters and requests from the department of education and posted them on a bulletin board where his professional staff could read and respond. He never read any of them. He realized that his job was to lead and form insights and build capacity in his district, not to read and respond to requests for reports. He also had the insight that the department, in their focus on tasks, had no capacity to enforce the requests and mandates that their personnel were so busy spending their time on. His district was in compliance because of his dedicated staff. He developed a team of leaders who worked together to help each other succeed. He knew they would make sure the compliance activities were being completed and would help each other with the tasks. The team determined how they could divide up the tasks so no one would have to bear too much of the workload. Often support staff can be used for many tasks that are completed by the professional staff. Although it must be recognized that tight budgets often limit the support staff in districts, leaders tend to be shortsighted in cutting support staff when their ability to help the administrators is extremely valuable. If administrators have more time for leadership activities, they can create more value for the students, parents, and the community. This added value can result in more financial support from the city or town and potential new revenue sources for the district.

In the worst cases, this superintendent received rare calls from the department of education stating that his school was not up to date on a report. On those rare occasions, the superintendent was able to meet the department's needs without any repercussions.

This same superintendent did not spend his time working on the published list of compliance tasks presented to superintendents each year. This list of over 100 items included reports due to the department, legal requirements for informing parents of their rights, and so forth, which all needed attention. However, this was a great list to give to his staff and spend very little of his own time monitoring. Unsurprisingly, this superintendent had more time to meet the challenges of his district than many of his colleagues. He always had time to talk about a new strategic idea on technology or a new partnership with a community organization that could help his students. This superintendent assumed the presidency of his state association, and always made sure he was up to date on all trends that could affect his school system. Every district led by this superintendent had very high scores in student achievement on all standardized tests. This same leader was the only superintendent in the state who attended a workshop from the Principal's Association on developing school teams with a group of principals, teachers, and parents. No other superintendent in the state had time to attend!

Following is a list of compliance tasks that become time consuming for administrators:

- Making sure that every request from the department of education is responded to immediately on the proper form that is requested
- Filling out all internal and external forms for the district on time and with extra attention to accuracy
- Personally checking on all tasks that are under the responsibility of each staff member; checking that each task is being done on time
- Reviewing the work of each staff person to make sure he or she is being productive each day
- Providing constant reminders to staff about the work they need to do and the deadlines
- Getting into classrooms every day to observe teachers or principals
- Reviewing all written documents and revising them to make sure they are completed as desired; making sure there are no mistakes on all written correspondence
- Ensuring that all rules in the system are being followed to the letter of the law
- Checking to be sure that each teacher is following all protocols and procedures that have been established
- Checking on all events to ensure no details are being missed; attending all events to show involvement and oversight
- Attending all school or system meetings to ensure that no mistakes occur

The world of technology has opened up new services for educational leaders. Many state associations have developed listservs for their members that allow colleagues to post questions using e-mail. The e-mails posted are mostly task-oriented or transactional in nature. Examples of postings have involved asking other superintendents for a copy of their residential policy or soliciting advice on how to handle a person in your office who uses too much cologne. The CEO of a corporation or a nonprofit would not spend time on these lower-level issues. Why should administrators?

THE IMPORTANCE OF RECOGNIZING LEADERSHIP STYLES

A principal in a suburban district asked the superintendent why he wanted her to spend more time in the morning with parents during the bus arrival and child drop-off time. The superintendent responded that her relationship with parents was poor and that the child drop-off time was a great time to build these relationships. On further examination of her own style, the principal decided that this morning time was not a good time for her to build relationships with parents. Her leadership style was often abrupt and direct on issues. If she saw a parent stressed out and worried about his or her child, she would be matter of fact in enforcing the regulations on proper drop-off procedures and would not show empathy for the concerned parent. Although this was proper procedure, it left a cold and impersonal perception with some parents. If she used the morning arrival time as a vehicle for building relationships, under a pressure situation her style could cause more problems with parents. A better approach would involve finding new ways to build relationships with parents that were more effective and fit well with her personality and leadership style.

The principal developed more thoughtful approaches to developing her relationships with parents. She was more effective in a group setting, talking to parents about her values for the school and participating in a dialog on how these values matched those of the parents and helped their children receive a strong foundation for learning.

Now, aside from a brief greeting time with students and parents when the buses arrive, the principal is able to organize her day more effectively in the morning. Her focus on organizing her own time and working with staff on professional development and finding more meaningful methods to engage parents in a thoughtful manner has improved her relationships with parents. Her relationship with parents is now being cited by the superintendent as a strength.

The principal was being a compliant leader by trying what the superintendent suggested. By effectively questioning the methods of achieving the outcomes, however, she was able to save valuable time in the morning and meet the goal more effectively.

As the characteristics of high-performance teams are presented, you will see that other styles and roles on the team may be better suited to certain accountability tasks. The principal cited previously has delegated the bus duties effectively to other staff members whose styles are more effective in making sure that parents and students are safe and treated well in their bus arrival experience. It is important that leaders decrease their time on compliance tasks and instead delegate these tasks to other staff members in order to meet the accountability needs.

Leaders will complete their goals more effectively by motivating staff in a vibrant positive environment rather than a punitive one, blaming, evaluating, and creating fear-based school cultures. Fear results in people shutting down their creative thinking sides and often becoming more compliant. An environment in which people feel they will be blamed prevents them from raising problems or mistakes early for fear of punishment or being fired. Creating a blame-free environment for identifying problems is essential to a culture of excellence (Edmondson, 2011).

In an urban district, a group of principals in fear of losing their jobs became very compliant as demonstrated by their calling the central office and asking about the requirements for format and font size for their school improvement plans. They were so focused on following the rules of how a plan should look that they neglected to focus on the quality and content of the plan. The fear prevented the principals from spending their time on ensuring that their plan was results oriented, thorough, and innovative. The principals were more concerned about making sure they did not make any mistakes on format and didn't omit any required sections than they were on the content. The central office did not receive any calls from principals about the content or quality of the plans, even after the office offered to be a resource to the principals. The plans that were presented lacked depth and substance, but they did follow the format requirements.

MOTIVATING PEOPLE INSTEAD OF ENFORCING RULES

Being motivational is an important trait of a successful leader. Actions such as walking around the school, interacting with staff, and getting to know people motivate each person to peak performance. Good leaders are clear in their expectations and do not tolerate people who sabotage results. They use motivational methods before they use the typical tools of evaluation to obtain results. When a principal writes a short note to a teacher about a positive statement from a parent, or the fact that the teacher's extra effort with a student in trouble paid off, it is very motivational to a teacher.

Today's movement is toward being tough on teachers and administrators with increased focus on evaluation to improve student achievement. Strong words are used that state that poor performance will not be tolerated. The anger and disdain for teachers who are deemed as low performers are creating an environment of blame that carries over to all teachers. Although it is noted that excellent teachers should be rewarded, the emphasis on the poor performers casts a shadow that can affect the entire profession. We need teachers to be motivated to do an excellent job and recommend the profession to others. The concern with all the talk of accountability and eliminating poor performance is that it is sending the wrong message to the very people we count on to help shape the lives of our children. It is important to evaluate teachers and to weed out poor performance (Dinan, 2009). However, evaluation is only one tool to improve performance. Successful leaders develop a teacher or an administrator into a high performer through a motivational and continuous-improvement approach. Creating a team culture is often more effective in producing results than a top-down evaluation process. In a team culture, people are encouraged to take risks and experiment with new ideas. They know that they have team members who will back them up and prevent them from failing. A strong high-performance team will actually show more accountability for results than a single supervisor can. Peer accountability is very powerful and the strong performers can both hold someone accountable and help that person succeed. This focus on team and team results is a powerful motivator for success. When a principal provides constructive feedback to a teacher on a situation right after it occurs, there is usually a positive impact.

An example of providing direct, real-time feedback occurred when a teacher was empathetic to a parent that was having a problem with her child. The teacher also promised to send the parent information on a new math program in the school. The teacher forgot to send the parent the information that was promised, and the parent complained to the principal. The principal asked the teacher to set up a meeting to talk about a complaint from the parent. In the meeting, the principal began by recognizing her great skills in empathizing with her fellow teachers, students, and parents. However, the principal did need to convey her concerns about the teacher's lack of follow through on promises she made and her inconsistency in meeting deadlines. The principal offered to provide some coaching services to help the teacher because she valued her skills in teaching and her interpersonal skills with people. The principal did not want her lack of follow through to affect her reputation. Although the teacher was not pleased with the negative feedback, she did appreciate the directness and the support of her strengths. The teacher was receptive to the principal's coaching and began to improve her ability to meet deadlines.

This demonstrates of how real-time, immediate feedback is more effective in improving performance than episodic feedback on formal evaluations that occur once or twice a year. The principal had developed a high-performance team of administrators and teachers that were able to discuss team and individual feedback on results. The members of the team were able to support each other and provide critical feedback to each other. This teacher from the previous scenario felt comfortable raising her areas for improvement within a team meeting, and she acknowledged her support of the principal for the effective way she delivered critical feedback. The principal's feedback was effective in improving performance for this teacher. The mutual accountability of the team was even more helpful in teachers building on their strengths and working on important improvements. A single evaluator may be able to point out areas for improvement but is limited in the day-to-day interactions and opportunities to both provide feedback to a staff member and to help him or her solve a problem.

School leaders live different lives than other educators. Their responsibilities result in high levels of stress every day as they try to meet the demands of a diverse group of learners. It is important for school leaders to align their personalities, leadership styles, and working environments to better manage their workloads and lead fulfilling lives.

INCREASING SELF-AWARENESS THROUGH LEADERSHIP INVENTORIES

How do these successful leaders become strong enough to receive critical feedback, resist the temptations of being task oriented, and cease to jump to respond to every request? They start by looking at themselves and becoming more self-aware of how their behavior affects others.

One must increase self-awareness by looking critically at one's own behavior. Once this self-awareness and openness is developed, the leader can hear critical comments and be motivated by the feedback. Too often people hear feedback and dismiss it or become defensive and block their own development.

There are many approaches to increasing self-awareness. The use of three leadership inventories will be cited throughout this text. In addition, other resources to increase self-awareness, such as emotional intelligence, that have proven to be very successful in many fields will be explained.

Leadership inventories allow us to see ourselves as others see us. We are often surprised when someone's reaction contradicts our intended result, and frequently dismiss the reaction as wrong or uninformed. If we really understood ourselves and how our behavior appears to others, we would realize that all reactions give us data that we can use for self-improvement.

Ken Blanchard's work on situational leadership states that we must alter our leadership approach to the needs of the situation (Blanchard, 2006). Each situation requires different leadership behaviors. It may be important that a directive approach be used in a crisis situation due to the urgency and short timeline for response. However, in a situation in which we require support from other people, a facilitative leadership style would bring out other points of view that could blend into a strategy that everyone could support. Although it is critical that we understand why we act differently in each situation, it is our deep understanding of ourselves that allows us to adapt to situations. We must understand why we tend to react to a situation and become more directive. Are we afraid that we might look weak to others, and that makes us more inclined to display power to control the situation? Another situation might require us to become more compromising rather than autocratic to ensure that no one has hurt feelings. We must understand why we act the way we do and what determines how we can improve as a leader. This knowledge will help us alter our approach in a manner that is personal and sustainable.

There are many theories about how to be an effective leader in education. These theories are often developed by interviewing successful leaders to determine their skills, characteristics, and qualities. In order to develop an improvement plan, leaders look at these lists of qualities and determine how their strengths and weaknesses match the proposed list. Equally important, however, is the hard work it takes to get to know yourself through personalized objective data and self-reflection to determine how to integrate a variety of leadership strategies within your personality. Behavioral change takes time and consistent focus. Each leader is different, and it is critical to understand yourself first before you develop a strategy to improve. Once you dedicate yourself to improving your own leadership you can help others improve.

The Myers Briggs Type Indicator

The first inventory used by the leaders cited in this text is the Myers Briggs Type Indicator (MBTI). The MBTI has been used since the 1940s and has been very successful in leadership development in both industry and the public sector (Center for Applications of Psychological Type, n.d.). Isabel Myers and

Katherine Briggs, a mother and daughter team, first used the MBTI to help women find jobs during World War II. It has since been used in many circumstances, including marriage counseling and matching college roommates. Today, the MBTI is published in 75 languages and used all over the world.

The MBTI is an excellent tool for individual leadership and team development. Knowing how other people solve problems is critical to working as a team. Patrick Lencioni's book *Overcoming the Five Dysfunctions of a Team* lists MBTI as the recommended inventory for team development (Lencioni, 2005). Each team member's knowledge of his or her own problem-solving style can be used on team challenges. One style may be better at brainstorming out of the box ideas to solve a problem. Another style might be better at developing a plan to execute a strategy for improvement.

MBTI is based on Jungian archetypes and has 16 different variations. Each aspect of the MBTI will be explained so the reader can assess his or her own leadership preferences. Your self-assessment can give you insights into your own behaviors as well as the behaviors of others.

Each person is plotted on a scale of the degree of his or her extrovert or introvert style. Everyone can exhibit each style of problem solving. People who are in the high zone tend to have minimal behavior in the opposite category. If they are close to the middle they are situational and can change their style in relation to the needs of the situation.

EXTROVERT/INTROVERT SCALE   The first area of measurement is the Extrovert/Introvert (E/I) scale. Extroverts tend to work well in teams and focus on building relationships with internal and external stakeholders. Introverts are much more reflective and tend to focus internally rather than work with external groups. They spend more time planning and focusing on in-depth implementation of a smaller list of goals. Table 2.1 contains some of the characteristics of the extrovert and introvert.

Extroverts are typically more effective in dealing with complex external educational challenges, especially in turnaround situations (Myers, Griffith, Daugherty, & Lusch, 2004). Reaching out for help and resources helps to resist myriad requests for a leader's time and energy. Extroverts' desires to form teams are also critical to success. Extroverts are more willing to hand over tasks to others in their desire to move quickly to get results. This text will outline (in Chapter 5) how introverts can adjust their style to move faster and still be thorough while achieving great results through team development.

SENSING/INTUITIVE SCALE   The second area of the MBTI is the Sensing/Intuitive (S/N) scale (N is used instead of I to not confuse readers with the I in Introvert). Sensing people are reality based and focused on short-term implementation. Data is important to the sensing leader. Intuitive people are always looking at the big picture. They want to know why something is not working before they move ahead to solve a problem. They look at the goal and plan back from the outcome to the current condition to develop an action plan. This process is often called *back planning*. Table 2.2 compares the sensing and introvert personality types.

The data cited in Chapter 1 indicate that we see better performance in leaders that are intuitive thinkers. It is easier for them to resist temptation to focus on short-term tasks. Intuitive thinkers tend to avoid focusing on the details of projects and initiatives that overwhelm those that have a sensing style. Intuitive types tend to put together long-term plans for success. They spend a lot of time on why things occur and have a better chance of determining insights for change that can be sustainable due to their long-term focus.

Sensing types focus on what is realistic in relation to current constraints. However, when the resources are scarce and the tasks are overwhelming, they have trouble stepping back and determining a path to success. The details take over and prevent them from seeing possibilities for new approaches. Although understanding reality is critical to making effective plans, the intuitive leader delegates more responsibility for implementation to his or her staff.

TABLE 2.1   Extrovert/Introvert Comparisons

Extrovert	Introvert
Thinks out loud	Thinks before speaking
Takes on many issues at one time	Works more individually and in small groups and focuses on each issue in depth
Tends to ask for input from many people before making decisions and expects a lot of personal communications	Communicates only when absolutely necessary
Forms large social and work networks	Sometimes believes networking is not genuinely substantive behavior and does not network unless there is a specific topic
Likes to work in teams	Does not like a lot of meetings, especially with large groups; tends to work alone
Speaks first and thinks later	Likes to be prepared before presenting to groups; speaks only when ideas are well thought out
Brainstorms ideas for new initiatives	Believes that brainstorming is a waste of time and lacks substance and depth
Takes on more than he or she can handle	Works on a smaller number of projects in depth
Can and will speak quickly on many topics	Would rather prepare before speaking on an issue
Moves on issues quickly	Tends to slow down implementation to make sure everything is being considered

TABLE 2.2   Sensing/Intuitive Comparisons

Sensing	Intuitive
Detail oriented	Big picture thinkers
Linear thinkers	Conceptually oriented
Factual and accurate	Focused on long-term strategic issues
Reality based	Always ask why before acting
Data oriented	Sees the whole as greater than the parts
Excellent implementers	System thinkers
Connects well to day-to-day issues	Assumes that the day-to-day activities will work themselves out

The intuitive person looks to the future and builds a plan for success. Many sensing leaders try to maintain the status quo and try not to lose ground. Being realistic is important, but the intuitive leader is better able to provide more direction to staff and is generally more motivational.

TABLE 2.3 Thinking/Feeling Comparison	
Thinking	**Feeling**
Task oriented	Values driven
Objective viewpoint	Relationship oriented
Analytical	Emotions are key to their work and passion
Tends to extract personal viewpoints and emotion out of the planning	Sensitive to morale issues; focuses on personal issues in planning and implementation
Can be very direct with people	Avoids conflict to make sure no one gets hurt
Very logical	Personalizes issues and does not let logic hurt personal feelings
Can cause conflict	May avoid conflict and hold onto personal feelings for long periods of time

THINKING/FEELING SCALE   The third area of the MBTI is the Thinking/Feeling (T/F) scale. The thinking person tends to be objective and does not overreact to emotionally charged issues. The feeling person is more relationship oriented and develops an environment that is focused on having a positive morale for staff. Figure 2.2 on page 39 shows the thinking/feeling scale for Mary, the case study leader featured in this chapter.

The data from Chapter 1 indicate that the thinking style is more effective in creating effective change in schools. The thinking type is able to objectively look at data and present an analysis without becoming sidetracked by other agendas. The thinking person is also less concerned with wanting to be liked and more focused on ensuring results. Individuals high on the thinking scale can create conflict and must learn how to be more sensitive to other styles. Table 2.3 compares the thinking and feeling personality types.

The feeling person is oriented to forming strong relationships. This is often the person who people come to when they have personal concerns and are having difficulty dealing with other styles of behavior. The feeling person may struggle with holding people accountable as he or she does not want to hurt his or her relationship with others.

JUDGING/PERCEIVING SCALE   The fourth area of the MBTI is the Judging/Perceiving (J/P) scale. People high on the judging scale are focused on results and the implementation of strategies that get results. They are outcome oriented and decisive people. Perceptive people are creative problem solvers. They are always looking for new ideas and innovations. They like to keep their options open, while the judging types like to focus on implementation.

The style that seems to be more effective in education is the judging style. Although the education world is filled with endless possibilities for new ideas and approaches to achieve success, the judging type resists temptation, chooses a plan of action, and stays focused. Such people develop and execute plans and are always outcome and results oriented. This has served our successful leaders well. They do not get sidetracked by tasks that take them away from their focus on results.

The perceiving types often have new ideas and get overwhelmed with the number of initiatives that could be implemented and therefore have trouble focusing on measurable results in short time periods. Their desire to keep options open can cause staff to feel unfocused. Table 2.4 provides a comparison of judging and perceiving types.

TABLE 2.4   Judging/Perceiving Comparison

Judging	Perceptive
Decisive	Creative problem solvers; may leave issues open and not make a final decision quickly
Results oriented	Explores options to get positive results
Develops and executes plans	Never lets past problems or barriers stop them from trying something new
Stays focused	Always see possibilities
Clear on expectations	Likes to keep options open and may not be clear on expectations
Deadline oriented	Finds new ways to do things; thinks out of the box
No means no	No means try another way to get a yes
Change can be disruptive	Change is exciting

THE ENTJ LEADERSHIP STYLE   The predominant profile we see on leadership teams that results in measurable results is the ENTJ profile. This profile has been seen in CEOs for many years, but the ENTP is becoming more successful in the corporate world. This sends an important message to educational leaders. Although the judging style of decisiveness and focus in education is key to turnaround situations, the perceiving person's creative, entrepreneurial style will prove to be more important in education over time. The need to develop new creative approaches to solve problems is becoming an essential skill in today's world of education as resources become more limited. Task-oriented leaders under pressure to comply and react will be less likely to bring in new ideas.

Each MBTI profile has its strengths and weaknesses. It is important that leaders know and understand their own strengths and weaknesses. Each leader can build a professional development plan to improve on his or her weaknesses and move toward success. In addition, examples of how these successful leaders build teams to complement their style will be outlined in Chapter 3. Some inventories, like the Gallop strength finder profile, believe that we should be strength based in our approach to develop leaders. Strengths are important and we should maximize their benefit. However, many leaders are blind to their weaknesses. In the strength-based approach, weaknesses are dealt with quickly through emphasis on a person's strengths that often, in extreme situations, can become weaknesses. These weaknesses, which are often not seen by the leaders but are seen by everyone around them, begin to erode their effectiveness. If a staff member has been a victim of a leader's weakness, it will be difficult to regain trust and restore his or her support for the leader.

For example, a leader recently lost his temper with his staff. This same leader was technically brilliant in the finance area. This leader saves the organization significant funds and has prevented financial problems from curtailing successful initiatives. However, the fear in the office was so great that the staff was afraid to bring up new ideas and there was significant staff turnover and low morale. This problem could not be handled from a strength-based approach only. This leader had to focus on his weakness and learn how to control his temper to sustain a team. His staff would not be productive just because their boss has strong technical finance skills. He cannot get their support by just working toward his strength. The negative behavior of lack of respect and anger problems must be stopped, and he will need to apologize to his staff for the office to function effectively.

The DISC Inventory

The DISC was created during the same time period as the MBTI by Dr. William Marston. Dr. Marston also used Jungian archetypes for his work. The validity and reliability of data is very high on the DISC. This inventory focuses on how we do the work in our jobs. It looks at the behaviors we naturally have at home and how we adapt them to the work environment. The DISC complements the MBTI well for educational leaders. A leader might have a particular style in the MBTI, but when he applies this style to the work environment it may differ from his natural style.

The four areas of the DISC are the following:

- Dominant (D): How people handle challenges
- Influence (I): How people work with others to handle challenges
- Steadiness (S): How people handle the pace of change
- Compliance (C): How people follow the rules

The DISC is growing in popularity in every sector except education. The corporate world uses this inventory extensively for hiring and leadership development. Nonprofit organizations and the federal government are beginning to use the DISC for their coaching programs for aspiring leaders (Bonstetter & Suiter, 2004). The DISC also has several specific applications, which are helpful in developing a leader's self-awareness. The ability of the DISC to show how a leader adapts to the work environment is especially helpful in determining how leaders are coping with new trends in accountability. The DISC is also helpful in telling us about the behaviors of leaders who are successful versus the behaviors of leaders who are not.

Studying successful leaders in education has produced a very consistent DISC profile. They have high scores on two major areas of the DISC.

1. The highest score is the influence area. Successful leaders have a high sense of urgency for results. Their focus on obtaining results is through coaching, empowering, and motivating people to succeed. They form teams around them to complement their skills and build capacity of others to succeed.

2. The second highest score for success is in the dominant area. Successful leaders motivate people to succeed and create positive environments for change using their influence behavior. However, when it is clear that they want the change to occur more quickly, they become more dominant and task and result oriented. Their high sense of urgency is clear when people deviate from the plan. If their staff does not respond positively to the coaching, training, and supports that are put in place for their success, the leader will become more directive.

3. The lowest behavior for our successful leaders is compliance. These leaders, as stated earlier, make sure that systems of accountability are set up in their schools or school systems. However, these leaders do not put very much of their personal time into compliance activities. They put very little time into filling out forms, writing reports, reviewing other people's work, editing their staff's documents, or micro managing.

4. The other low area of behavior is steadiness. This means these successful leaders move quickly. They do not spend a lot of time in committees studying data and making sure everyone is comfortable with the next steps. They gain input from people as part of a team development process and then they act. They try new approaches and learn from implementation. They are not afraid to make mistakes. They never are paralyzed by overanalysis. They are risk takers, but are not reckless.

As you can see, the profiles of our successful leaders are predominately influence and dominant. These people have a high sense of urgency, act quickly, and hold themselves and others accountable. These leaders do this work in a positive, high-spirited, engaged, and low-blame environment that they create and foster. These high-performance leaders do not support the idea that change takes several years. They believe that with the proper leadership and teamwork, change can begin now (Reeves, 2011).

Now we are getting a clearer picture of the profiles of successful leaders. The ENTJ takes charge, reviews the data, and puts together a plan that is focused on results. These leaders' behavior profile in the DISC allows them to build a team by finding and developing leaders that complement their style. These leaders move quickly and are not paralyzed by data, rules, mandates, criticisms, and other people's agendas.

In educational environments, results are paramount, but a positive climate for staff is the key to success. Strong leaders must build a team to balance their weaknesses. They must not let their egos prevent them from admitting their weaknesses and receiving critical feedback to help them improve.

The Workplace Motivators or Values Inventory

Understanding one's own motivations is key in developing a strategy for success. Why do we make certain choices, and what makes us passionate about specific issues? Understanding a leader's values is important in creating a plan for sustainable change. If leaders are asked to change in ways that are contrary to their values, they will not stay committed to the change. Values are a set of beliefs that a person has that govern one's own behavior and the behavior one wants to see in others. Values, by definition, do not change and we cannot change the values of others. However, we must understand how our values cause us to act. This final inventory focuses on values.

The Workplace Motivators or Values inventory helps us realize what motivates specific behaviors. We cannot just do what other leaders do to be successful. We are all different and our value systems are unique. Any plan for improvement has to work well with your own values or it will not be sustainable. Typical mentoring programs miss the key to sustainable change. A mentor might say, "If I were you, I would do it this way." However, the mentor is *not* you and he or she does not know and understand your value system. The mentor does not usually take the time to understand who you are because the mentor sees his or her role as helping the leader deal with the tasks that need to be done. A mentor should understand the mentee's values before they begin their working relationship. However, leaders' key to success is knowing who they are and why they do what they do. One consultant, Guy Finke from Vistage Inc., an organization that facilitates CEO groups in the private sector, stated that people get hired for their skills, abilities, and experiences but get fired for who they are. Getting to know and understand why you act in a certain way is hard work and daunting at times. If you become more open to this analysis it will serve you well. The Values inventory delves into who we are through the areas described in Table 2.5.

The Values inventory has produced a less specific profile of successful leaders. This inventory is particularly helpful for the leader when choosing strategies for change and improvement. Strategies must be consistent with values or they will not last. For example, a leader that is not overly effective in building a team believes that her staff should not socialize at work. She believes that personal time is for the home. Faced with a racially, culturally, and generationally diverse staff, her values are not shared. Her staff believes that she is judgmental and micro managing them by watching and critically commenting on their personal behavior at work. They have a value system that supports their enjoying their work and building social time into their day. This conflict is resulting in major morale issues and high staff turnover. The staff has complained to their department leader's boss about her oppressive behavior. Many of the staff members are frustrated and are looking for new employment.

Highly effective leaders have a clear understanding of their value systems and how they affect their behavior when working with other people. If one tries to change or challenge another person's value system, the response is often emotional and defensive. An attempt by one person to show how his or her values are better or more important than those of another person will not be successful.

TABLE 2.5	**Values Inventory Definitions**
T: Theoretical	This value is very important for educational leaders. It is about the search for why something is occurring. Delving into data and research for root causes is a key element of this value.
U: Utilitarian	This value is about money and return on investment. This can also be about the investment of time.
A: Aesthetic	This value is about the beauty and harmonious world and environment in which we live and work. Aesthetic leaders want to make sure that the work environment is pleasant and conducive to productive work. They also want a harmonious work environment without excessive conflict.
S: Social	This value is about people who want to make a difference in the world. In the educational world, it translates in wanting to make a difference in kids' lives.
I: Individual	This value is about power to influence and control people's actions. In education, this often translates into making sure that the data on achievement for all kids is really being addressed and/or making sure that there is equity in educational opportunities for all students and families.
T: Traditional	This value is very interesting in the educational world. It is about the leader's belief that there is a wrong and right way to behave. This can be based on personal, and/or family values. This often translates into a leader's work ethic. This value can result in the leader's intolerance for behavior that is different from his or her value system.

Threatening the core of who we are often results in an extreme reaction that moves one away from the problem-solving and solution-oriented style needed to get results. It is important for leaders to understand what motivates them to higher performance. If leaders know that their values involve the need to search for knowledge and data on root causes for improving student achievement, it will help them deal with others who do not share their value system.

For example, if a superintendent tells a principal who has a high theoretical value system that the principal does not need to develop actions that are research based, the principal will become very frustrated and lose motivation. The awareness by the principal that this research base is core to his belief system allows the principal to talk about this issue with the superintendent. Instead of making a negative judgment about the superintendent, who appears to be making snap decisions that are not anchored in research, the principal can discuss his value system openly with the superintendent. The superintendent might be lower in the theoretical value and higher in the utilitarian value. The superintendent needs to be respected for her values of wanting to move faster on actions so she can show the use of the public's tax dollars. She may view the the principal as too immersed in data and slow to action. If a discussion of both value systems occurs, the two parties can work out a solution to move ahead in a manner that is motivating to each leader. The superintendent could agree to a slightly extended timeline for gathering research on key areas, and the principal can help focus the research collection to move more quickly in an acceptable timeline. The other compromise could be to move ahead on an action and agree to gather research that could be used in implementation or to change direction if necessary. The superintendent and principal learn that a team of different values that are respected can obtain a better result for students.

CREATING AND LEADING HIGH-PERFORMANCE TEAMS

Now that we have reviewed the basic profiles of our most effective educational leaders, it is time to emphasize the importance of building a team. It is important for leaders to hire the best people, recognize the strengths of others, and revel in the success of their staff. A leader should constantly look for talent outside the organization and within the staff, and work relentlessly to get the best out of every person. This is done by coaching, developing individuals, and forming a strong interdependent team focused on common goals and outcomes. This characteristic of building and developing talent is consistent with the influence behavior in the DISC inventory.

The development of high-performance teams (HPT) outlined in this text builds on the work of Lencioni (2005) and the characteristics of high-performance teams in industry by adding the personal and professional development of the leader and the use of the inventories for true high performance. This text will show how the work of team development can be applied to education to provide the missing piece of educational reform and ensure that results are sustainable.

Leadership teams in most sectors are usually anywhere from 7 to 10 people in key leadership roles in the organization. On some occasions, there could be up to 15 members on a leadership team. The high-performance leadership team in a school or school system works in concert with the leader to focus on three areas:

1. *Operational:* This ensures that the day-to-day activities of running a school or school system are seamless. Effective operations result in deadlines being met, staying within budget guidelines, meetings having clear agendas and staying on time, schedules being accurate and realistic, and the buses running on time.

2. *Strategic planning:* The short- and long-term direction of the school and school system is in writing and clear to all constituents. This is usually in the form of a strategic plan for a school system and a school improvement plan for a school. The plan needs to be for 18 months to 3 years and cover all aspects of the organization.

3. *Leadership development:* This ensures that everyone in a school or school system is focused on continuous improvement in their leadership roles. This involves teachers, administrators, school committee, custodians, aides, and so forth.

High performance is measured in several ways, such as:

- Test scores for students
- Job satisfaction for teachers, administrators, and other staff
- Ability to develop the whole child (social and emotional aspects)
- Community satisfaction
- Financial success
- Parent satisfaction
- Developing new leaders from within (succession planning)

If a school's focus is on instructional leadership only, it will miss several of the measures of high performance. If leadership teams instead look at all areas of high performance, the focus will remain on instruction but will add the other elements of high performance that deal with parents, community, talent development, finances, and so on.

Many leaders believe they have developed a leadership team. However, what they really have formed is a working group, not a real team. Table 2.6 shows the differences between a working group and a team.

TABLE 2.6   Differences between Working Groups and Teams

Working Group	Team
Strong, clearly focused leader	Shared leadership roles
Individual accountability	Individual and mutual accountability
The group's purpose is the same as the broader organization mission	Specific team purpose that the team itself delivers
Individual work-products	Collective work-products
Efficient meetings	Open-ended discussion and active problem-solving meetings encouraged
Effectiveness measured indirectly by its influence on others (e.g., financial performance of the business)	Performance measured directly by assessing collective work-products
Process for accomplishing goals is discussion, decision, and delegation	Process for accomplishing goals is discussion, decision, and sharing of actual work

In *Peak Performance,* Dr. Charles Garfield (1987) outlines how high performance is a step beyond team development. Garfield outlines six characteristics for high-performance teams—a team mission statement, "real time" results, self-management, a dedication to building teams, no fear about making changes, and a view of setbacks as learning experiences for working toward the future. This list outlines how high performance is a step beyond team development. A high-performance team becomes self-directed in getting results and holding members accountable for behavior that is needed to reach goals. HPTs can admit mistakes and are dedicated to continuous improvement. They are committed to making sure other HPTs are developed throughout the organization. Although they are self-directed, they are respectful of authority and ensure that their work is aligned with the goals throughout the organization.

A leader who builds an HPT needs to be willing to allow each member to think and act beyond the member's own job function and fully invest in the success of the school and school system. A member of an HPT is on the team to look at the whole school or school system, not just to represent the member's area or function.

Looking at the Big Picture

One of the greatest problems in school systems today, and in many organizations in all sectors, is people working in their own silos. School systems do not operate like assembly lines. To aid appropriate transitions for students from elementary to middle to high school, for example, leaders must look at the big picture of the whole system. Parents, as well as school leaders, being key partners in their students' education, need to understand how to support students through these transitions to ensure academic, social, and emotional success. If a leader remains focused only on his or her own high school he or she could believe that if his or her own school is successful, his or her goals have been reached. However, that leader may have lost an opportunity to learn from another principal who has great skills in motivating teachers or to learn about the key issues of the middle school that will present proactive opportunities for the high school to help students as they transition to a new culture.

Principals of each educational level need to understand how the other levels work. How resources are allocated needs to be a systemic decision. A first-grade teacher supports a third-grade need for resources; a high school principal provides more resources for the elementary schools in language arts to form a foundation for the high school courses that will need to build on the foundation set in early grades.

The formation of leadership teams that care about the whole school system is critical to success and meeting the myriad challenges facing schools. In an HPT, one member might team up with another on a set of tasks that are outside their area of expertise in order to support the team. Team members work together and cross-functionally on goals to add capacity and resources to help each other's areas succeed. Staff members have an opportunity to gain new skills by working in areas that are outside their expertise or comfort zone.

Developing the Team

How does a leader develop an HPT? He or she must first choose a team. Usually the team represents the leaders of each functional area. However, we encourage leaders to add to their team the best talent for overall success. This could mean teacher leaders, union leadership, and other talent in their organization.

Now the leader must create an environment of openness and trust. Trust is fundamental to the development of a real HPT. Trust is a difficult word to define and is difficult to measure. When a relationship breaks down and a team is dysfunctional, lack of trust is usually mentioned as a fundamental problem. Trust can mean fear of people betraying you or fear that you cannot count on people to complete the work that they agree needs to be done. Trust can also take a long time to build but can be lost quickly. Once lost, trust can be hard to recover. The leader must begin the process of developing trust by having a team of members that are free to speak the truth without any repercussions. The leader must demonstrate that he or she is willing to look at his or her own strengths and weaknesses, and thereby encourage others to do the same. The review of the inventories for the leader helps set the tone of openness and honesty. In most cases, it is beneficial to ask the members of the leadership team to complete the inventories. This allows everyone to be equal in looking at themselves first before working on the improvement of the school or school system. The inventories build a personal knowledge of each member's leadership style to ensure that the relationships are strong and that the team can discuss issues in a manner that can include the role that each person plays in moving an issue ahead, or how someone may be a barrier for progress. The inventories present a group profile that will show the strengths and weaknesses of the team.

If a principal understands the profiles of the members of his or her team, he or she can fill gaps and build on people's strengths. For example, a principal may be great at solving immediate problems that occur in the school. His or her style is to focus on short-term problems and to be decisive in making decisions. However, the school needs a school improvement plan that is comprehensive and needs to be able to integrate curriculum issues with behavioral management and child development issues. Turning to team members that have profiles that are more comfortable with strategic thinking and reaching out to other faculty for ideas to build a systemic plan will result in a more successful school improvement plan. Knowing one's style and gathering team members that provide complementary styles and abilities forms a strong high-performance leadership team. It is also helpful to understand the profiles of a team around key issues such as sense of urgency. If the principal is in a situation that warrants major turnaround and a high sense of urgency for change and action, it is critical to know which members of the team have traits that work well in a high-urgency environment.

Everyone does not need to have a high sense of urgency, but it is imperative to know who to count on to move actions quickly and who will react negatively to too much pressure. This knowledge allows the principal to coach people in a motivational manner toward clear expectations for change and be supportive of each person's ability to make a contribution to the turnaround effort.

The knowledge of styles on a leadership team is very important. However, creating a safe environment for people to talk about their styles is another matter. Therefore, the characteristics of self-awareness and being able to receive critical feedback are very important in team development. If members hold back on issues or are afraid to raise a concern that is critical of another team member, the discussion on the issue is missing key data that may be essential to developing the right strategy for success. Establishing blame-free, constructively critical environments for working on issues is essential to success.

Building trust and relationships that can withstand critical feedback takes time. It also takes training on giving and receiving critical feedback. Leaders must constantly work on this open and honest behavior. Autocratic leaders focused on their own egos are not open to critical feedback. These leaders miss key information and ignore perspectives that are important to identifying issues early and solving problems in a sustainable manner. Their staff members hold back information based on fear or because they do not believe their point of view will be considered. Strong leaders of HPTs have staff come to them with problems and they know that they will be dealt with quickly and thoroughly without blame. HPT leaders use all problems and critical situations as learning situations for future growth for themselves and their teams.

Forming leadership teams is the key ingredient to accomplishing seemingly insurmountable goals. Maximizing the human capital in organizations has become a growing trend in organizations outside education. An organization will determine that investment in human capital will provide a competitive advantage in the marketplace. If the organization hires the best people and invests in their development, it will have an advantage over a competitor that has a weakness in a particular area of performance. Although education does not think about competitive advantage, the term does have application to today's educational environment. In order to get the best candidates for superintendent, principal, special education, or other teachers, the culture in the school system involving how people are treated and respected and the commitment to their professional development is critical to attracting the best people. With high-stakes testing and accountability, having the best staff makes a difference in performance of the district (Myers et al., 2004). As education faces challenging goals of increasing student achievement, and as budgets shrink throughout the country, it is critical to place more focus on team development and begin using a team-based framework to increase capacity in schools.

In his book *Overcoming the Five Dysfunctions of a Team* (2005), Patrick Lencioni states that "Teamwork remains the one sustainable competitive advantage that has been largely untapped" (p. 3). He lists five team dysfunctions:

1. Absence of trust
2. Fear of conflict
3. Lack of commitment
4. Avoidance of accountability
5. Inattention to results

As teams move through their development stages toward meeting their goals and achieving results, the leaders must have the strength and the commitment to putting their teams ahead of themselves and using each person's talents to the maximum.

CASE STUDY

MARY

Overview

Mary M. is a high school principal in one of the largest urban high schools in the United States. The New York City community is culturally diverse and predominately working class. Her students are resistant to learning, there is little parental involvement, and violence in the community and the school prevents her from improving student achievement. Mary is fortunate that she has myriad excuses for why she cannot improve student achievement in this poor urban school environment.

Mary chooses not to use them. Instead, she chooses a determined focus on success for every one of her 5,000 students. She chooses to motivate, rather than punishing poor behavior. She does not openly criticize her faculty for mistakes or threaten to fire them for poor performance. When she began her work at the school 9 years ago, Mary faced extremely low standardized test results, poor teacher morale, and low expectations.

The school is now ranked high for standardized tests results of all high schools in the state and has a high teacher's satisfaction rating. Mary knows that there is urgency for results on behalf of every student, but her instincts and leadership style cause her to have a different but very effective approach to success. Mary balances the need for a focus on accountability by increasing her time for self-reflection, community involvement, teamwork, developing school spirit, and a determination for results and success for all students.

In 9 years, she has only fired one teacher who chose not to accept the help provided to succeed. The idea of firing poor performers did not resonate with Mary. She knows that many teachers care about kids and want to do a good job, though they frequently lack the necessary leadership to show them how to succeed.

Mary focuses on data and accountability by working with her staff in teams to understand what the data tells them about each student. She creates an exciting and colorful environment in the school. She works with community leaders to become partners in the school's community. She hangs posters that state new expectations and flies banners with messages of success at the front of the school.

Is Mary centered on clarifying her role as leader of the school? Yes, everyone knows she is in charge. However, she always puts the students and the teachers in front, not herself. In fact, she recently developed a video on her school in which she only appears once midway through introducing her staff. The video opens with the students, displays of team spirit, and the demonstration of the vibrant community. This high-performance leader is not ruled by her ego to get the most attention. People perform better with a more understated leader, as noted by Jim Collins in his description of level five leaders in his book, *Good to Great* (2001).

How did Mary know how to turn this school around to get such extraordinary results? She probably cannot even tell you exactly how she does it. However, her leadership profile is ideal for becoming a successful leader.

Mary and the MBTI

We administered our three leadership inventories to Mary. In the Myers Briggs Type Indicator, her results are ENTJ. Mary's clear score as an extrovert on the E/I scale accounts for her great communication both internally with her staff and externally with parents and the community. Her high score on the intuitive scale means that that she is strategic and able to make both short- and long-term plans (see Figure 2.1).

Mary's thinking score shows that she is objective, but since the score is not extreme it indicates that she will be sensitive to the feelings of others. Her judging score is relatively high, supporting her focus on results. The score is not so high that it indicates rigidity (see Figure 2.2).

CASE STUDY *(continued)*

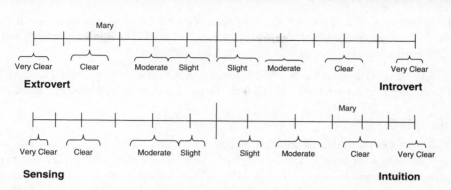

FIGURE 2.1   **Mary's Scores on the Extrovert/Introvert Scale and Sensing/Intuitive Scale**

As an extrovert, Mary tends to engage people in conversations about a variety of topics. She also takes on several issues at one time. She will likely visit classrooms on a regular basis and frequently interact with parents and community members. As an intuitive individual, she is able to focus on the big picture. She looks at both short- and long-term plans for her school's success. She sees the school as part of a larger community. Her focus on improvement involves developing a clear vision for success. When she sees a problem, she wonders why something is wrong and challenges herself to find the cause. She craves a deep understanding of each problem.

As a thinking person, Mary is objective, analytical, and does not take issues or concerns personally. She has a thick skin, can handle criticism, and stays the course despite the pressure. Her high score on the judging scale indicates that she focuses on results, developing and executing plans, making clear decisions, setting expectations, and closing issues rather than leaving loose ends.

Mary's weaknesses, and those of all ENTJ leaders, are the following:

- She might be insensitive to personal issues with staff. This involves the T style versus the F or feeling style.
- She could have trouble with change. This involves the J style, which is less open to change than the P style.
- Mary could miss details and stretch a group beyond their resource capabilities. This involves the N intuitive score, which is not detailed oriented, and the S score, which is focused on details, realistic goals, and more linear thinking.

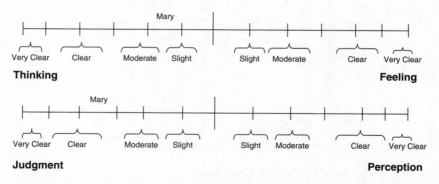

FIGURE 2.2   **Mary's Scores on the Thinking/Feeling Scale and the Judging/Perceiving Scale**

(continued)

- She could take on too much and not slow down to make plans on the school's future or key initiatives. This involves the E characteristic, which takes on too much, versus the I that is more thorough and more plan oriented. Extroverts can also be seen as only focused on themselves.

Mary's strengths lie in her approach to turning around the performance of her school. However, what about her approach to dealing with her weaknesses? How does she prevent them from curtailing her success?

Mary and the DISC

The answer to Mary's success in dealing with her weaknesses is found in her DISC results. Figure 2.3 shows Mary's DISC profile. Any score over 50% in the bar chart is considered a high score. It is evident that her scores are highest in the influence and the dominant areas. The right side of the bar chart indicates her natural behaviors and the left side indicates her adaptation to the work environment. The adaptation score indicates how she changes her behavior to be successful or cope with her workplace. Mary's scores are relatively consistent between natural and adapted. Her steadiness score, which involves the pace of change, does drop significantly from natural to adapted scores. If there is a drop or rise of more than 25 points from either the adapted to the natural or vice versa, this indicates the beginning of a high-stress area. In Mary's case, she is moving very fast with less focus on involvement of her staff. She could work on slowing down and allowing her team to take more of the lead on key issues; she has built a team and now can delegate. The low steadiness score could also indicate a lack of focus on systems development in the school. She does tend to value systems and delineates tasks such as scheduling, data analysis, and operational planning to others who are more detail oriented.

Figure 2.4 shows the areas in which Mary spends more of her time at work. Mary spends most of her time interacting with others. She spends the least amount of her time organizing her workplace and analyzing data. Although data is very important to her, she does not spend a lot of her time on the analysis. The low score on organizing her workplace does not mean she is disorganized; it only means that she does not spend a lot of time on this behavior.

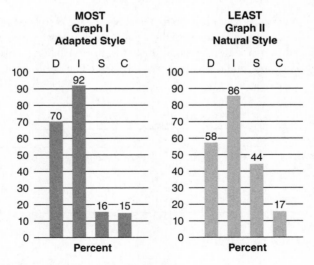

FIGURE 2.3   Mary's DISC Bar Chart
Source: Copyright © 2012 Target Training International, Ltd. Used with permission.

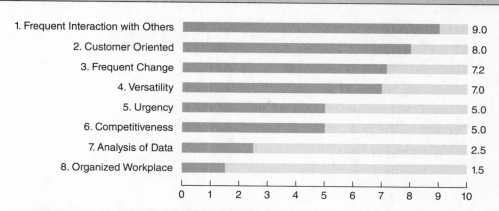

FIGURE 2.4   Mary's DISC Hierarchy of Behavior
Source: Copyright © 2012 Target Training International, Ltd. Used with permission.

The DISC measures Mary's natural and adapted behaviors. Here is what the DISC tells us about Mary:

- Her highest score is in the influencing area. This means that she believes in creating results through influencing people's behavior. This is done through coaching, motivating, and inspiring people. The focus of a high influence leader is to develop a team of people that help each other succeed.
- Her second high area is the dominant area. This means that she has a high degree of urgency in getting results and solving problems. She will see a problem and pull people together to clarify roles and develop actions to get the result quickly.
- She has a low score in the steadiness area. This means that she wants change to happen quickly. The pace of change and actions would be faster than in most educational institutions.
- Her lowest score is on compliance. Compliance behaviors include filling out state and federal forms, checking to make sure people are doing things right, and following the rules. Mary spends very little time on these activities.

Mary's behaviors do not change very much between her natural way of working and how she spends her day as a principal in her school. The fact that there is very little change in her behavior matches other successful leaders who have completed the leadership inventories for this text. Mary's DISC results work in accordance with her MBTI results.

Mary and the Values Inventory

The Values inventory is the last piece of the puzzle. Mary's Values inventory bar chart appears in Figure 2.5. Her high score on the social scale shows her passion for children, and her high score on the individualistic scale demonstrates her desire to be a leader and create change. Her desire for power relates directly to the social score. For her, power is related to making a difference for students and families. Her theoretical score is just below average, indicating that she does have a desire to analyze data to find the root causes for why a child is not learning, but it is not an area in which she spends an inordinate amount of time. Her utilitarian score is low, meaning that she is not motivated by money or return on investment for her time. Like many educational leaders, Mary did not choose her career path because of money. Her return on investment is the success of her students. Her aesthetic score is low, meaning that how things look and harmony are not critical to her motivation. She places little focus on the beauty of the school environment. Her choice to display pictures and banners in the school shows

(continued)

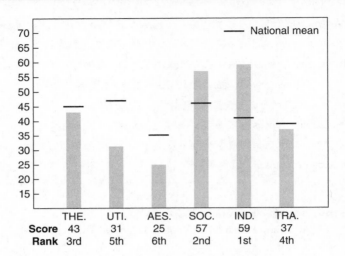

FIGURE 2.5   **Mary's Values Inventory Bar Chart**
Source: Copyright © 2012 Target Training International, Ltd.
Used with permission.

that she is motivated by her competitive, individualistic leadership style. She also has a relatively high score in the traditional area. This means that Mary has a high value for a strong work ethic. She has trouble relating to people who are not doing their best for kids.

Mary and the Seven Competencies

Mary matches the competencies we have developed from our data on high-performing leaders.

1. *Challenges the status quo.* Mary has resisted breaking her large high school into smaller units even though the research shows that breaking into smaller units is better, based on research 2 times in one sentence research (Toch, 2010). She believes that creating a sense of community is achieved by creating an identity of oneness within the school. Although Mary frequently uses data for planning and determining the success of her school's strategies, she does not dwell on data analysis. Mary does not ask her teachers to teach to the standardized tests.

2. *Builds trust through clear communications and expectations.* Mary is very clear in her communications and expectations. She is focused on every student's success and motivates her faculty to view each student as their customer. Her expectations are clear that everyone must put forth his or her best effort and that there are no excuses for failure. However, she does not blame people when failures occur. She supports her staff to do a better job and accepts her responsibility for improving the school's efforts.

3. *Creates a commonly owned plan for success.* Mary has a plan and everyone in the school knows, understands, and follows the plan. The staff participated in the development of the plan and it is based on the needs and goals of the school system and the school.

4. *Focuses on team over self.* Mary is the ultimate team player. Although she has a strong ego and those who do not know her might think she is a self-promoter, this is not actually true. She makes everyone around her better and gives them the credit for the success. She would like to help the other schools in the district succeed, but the other principals are often jealous of her success and do not want her help. This is a team development issue for the school system that she would gladly welcome as a challenge.

5. *Has a high sense of urgency for change and sustainable results in improving student achievement.* Her sense of urgency is her greatest strength. She will not tolerate one child getting a poor education and not succeeding. Her positive energy regarding success is infectious and builds a spirit of success that is unmatched. Her school's test scores keep rising, whereas the other schools in the district have not been successful in raising test scores.

6. *Commits to continuous improvement for self.* Mary is always open and thirsty for learning and personal and professional development. She completed the inventories immediately and was open to learn about her strengths and weaknesses. With all her success, she could easily adopt a stance that she cannot learn from many people. Instead, she is open to learning from other educators and people from the private sector.

7. *Builds external networks and partnerships.* Whereas most educators are being told to focus within their schools and a school system to improve student achievement, Mary is the gold standard for building networks and partnerships. She has an amazing network of resources nationally and travels frequently to spread the word to other leaders on what she has learned to help students achieve. Her school improves every year despite her travel schedule. This demonstrates her development of a culture of success and a team that can carry her vision every day to every student.

Action Plan for Improvement

Although Mary is very successful as a principal in every area of measurement, there are still areas in which she can improve. She is always looking for new ideas and partnerships to improve her school. Mary does not have a desire to be a central administrator or superintendent. She enjoys making a direct impact on students' lives. She is interested in the leadership inventories because they provide feedback about her leadership. She wants to see how other leaders who are successful are rated in each area of the inventories. This data helps her reflect on her style to determine where she could improve.

Her action plan involves spending more time coaching people in her school to improve their impact on students. She will be working on more formal team building efforts to draw more initiative from her staff. She does realize that her style can be intimidating to others, and that she needs to find methods to tone down some of her statements to help others learn at their pace. Her action plan will be to work with colleagues on supporting their ideas to help them meet the goals for the school. Many people in her district are jealous of all the attention she and the school get from high-level state officials. Although Mary is not concerned about others' opinions, she does need to put more effort into helping them achieve for the good of all the students in her district.

The Final Story

How does Mary get permission from the superintendent to not just follow the rules and spend her time on compliance activities? Her superintendent knows that her results tell the story, and interfering with her approach could be detrimental to success. Her success is also the superintendent's success, and he knows and supports her efforts.

Mary speaks to educational leaders around the country on how to turn an underperforming school around, even in an urban district in which the population is of low socioeconomic status. She speaks about forming teams of teachers to assist students in learning based on clear data analysis of test scores. People who try to duplicate her activities learn some of her approaches. Many improve their situations but most have minimal results.

Why is this? The answer is that we need leaders with Mary's profile to turn schools around. We cannot change someone's profile, but we can help leaders develop teams to support them. People like Mary have the

(continued)

CASE STUDY *(continued)*

instincts to be successful. However, true to her style, they always want help and are open to learning. They have a built-in desire to improve every day.

Can leaders with different profiles get the same results? Yes, they can, but the speed of change will be slower. In the following chapters, case studies describing leaders with other styles who have achieved success will be discussed. However, Mary's style is consistent with other high-performing leaders we have outlined in this book. Mary is the ultimate example that it is not enough to be an instructional leader who focuses internally on student achievement and spends most of her time in classrooms holding her teachers accountable. Mary understands best practices in instruction and assessment, but also is a high-performing leader who builds capacity for leadership to occur at the teacher level. She knows that her role is broader than instruction and that her ability to build and use external networks and demonstrate the competencies of a true organizational leader will result in continuous improvement in student achievement. She has the courage and commitment to stay in her school through good and bad times and not blame others for failure. She could become a superintendent anywhere in this country. However, she stays committed to her school, faculty, and the students in her community.

Reflective Questions

Answering these questions will help you begin to apply what was discussed in the chapter and the case study. This will allow you to begin to see what it takes to be a high-performing leader.

1. How would you rate Mary on a scale of 1 to 7 (7 would be the highest) on each leadership competency?
2. What are Mary's areas of strength as a leader? How do you know they are strengths? How can you learn from Mary's profile?
3. Reflecting on your leadership style, how much time do you spend leading versus doing?
4. Who is on your leadership team and what are their styles of problem solving?
5. How do you believe you can adjust your leadership style to delegate more to your team and decrease your time on compliance tasks?
6. What are the tasks that need to be completed and how can you match them to people's individual styles?
7. How could technology be used more to decrease the time spent on details and compliance tasks?
8. How would you begin to develop a high-performing team?
9. If you had more time for leadership, what would you do first?

3

Who Are You As a Leader?

Appearances Aren't Always the Real Story

I t may appear that a school or a district is doing everything it is supposed to do, but it still isn't successful. School leaders are being told to focus on instructional leadership and narrow their initiatives to implement the programs that the school board, public, federal government, and state believe will get results. In the Obama administration's Race to the Top initiative, school leaders were being told that teachers must be evaluated with stronger, more airtight forms and processes to weed out the poor teachers. President Obama clearly stated, "I've got to be honest; we've got to do a better job of moving bad teachers out of the classroom" (Obama, 2009). The public believes that teachers need to understand that they must perform better and dramatically improve their students' results on standardized tests. The media often reports that we are losing ground to other countries in academic achievement. Superintendents are being told by state and federal governments to focus internally on improving student achievement by getting out to schools every day to observe that the key initiatives that are being recommended are being implemented with rigor (Guggenheim, 2010).

The secret is that if you do everything you are told to be a success, it might work initially but could unravel very quickly. The best instructional programs cannot be sustained if the principals are autocratic leaders who do not know how to develop a collaborative team culture in their schools to support teachers' collegiality. If the principal is directing the teachers to implement a new instructional program and they are just complying because they have no choice, there will inevitably be problems. The teachers will most likely do the minimum in implementing the program. The principal will not have the benefit of the ideas the teachers have on how to adapt the program to meet the needs of their students. The superintendent who is getting out to schools every day could be negligent in developing key relationships with the community or municipal leaders. These relationships will prove critical in gaining support for the superintendent's vision for the school system and the budget to make needed change sustainable. The teacher evaluation process may add more teeth to removing poor teachers. However, the process will not motivate teachers to go the extra mile for their students as they strive to reach their potential. Teachers who are new and developing their skills need time and support to take risks and should be encouraged and supported instead of focusing on their evaluation to improve performance.

BECOMING A SYSTEMIC LEADER

Discreet initiatives such as new teacher evaluation forms or new literacy programs are being implemented in many states around the country. This piecemeal approach to improving student achievement is being labeled as a systemic reform effort. Many leaders at the state and federal levels believe that these initiatives will be integrated and create systemic change. However, the secret they do not know is that the school or district's ability to integrate discreet initiatives is dependent on the leader's skill to connect these efforts to a plan that motivates staff to achieve extraordinary results. Educational reform will work if the leader knows how to think systemically and can build a culture of teamwork in the school to sustain positive change. The implementation of very sound initiatives can appear to be the key to success, but if implemented in a nonintegrated manner they will be destined to fail. An example of this occurred a year ago in a suburban district. In an effort to communicate more effectively with parents, the school committee and the superintendent instituted a new policy and practice for the district. Teachers would provide their e-mail address for the parents to ask questions, with the expectation that the teachers were to respond as quickly as possible. The community is known for parents who feel entitled to attention from the school. The new e-mail policy, intended to improve relationships between teachers and families, created the opposite effect—teachers appeared less credible to parents and communications became strained instead of effortless. No one had thought about how this communication initiative was to be integrated within the new block scheduling of classes. The block scheduling created longer periods of time for classes. Therefore, the teachers did not have as many occasions to check their e-mail and respond to parents. The parents would e-mail the teacher during a class; when the teacher did not respond immediately, a subsequent call was made to the teacher. The teacher, who was still in class, did not respond. Parents became very frustrated by a lack of response and would then call the principal to complain. This was poor implementation that originated from an initiative that was not tied to other goals and plans for the school.

It will be demonstrated later in this text that most educational leaders are not systemic thinkers. The lack of systemic thinking caused the problem with communication. As new initiatives are being introduced by the school leadership, they are implemented as discreet programs that are not being tied to overall strategies for improvement.

FOCUSING ON INNOVATION IN EDUCATION

Another example of a potential initiative that could be very important to effective change is the focus on innovation. This new focus is a key part of the Race to the Top funding from the federal government. Race to the Top funding rewards the highest performing districts with federal funding to implement innovative programs to improve student achievement (Obama, 2009b). The message being sent from the U.S. Secretary of Education is that it is time to find innovative ways to change education because the standard approaches obviously haven't worked.

Innovation is a term that is creating confusion throughout the country. Innovation is a skill, an attitude, and a perspective that leaders need to possess to be successful in today's society. Innovation is an overall umbrella concept that applies to all aspects of a school or school system. It is not a singular act or a project. Examples of innovation are looking at and evaluating current educational practices and determining whether there is a more efficient way to use resources or a different approach or mentality that must be taken. The idea may be brand new or it might be a different application of a current process. Both can be innovative!

Some people believe that innovation means that every idea must be new and have no history of prior use. Other people are doing the same things they have always done with slight incremental change and calling it innovation. Innovation is becoming another discreet initiative to add on to the list of changes schools must make to be successful. Many educational leaders are not trying to be innovative, but are interested in finding ways to appear innovative to obtain added funding from the federal government. It is critical to show in proposals that the improvement in schools is innovative.

In some states (e.g., Massachusetts, where the Massachusetts Innovation Schools Act of 2008 was designed to provide a pathway for schools and districts to develop and implement innovative practices) "innovation schools" are being formed to indicate that new ideas are the key to success. In many cases, however, the people involved have not spent time defining innovation. They are putting a label on their work to help obtain funding and to look like they are more unique than other efforts to change education. The real work is to define innovation and to train and support leaders in the innovation process. It would be helpful for educational leaders to view innovative practices in other sectors and to form alliances with innovative educators and leaders from other areas. The motivation is often to obtain new money, not to commit to the importance of innovation to improve results.

Technology is a great resource for innovation. Leaders who step back from their daily processes and bring in a technology application to dramatically change an aspect of the learning process are being innovative. Innovation is not a new initiative. There is a long history in education of great new programs that were supposed to make a major impact on student achievement. These programs started out with a lot of promise for new results. However, many of these programs did not make the impact they were touted to accomplish. Instead, they tended to lose support and funding and finally died. For example, school districts are trying to reduce costs to maintain their current programs during these very challenging economic times. A strong leader looks at key expense areas and determines whether there are innovative ways of getting results that could reduce costs. An example of a question being addressed in every district involves whether special education can change dramatically and reduce costs and still meet the needs of the students (Cromwell, 1997).

Another innovation that some districts are considering is switching from using textbooks to e-readers. This innovation cannot be implemented successfully if it is a separate initiative. The leader must think systemically and use a variety of skills to implement this change effectively. The leader must be courageous in order to change from the standard usage of printed textbooks. The leader must be able to motivate teachers to change teaching practices and increase their use of technology. There are many people that will say that print books are key and cannot be replaced. The technology will be criticized as being inadequate in creating the love for reading that many educators, parents, and community members believed was crucial for their own learning (Boss, 2008). The leader must be able to listen to concerns and be persuasive in challenging people to try this new technology. Some people will be supportive if it saves money. Others will not care about the money and will be fearful about technology taking over and ruining the feeling of curling up with a good book that they experienced when they were young. The leader must convince their team members to support this change and alleviate the fears and concerns of the many critics they will encounter.

A superintendent in Massachusetts recently attempted to rethink special education to find cost cutting opportunities. In his analysis, he reflected on how special education began and realized that it was set up on a premise that does not fit today's society. He stated that the premise of special education is that we need specialists to educate students with specific disabilities. The premise of needing specialists led to removing students from the classroom for their education. However, the process of removing students from the classroom to work with specialists has created major problems for funding and for providing the most effective educational opportunities for all students. Based on his reflection and analysis, this superintendent decided that the best way to improve special education was to develop teams of regular education teachers, specialists, and special education teachers. He has also asked his staff to determine what approaches are most effective in improving achievement in their students, rather than assuming that everyone was providing the best possible services. By becoming outcome oriented and not assuming that the best possible services are already being provided by his dedicated staff, he has been able to streamline the process for special education. This approach has reduced costs and the team approach has improved student achievement. This superintendent thought systemically and broadened the initial focus from cost saving to improving the services for special education students. He was able to think in an innovative and reflective way, which resulted in both short- and long-term results. He could have just reduced costs and appeared successful, but that would have been insufficient to produce sustainable results.

PRACTICING HIGH-PERFORMANCE LEADERSHIP

In order to sustain improvements in student achievement, leaders must develop the leadership capacity in the school or school system. If a school has a strong base of leadership in its teachers, and they are able to work in a team environment, their ability to integrate strategies for improvement into the school culture is much greater than just counting on one principal. If all the teachers and support staff are open to new ideas, are supportive of the development and the success of their colleagues, and are committed to continuous improvement, the school will improve and become a sustainable learning community. In order to create a true learning community, leaders need to practice the characteristics of high performance to obtain the support of the team. The following are the author's 12 principles of high performance that were developed from consultation with over 700 education, corporate, government, and nonprofit clients. These principles can guide the leader's systemic change effort.

1. *Embrace conflict.* Increase your skills and comfort in dealing with conflict. Conflict can be a gateway to true innovation.
2. *Communicate in an open, honest, and direct manner.* Always go directly to a person with your concerns. Gossip behind the scenes and secrets can kill an organization.
3. *Overcommunicate.* Make sure your message is heard. Don't assume that once you have sent an e-mail, it is out of your hands. Make sure your message is heard and understood.
4. *Don't use confidentiality as a shield.* Confidentiality is about personal issues. Organizational issues can be harmful if they are kept confidential.
5. *Use the MBTI, DISC, and Values inventories as tools for communication and results.* Personal and team assessment data are very helpful in communication and in dealing with conflict.
6. *Deal with concerns immediately.* Catch problems early, before they blow up and cause severe damage.
7. *Focus on solving problems analytically, not personally.* Objectivity is essential in solving organizational problems. Some people have difficulty removing the personal element from the discussion.
8. *Put yourself in the other person's shoes.* Think about the other person's perspective before you criticize him or her.
9. *Value your team first, and your specialty or function second.* High performance is about looking at the whole school system and school instead of advocating for your own interests.
10. *Remember, you are the problem.* You must take personal responsibility for a problem before you look at others.
11. *Everyone is a leader and a follower.* Support others and do not concern yourself with always being out in front.
12. *Assume positive intent.* People usually are trying to do their best and you need to begin with the assumption of positive intent rather than accusing people of being negative.

Leaders should work with their teams to review these 12 high-performance principles and decide which ones apply to a particular challenge. The leader would then use the appropriate principles with the team to devise a sound strategy for success. For example, embracing conflict and maintaining open, honest, and direct communication are two principles that would allow critical comments to be stated and taken seriously without any repercussions from the team or the leader. The overcommunication principle is helpful because it will guide the communication strategy to ensure that everyone impacted by the change is heard and that clear understanding is achieved. Although other principles will also apply, it is critical that number 12 (assume positive intent) is used. People can be very critical of an initiative you present as a leader. It is important that you realize that they have positive intent. They care about the students' values and may value a particular tradition. The critics need to be recognized for their positive intent even if they are against your change. It is through this acknowledgment that true compromise and support can be achieved.

THE CONTINUOUS IMPROVEMENT PROCESS

A school district could look good to the outside public if it has many technology programs or several ways to cut costs in education. However, if this technology is not tied into a plan for improving instructional practice or the cost cutting efforts are simplistic and short term, they could be harmful to the overall success of the school system. Successful leaders have the skills and commitment to go beyond the minimum that is required to look good. They think and act in a strategic manner and develop plans to be successful for both the present and the future. Leaders like Mary, the case study in Chapter 2, do not respond to every initiative or new innovation that they are being told will produce results. Mary's profile and actions are systemic, courageous, and motivating. Mary always has an integrated plan for implementation that may include new ideas or an innovation that is being implemented in another school. Mary has created a culture of success in her school through the development of teams of teachers focused on common goals. This approach allowed key initiatives to be implemented in a comprehensive way and have an impact on all aspects of her school culture.

Successful leaders create a positive team culture, cultivate their staff, think short and long term, and always look for continuous improvement. The continuous improvement process requires asking questions every day and often leads to finding innovative approaches to solve lingering problems or improve results. Leaders focusing on continuous improvement regularly ask themselves this question: How can I change what I do today to improve results tomorrow? This questioning process energizes the successful leader to try new ideas and look for examples of success from other colleagues. The continuous improvement leader energizes the leadership team to ask the same questions about their work and to use this continuous improvement attitude with their staff. Leaders must be learners to create a high-performance team. As stated by Frank Siccone (2012), "Your role is to be 'learner in chief' so that you are demonstrating by example that the learning process can be as challenging as it is exhilarating. By increasing your knowledge, setting professional goals, practicing new skills, expanding beyond your comfort zone, and gaining greater confidence in your capacity to be an effective leader, you have the power to inspire the rest of the school community to learn to love learning" (p. 2).

A leader that helps establish a positive environment for learning and teamwork can begin to develop a group of leaders who can provide direction for a school or school system. A team that has trust can begin to admit mistakes and talk about challenges that are impeding progress on goals. This open and honest dialog can allow a team to set goals for the school that are challenging and necessary to achieve results.

The leader can then work with the team to clarify the current condition in the school and the barriers to change. The team can begin to talk honestly about what is blocking change and can feel comfortable admitting areas in which members' own styles and behaviors could be barriers. Now true and substantive strategies for change can be developed and monitored for success. Once a team can honestly realize what it needs to do to succeed and who can help in the journey, the team is well on its way to being a high-performance team.

This HPT can even meet without the principal because its members are committed to change and improvement and are able to understand the direction that is needed for the school. This team can begin to hold each other accountable and begin to build accountability for success within the school. That accountability becomes more about motivation and pride and less about fear and consequences.

A true HPT is able to function openly and honestly in meetings and every day in its regular work. People become self-directed to meeting goals without someone checking in on their progress. The team members are committed to their own learning and are able to ask for help and training to improve their skills. They know that everyone is important in the team and they want each person to be successful. They see that they must challenge all assumptions to be the best for their students. The leader and each team member continuously challenge the status quo to make needed change.

HOW YOUR LEADERSHIP PROFILE AFFECTS YOUR TEAM

A leader who has a profile that is more focused on maintaining the status quo tends to defend current practices and often struggles with the concept of continuous improvement. This profile is usually the ISTJ or ESTJ in the Myers Briggs or the steadiness and compliance person in the DISC. These profiles are usually focused on maintaining today's conditions in education (Berens & Isachsen, 1988). They are often frustrated by new ideas and concepts that seem to be unrealistic based on a lack of financial resources or time to effectively implement change.

The steadiness and compliance profile is commonplace in education, which creates friction with leaders who are trying to create a sense of urgency for change. These same educators are often overwhelmed by constant change, and the prospect of continuous improvement is viewed as lack of recognition that people are already working too hard and cannot do one more thing at a time. Creating a culture in a school or school system that is dedicated to continuous improvement may produce more results than any initiative being touted for success. Strong leaders must help their leadership teams and their staff to realize that continuous improvement will not add to their plate and is not a criticism of their current or past practices. This requires commitment from the leaders to establish blame-free, team-oriented environments in which it is okay to make mistakes. Leaders need to have confidence in themselves and their teams that each mistake can be used as an opportunity to learn. This requires full support by the school board and the superintendent. One cannot assume that people will support a change if they are not part of the planning. Lack of involvement prevents support because key groups do not understand or appreciate the challenges and the risks involved for effective implementation. Parents, the media, and the one critical member of the school board will always find the one mistake that can be used to criticize a leader and the staff. It is paramount that the leadership stays strong and confident in their commitment to learning from mistakes. It is advisable to tell the critics that mistakes, when used as a vehicle to learn, often produce the greatest innovations. Mistakes can become a great source for learning and even for innovation and change.

Educators cannot make mistakes with kids' lives. The status quo leader shuts down any possibility of learning through his or her negative reactions to examples from other sectors. Leaders begin by asking questions instead of making judgments. How can I create a blame-free environment in my school or school system? This question energizes strong leaders to be creative in improving their approaches to gain results. As Warren Bennis, a well-known author in organizational development, states: "Successful executives are great askers" (1985, p. 96).

TEACHER EVALUATION: WILL IT IMPROVE STUDENT OUTCOMES?

As mentioned previously, another example of challenging our assumptions relates to the current movement in education to produce stronger teacher evaluation forms and processes. The status quo leader stays the course of implementing the new evaluation processes. The successful leader realizes that the teacher evaluation process could increase the teachers' fears of being blamed and decrease the teachers' abilities to support the concept of continuous improvement. The successful leader then asks another question: How can I motivate teachers to want to improve and still implement a teacher evaluation process to remove poor performers? This question leads to a second question: How can I hire the best teachers that will make the evaluation process a secondary issue for success?

Southwest Airlines is a very successful organization by most standards. The company is a leader in the airline industry in customer service and financial results, and it is recognized as a great place for employees to work. If the CEO or any manager at Southwest were interviewed and asked what the key to his or her success were, what do you believe that person would say? He or she certainly would not list the staff evaluation process and ability to weed out poor performers. Southwest undoubtedly has a good staff evaluation process. However, their focus is on hiring the best people and motivating them to perform at the highest level (Taylor, 2011). The managers create a culture of positive success, not a top-down, punitive process to remove poor performers. This more strategic and comprehensive approach to success is what makes Southwest a leader in the airline industry. This is also applicable in education.

Skeptics are probably questioning the relevance of the example because Southwest can remove poor performers easier than educational leaders can in this union-based and litigious environment in education. Remember that Mary, the high-performing leader studied in Chapter 2, only removed one teacher in her change process in a very large urban high school. Strong leaders put their effort into hiring the best people, cultivating their staff, and providing clarity on direction for success. This approach is clear to the poor performers. They get the message that they must change or leave. Mary did not punish the resistant people. She continuously provided resources to help them improve. They were not told to leave, but they also could not hide and ignore the direction set by the principal for success.

CONTINUOUS IMPROVEMENT: A KEY TO HIGH PERFORMANCE

High-performing leaders never accept success as the end of their process. They always try to improve and look at what challenge is around the corner. A very successful math teacher in a major urban district recently stated that his key to success was to recognize that students come to school bored with very little excitement to learn. This teacher embraces the continuous improvement approach and comes in every day and thinks about how he can be a better teacher that day than he was the day before, and how he can make math exciting for his students. This teacher pays very little attention to the standardized tests and the initiatives that the district tells him are the key to success. Instead, he focuses on learning, discipline, engagement, and continuous improvement. This teacher does not focus on complying with the mandates for successful change. The results of the students in his classes are remarkable! His students are performing higher than most students throughout the state. His success is recognized in his district, and he is continually asked to train and mentor new teachers and show how he became so successful. In a recent interview, he talked about some of his noncompliant and innovative practices. He stated that he focuses on learning and not just teaching, and he gives group quizzes and makes the homework due right before the test. He believes students need to focus on the learning process. The testing and evaluation process puts too much attention on the teaching and the teacher rather than on the learning. He states that students must learn to work in teams to prepare for the world ahead of them by learning from others not just performing on their own. He has conversations with students about their lives and often shares some of his own experiences in his education. He often tells students that he was not a high-performing student. He joined the military and learned about commitment, discipline, continuous improvement, leadership, and the importance of teams. Now he applies that learning about leadership to his classroom. Although he does not focus on compliance to what he is told to do, he does not ignore the school system initiatives. The initiatives that the district supports are important resources to him as he develops plans for each student to improve their performance. The secret that this math teacher knows that is rarely told is that it is important to focus on the results and impact we want to make, not the variety of inputs or methods that people tell you will make the difference. He is focused on the goals and outcomes, and he is free to create new ways to educate his students that are different from the typical well-established methods of testing and instructional practice.

This math teacher comments further on his meetings with younger new teachers. He states that they are looking for what approach works best and how they can meet the requirements of the myriad of programs for change in the district. They are so overwhelmed and are looking to him to tell them what to do. He instead talks to them about their beliefs and values and how they can have the attitude of continuous improvement. He ends his sessions with new teachers with one question: How could I have done a better job mentoring you today so I can improve for the next time we meet? The teachers continually ask him why he would have to change when he is the example of success. He answers that no one is the example for success. He states that no one can tell you how to succeed. The teachers need to look at who they are and what they believe is the best approach to prepare students for the challenges they will meet. He is committed to making the effort to help his profession improve. He does state, however, that the educational environment is slow to change, and he understands that great leaders and great teachers focus on developing their own plan for success, being self-aware, and committing to teamwork and continuous improvement.

UNDERSTANDING WHO YOU ARE AS A LEADER

If leaders are committed to continuous improvement, they are well on their way to beginning the hard work of understanding who they are. The curiosity involved in looking at new ideas or practices and determining whether they could be helpful in getting results, as well as understanding how one needs to change, is the beginning of the self-awareness process. Educational leaders have to become self-aware and focus on learning how to be better leaders before they can navigate the treacherous waters in education today. If they know who they are, are open to critical feedback, and are committed to continuous improvement, they will be able to stay focused despite all the new methods of teaching or new programs that they are being told are the keys to success. They know they can't do it alone and must develop leadership teams to complement their skills and support their weaknesses. Leaders need to constantly assess their own leadership style and effectiveness using tools similar to the inventories presented in the book and other methods, such as 360 reviews or emotional intelligence assessments.

The 360 review process, which is more commonplace in industry and health care, can be very helpful to a leader. The 360 process involves asking questions about leadership qualities and practices of people above the leader, their colleagues, and their staff. It is important for leaders to understand how staff and colleagues react to their leadership style and behavior. Leaders can spend too much time meeting the needs of their bosses and neglect the needs of their staff. Some leaders focus too much on their school and neglect building relationships with their colleagues. The 360 process provides feedback on how each group responds to your leadership qualities. The data will allow you to develop a plan to meet the needs of all the groups that are important to your success. It is difficult to keep everyone happy all the time. You may be setting high expectations for your staff, which could results in negative comments on your review. Although this may be understandable, the review process will allow you to determine how you can improve your relationship with staff in a manner that does not lower your standards for performance.

The data from the 360 are analyzed and presented as a professional development tool for improvement, not for evaluation. If the data are used for evaluation it could be misleading and not understood in context of the current situation for the leader. The reason for the development focus is that one could receive better ratings from people above than from one's staff. If this happened, there could be a good reason this has occurred based on a particular issue, such as the leader increasing accountability for the staff. The data from the 360 is helpful to the leader when used with a mentor or coach for improvement. The leader could use data from the 360 review or other inventories to discuss with the team how he or she can lead more effectively. This modeling by the leader also can help members of a leadership team be willing to use the same approaches with the staff for their own improvement.

Even the most successful leaders make mistakes and often get caught up in the urgency and accountability involved in implementing discreet initiatives, or they focus too much on complying with state and federal mandates for change. They can become overly focused on wanting to look good to the public and their colleagues. However, since they know who they are and are always open to change, they can catch problems before they become a crisis. They will not accept the appearance of success even if they are used as an example for others. The math teacher mentioned earlier never accepts success or stops his learning process.

A NEW ATTITUDE FOR TODAY'S LEADERS

The math teacher discussed previously was in the military and had a broader view of his role in educating students. He knows that who you are and how you think are key to living and being successful in today's global community. Educational leaders today need to adopt a new attitude to become true global leaders. Although policymakers may focus on internal instruction, leaders' ultimate success will be to embrace the United States' role in being part of a global community. We are living every day with the effects of a global economy and society. Among other things, we need to prepare our students for a world that uses technology to interact with people in other countries as they do with people in their own country.

To lead in today's world we must be outward looking to bring in the myriad of resources that are available to us to educate children. This means being a leader that wakes up every morning with a love of being an educator and of learning new ways to improve and open new doors for student learning.

Global leaders in education need to be continuously networking with leaders in many sectors to learn new practices and form new alliances. Leaders should never close down opportunities to learn and improve their craft of leadership. A superintendent once told the author that she wanted to be in a CEO group with non-educators because their work is to study leadership, not education.

This openness and creativity will rejuvenate education and create positive cultures for sustainable learning. This does not mean that all new ideas need to be pursued. As stated earlier, developing a focused plan for improvement is critical and building a team for leadership and implementation is imperative.

Global leaders are team oriented. They realize that being the expert is an antiquated concept. The leaders must create an environment in which people learn from each other and in which all strengths are recognized and weaknesses are supported for growth.

The global leader spends a balance of time externally and internally. The data on successful leaders gathered for this text indicate that the best leaders in improving test scores do not spend all their time internally. Principals and superintendents who belong to networks for leaders and focus on staff learning and support get the best results.

A recent college student at the University of Texas suggested that his former principal read about the leadership qualities he heard presented in the business school. The principal stated that in education today, the leadership qualities that this presenter was reviewing did not apply. The principal stated that educational leaders have to be focused on their own schools and the curriculum. The student was surprised; he thought the business presenter was motivating, and he thought the ideas would inspire this principal. Instead, the student heard a parochial response from someone he admired.

The 10 characteristics that Bob Johansen presented to the business school at the University of Texas are from his book, *Leaders Make the Future: Ten New Leadership Skills for an Uncertain World*. Although Johansen typically makes presentations in the corporate world, he is working on a project to help education. Although the terminology may sometimes be new and confusing, you are encouraged to seek out authors from outside education to provide new perspectives. By dismissing the ideas presented by a business leader as not relevant, educators miss an opportunity to expand their viewpoints.

Johansen began his speech in Texas by congratulating the faculty at University of Texas for the rigor and relevance of their curriculum. He stated that top traditional business schools were often too theoretical and were teaching to the past. He was recognizing the faculty for being progressive and broad based in their teaching. It is important that leaders in K–12 education have the same broad perspective as the professors of the University of Texas, which has become recognized as one of the highest ranked business and education schools in the country.

Following are Johansen's 10 characteristics and how they could apply to education:

1. *Maker instinct.* Leaders must understand how programs or services operate in order to judge their effectiveness. For example, if leaders really understand how the special education services are provided from a parent's point of view, they will be able to assess needed changes more effectively.

2. *Clarity.* The ability to communicate clearly in confusing times is critical for education. Too often leaders are stating the problems with funding and demands and not clearly presenting their point of view for success to the multiple constituencies they must serve.

3. *Dilemma flipping.* How can education leaders not complain about lack of funding from state and federal sources and use the opportunity to seek out new alternative sources of revenue? The state and federal picture for funding will never be enough and is not worth all the effort leaders place on hoping it will change. A superintendent used this opportunity to obtain a $1 million donation from an individual who was concerned that the focus on STEM (science, technology, engineering, and mathematics) would not receive enough funding for students in the community.

4. *Immersive learning ability.* How can educational leaders immerse themselves into the world of social networks to fully understand how they could be used to advance their goals? Instead of fearing them and seeing the downsides, such as lack of privacy and control issues, it is important to really understand this new power of building networks for positive action.

5. *Constructive depolarizing.* The ability of leaders to facilitate diverse parties within the school or school system and in the community to achieve common goals is a critical skill now and for the future.

Too many educational leaders get caught up in control issues and wanting to move their agenda ahead without having the skills or building support from outside groups that tend to polarize issues.

6. *Bioempathy.* The skill and commitment to engage in green activities is negated by many educators as being too futuristic. It seems too costly to meet environmental goals that could cost more than current budgets allow. However, there are more opportunities for grant support and public acclaim for meeting environmental goals. The commitment to this effort can bring in new partners to support educational efforts in funding and instructional support.

7. *Quiet transparency.* The ability to be open about the budget and issues within a school system is very important to increase credibility in the eyes of the parents and the community. Leaders do not have to be too self-promoting to let people into the world of how education works. The leaders who are more transparent are gaining in credibility in a world that tends to lack trust in its public officials.

8. *Rapid prototyping.* Having a high sense of urgency means trying to move initiatives ahead faster and taking more risks. Learning how to build parents or school board members into this process of understanding and sharing in responsibility for risks will pay off in increasing creativity and innovation and getting faster results. The current world of caution prevents this rapid prototyping from occurring.

9. *Smart mob organizing.* This competency involves building networks of support using media, social networking, and community organizing to advance goals. This does occur in some school systems, namely in municipal meetings when parents and students show up to prevent budget cuts. However, this organizing can be more useful and involve more people if the leader understands how to build brand support as a regular activity for goal completion.

10. *Commons creating.* This is tough one for education. This competency involves forming public and private partnerships to meet common goals. Education is very reluctant to form partnerships with the private sector in industry and with charter schools. The fear of competition creates isolation. Learning how to build partnerships with competitors and people educators are currently uncomfortable dealing with will open up new sources of revenue and support and increase learning opportunities for education and the private sector.

It is not the position of this author that Johansen's characteristics are the right answer. Some may apply better than others. However, being open to learning from someone who is presenting a new idea or concept might be of benefit to your learning. Listen, don't criticize, and take what is valuable to help you lead in today's world.

There are many educational resources that provide lists of skills and competencies for educational leaders. There have also been several efforts to provide national standards for leaders in education, such as those created by ISLLC (Interstate School Leaders Licensure Consortium). Although these have great merit and value, they often do not include a review of leadership perspectives from outside education. Educators need to be leaders in their communities and on a global stage and must be able to speak the language of leadership that is part of the lexicon of other sectors.

APPEARANCES ARE OFTEN MISLEADING

The case study in this chapter is about a superintendent who has done everything imaginable to be successful. She has been able to change her district to a culture of excellence, and from the outside everything is perfect. Her story will illustrate the point of this chapter that what you see isn't always what it appears to be. This superintendent has the profile for success that we are promoting (ENTJ, high influence and dominance, and low steadiness and compliance). She appears to be meeting all the compliance standards that are required to be successful.

She has hired the best people through the normal school system hiring process. The school system is financially managed very well, and there is no apparent conflict within the school system or with the community. The board supports the superintendent and the senior leadership team. The school system has training programs to build future leaders. The standardized test scores for students are high and improving. People want to work in the school district and it always attracts a large pool of applicants for key positions. The district is rarely cited for problems on compliance issues by its state department of education.

CASE STUDY

KATHY

Overview

Kathy is the superintendent in a fast-growing suburban district in the southwest. It is 20 minutes from a major metropolitan city and the district has 30,000 students. She is a charismatic leader who engages everyone she meets in a manner that makes people want to be a part of her story of success. She is confident (but not at all arrogant), energetic, listens well, thinks systemically, and uses every opportunity to learn from whomever she meets. When you meet her, you believe that you are the only one she wants to talk to and that she values everything you are saying. She focused on hiring the best and has formed a formidable team of central administrators and principals in the schools. She also has added a major focus on customer service, and her high level of organizational skills has served as a model for everyone.

She is very driven and expects more than 100% from herself and her staff. She is creative and entrepreneurial. She moves quickly and is very focused on results. The regulations, constraints, and limitations are merely minor obstacles as she moves quickly to improve student achievement for all students. She finished second in the superintendent of the year voting, which seems impossible when you meet her. How could anyone get more votes? On first meeting her to review the results of her leadership inventories, she takes out a notebook and immediately asks what she can do to be a better leader. As the inventories are explained, she gives specific examples to support the critical feedback and looks determined to deal directly with these areas for improvement. Kathy is a master at building relationships and is very self-aware and determined to make her system the best. She shows humility and is very modest about her accomplishments and always gives credit to others.

Her attitude is only about success and is contagious to all who meet her. She sees all of today's challenges as opportunities and talks about today's educational environment as an exciting time. Her school board, which has been fractured in the past, is completely behind her and is focused on the big picture and the development of policies to support the district's success. The micromanagement and politics are still there, but Kathy navigates these waters with respect and grace.

She has formed many partnerships and built alliances with organizations in her community and outside her district. One key initiative that has improved test scores is a comprehensive instructional leadership program for principals. This program has been led by one of her central leaders. She believes that the instructional leadership program will produce leaders who can focus on improving student achievement. She also believes that the leaders will be open to learning new ideas for improvement and will fully integrate all aspects of the school system into their leadership approach.

Kathy believes that teams are responsible for success and that leadership is about building a spirit of confidence and positive attitude that engages staff in the importance of their work in educating all students. She believes that everyone on the team must work together and that all functions must be interdependent to get sustainable results.

If one area of the school system fails, all other areas must move resources to help that function or the entire system fails. She does not support a silo approach in which each area is an island and only cares about its own success. The whole is greater than the sum of the parts is a core belief. She believes that administrators cannot exist on their own and must be leaders in the integration of the work across the system to achieve maximum results.

Kathy's district has enjoyed a lot of growth and the finances have provided a distinct advantage. However, there are signs that this resource base is eroding. Kathy will not wait and is looking at a number of entrepreneurial initiatives to bring in alternative sources of revenue. She looks at the assets of the school system and the community and is determining a way to leverage her success to help other school systems and bring in new resources.

Kathy is always strategic and does not get bogged down in the tyranny of the task. She delegates very well to her capable administrators. She oversees all issues in the system without delving into specific issues unless there is a concern. Kathy believes that her central leadership team is thinking systemically and not just concerned about their personal success.

The next challenge is to engage strong, individually driven, successful leaders in a new activity of team building and capacity building. This will be critical for their success and will be essential for their individual functions and capacity for sustainability. Kathy has begun the team building process and has used the leadership inventories for herself to determine how she must adjust her leadership style. She is also committing her team to the same process for team members' development.

As Jim Collins states in his book *Good to Great* (2001), "Success is the enemy." Organizations and leaders who believe that their success can be maintained as times change often move quickly from the top to the bottom. Leaders who realize that they must always read the signs of change internally and externally and adjust their style will be able to manage change and transitions (Collins, 2001).

Kathy and the MBTI

Kathy is an ENTJ. Her style is almost exactly the same as Mary, the principal in the Chapter 2 case study. She is externally driven and spends a significant amount of time in the schools and the community communicating her message to each constituent group. Kathy is highly intuitive, which means she is strategically oriented. She maintains her focus on vision, mission, and goals and not on day-to-day transactional issues.

Kathy is a thinking person. Her score is not that high, so although she is objective, analytical, and does not often take things personally, she is sensitive to people's issues during change. The thinking style allows her to determine how to change without worrying too much about what people will think of her. She is more focused on what she has to change and whether it will be effective.

Kathy's judging style means she is very focused on results and follows plans to execution. This has worked very well for her up to now because she is steadfast on executing her plans for improving student achievement. She has also been able to support her senior staff to stay on course as they get pulled in new directions.

The major issue Kathy must change involves her judging style. She must change her approach to leadership, which can be difficult for her when the current approach is working. However, her intuitive style and her extrovert style are providing new information that she must consider. Kathy has reached out, in her true external style, to resources that are credible and which have counseled her that her success is very vulnerable in the long term. She is strategic and looks at the long-term success and must adjust her style to sustain the success that has been built over time.

Kathy's MBTI E/I and S/I scores are shown Figure 3.1. Her extrovert score is clear and accounts for her ability to communicate to multiple constituencies. Her intuitive score is also very clear, which explains her style of developing a vision for her district and raising strategic issues for her team on issues such as instructional goals and community involvement.

(continued)

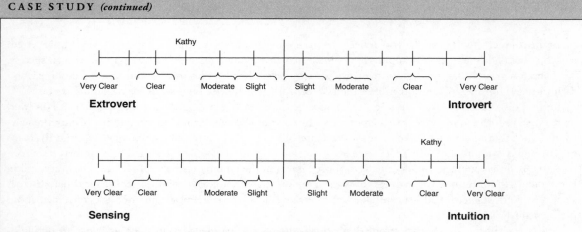

FIGURE 3.1   **Kathy's Scores on the Extrovert/Introvert Scale and Sensing/Intuitive Scale**

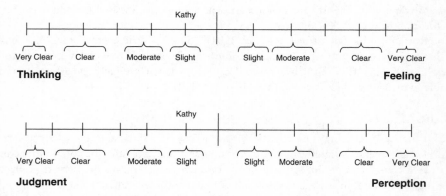

FIGURE 3.2   **Kathy's Scores on the Thinking/Feeling Scale and the Judging/Perceiving Scale**

Kathy's T/F and J/P scores are shown in Figure 3.2. She is a slight thinker, which means that she is objective and analytical and tends to not take issues personally. She is slightly judging, which accounts for her focus on results and outcomes. The judging score is slight, which allows her to be open to change if necessary to improve student achievement.

The MBTI results for Kathy's leadership team provide more data that explain both the challenges ahead for the team and how they can improve. On the introvert and extrovert scale, the team is balanced (see Figure 3.3). A high-performance team should have people at the extremes on each axis and an even distribution of profiles on the grid. The introvert and extrovert grids are ideal for a high-performance team. If the team works interdependently, there are extroverts that will move issues quickly and introverts to raise concerns about priorities and quality.

The sensing and intuitive scale also has relatively good balance (also shown in Figure 3.3). The only concern is that the superintendent is one of only two members that have a style that is strategic and would think from a systemic point of view. As noted earlier, the most successful leaders think systemically. The fact that the leaders are more on the sensing side adds to the overall problem of being silo oriented. Sensing people are focused on short-term results and usually tend to concentrate on their department rather than the entire school system.

CASE STUDY *(continued)*

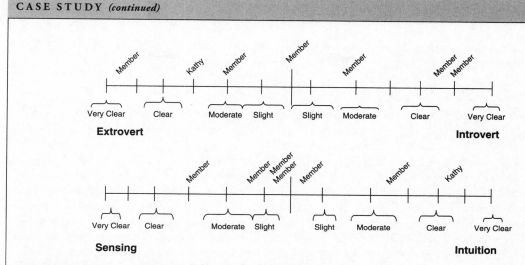

FIGURE 3.3   The E/I and S/N Scores for Kathy's Leadership Team

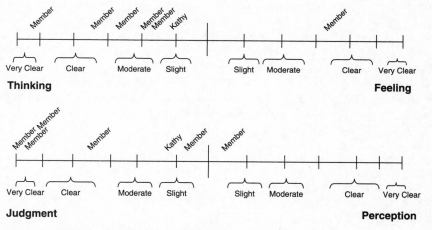

FIGURE 3.4   The T/F and J/P Scores for Kathy's Leadership Team

The entire team is on the thinking side of the scale (see Figure 3.4). This indicates that the team members are very objective in their thinking and problem solving. The only feeling-style person is the executive secretary. This is positive due to the importance of looking at data objectively and making difficult decisions for the district. However, the lack of the feeling style is an indication that the team members would not work on improving their relationships. This also presents a challenge around conflict that could be difficult because each person may tell the others to stay out of his or her work.

Finally, most of the team is on the judging side (also shown in Figure 3.4). This makes the team very results oriented. The only concern is that people are results oriented for just their department. The judging style allows them to focus on implementation. However, the team is not open to change, which makes the challenge to

(continued)

build the team a major challenge. The fact that the team members have been successful makes it more difficult to convince them to be open to change.

Kathy and the DISC

Now let's look at Kathy's DISC scores and see what they tell us about her need to change and how she can do this effectively (see Figure 3.5). Her natural high scores are in the influence and the dominant areas. However, in her adapted style, she has become more dominant than influence oriented. Kathy's adapted style shows the beginnings of her problem with her team. Her adapted dominant score has increased and her influence score has decreased more than 25 points. This indicates that her current behavior is to force more urgency and that she is potentially moving her plan ahead without getting the full support of her team. Her steadiness score has decreased, meaning that she is moving even faster than normal. Her compliance in the adapted chart, while still low, shows that she is exhibiting some concern over whether what she wants is being done correctly by her standards. This means she is driving some results more directly due to what she sees as reluctance and resistance from some of her senior managers. Because she has already developed the relationships internally and externally, she has now become more focused on tasks and results. This behavior is providing some warning signs that need to be reviewed.

Her behavior is showing that she is losing her confidence in her team to drive results and believes she must become directly involved. This is beginning to create a conflict between her and her team. Remember, she has hired strong successful leaders who are more silo oriented. Now she is becoming more directly involved in driving results with a high sense of urgency. This is beginning to cause a problem for her team. Team members wonder why she is suggesting new approaches and why she is suddenly becoming involved in their work. They are concerned that she now questions their ability to get the job done.

Kathy's own success has set her up for a new problem. She has created a well-oiled machine in terms of getting results under the current conditions of the school system. However, now she realizes this will not be sustainable as times change. How does she get her team to buy into change when the team is succeeding and the members are working so hard individually?

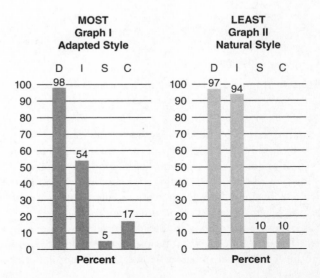

FIGURE 3.5 Kathy's DISC Bar Chart *Source:* Copyright © 2012 Target Training International, Ltd. Used with permission.

CASE STUDY *(continued)*

Kathy must change her approach to building her team. Her current approach was to focus on the work, express support for her team, and let them have a lot of latitude on the work in their functional area. She would jump into situations when she thought they were missing some key issue that related to political or other system-wide issues. The change of style would mean going back to her influence side in the DISC and lowering her dominant behavior. Her team must buy into this approach. However, it won't be easy. It will take some time to turn them around and realize they need each other and the superintendent's new approach to sustain results. They must change their approach from a focused implementation of tasks to leading people and building capacity to get sustainable results.

Kathy is also low on steadiness and compliance. This focus on quick change is both an advantage and a disadvantage for the need to change. She will want change quickly and will need to be more patient. She will tend to pay less attention to what her team is currently doing and will want to look at new behaviors too quickly.

The profile of Kathy's team shows that the members are relatively dominant, which means they also have a high sense of urgency. However, they are all very compliant. The ability of Kathy to delegate and put her time into strategic issues has been a great success but does have a cost. Her team has assumed the compliant work of making sure all regulations and requirements are being followed, and team members' personal time is put into checking that all work is being done right. Now her team is facing burnout.

Kathy did not realize that her style would create a silo-oriented team that is doing too much compliant work themselves. Her top leaders have not built high-performance teams and have not distributed leadership the way she did with her team.

Now her team believes there is no time to change and build a new team in each of their areas. Team members believe they must stay the course to maintain success. Kathy must be determined and patient to help her team realize and embrace change individually and collectively to ensure long-term success.

Kathy must use her influence behavior on her own team to engage them in this new work of building a high-performance team for the senior level and in each of their departments. This will take some time and focus for Kathy and her team. She can use the team members that understand and are committed to this work to influence the others. However, she is concerned about one major risk. If she pushes some of her team members to change course and they continue to resist, does she become more dominant and direct them to embrace this new team approach?

She fears that her highest performers, who are so busy, stressed, and driven, would comply and lose their motivation, resist, and then quit. She now has a dilemma. She could just stay her current course and rely on the fact that everything looks fine from the outside. However, she knows that their success could unravel over time. If she left, no one would blame her. She could leave with a clear conscience and it would be the next superintendent's problem to rebuild the system.

Kathy's DISC Hierarchy of Behavior

Kathy's DISC behavioral hierarchy (see Figure 3.6) shows that her highest areas for behavior are urgency, competitiveness, versatility, and frequent change. Her scores are all 10s. She is very comfortable with change and sees every barrier as a challenge to overcome. She is dedicated to being the best.

Her lowest scores are in data analysis and organizing her workplace. Kathy has built a team that is very strong in data analysis and has an assistant who is exceptional at organizing her workplace.

Kathy's DISC Wheel

The DISC wheel plots each person's natural and adapted behavior. The wheel is divided as follows:

- Promoter: An enthusiastic and creative force who engages others through optimism and enthusiasm
- Relater: A thoughtful team player who strives for balance and harmony

(continued)

CASE STUDY *(continued)*

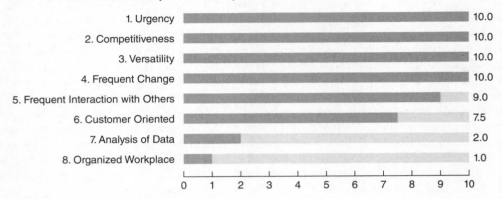

The Behavioral Hierarchy graph will display a ranking of your natural behavioral style within a total of eight (8) areas commonly encountered in the workplace. It will help you understand in which of these areas you will naturally be most effective.

1. Urgency	10.0
2. Competitiveness	10.0
3. Versatility	10.0
4. Frequent Change	10.0
5. Frequent Interaction with Others	9.0
6. Customer Oriented	7.5
7. Analysis of Data	2.0
8. Organized Workplace	1.0

FIGURE 3.6 Kathy's DISC Hierarchy of Behavior
Source: Copyright © 2012 Target Training International, Ltd. Used with permission.

- Supporter: A value-focused and loyal team player who builds long-term relationships
- Coordinator: A reliable and conscientious planner who is well-organized
- Conductor : A decisive and goal-oriented person who ensures that deadlines are met
- Persuader : An eager and tireless visionary who takes action
- Analyzer : A detail-oriented information gatherer who ensures integrity in decision making
- Implementor: A disciplined monitor of the tasks at hand who ensures control and objectivity

Kathy's DISC wheel (see Figure 3.7) shows that she is still operating in the model suggested for a successful leader. Naturally she is a persuader, but she has adapted to being more of a conductor. Her natural and adapted scores are relatively close together. This has proved to be an indicator that she is still successful and not overly stressed. However, the large drop in the influence is the warning sign.

The key to being a successful leader is to know yourself and be able to read those early warning signs that your behavior needs to change. She realizes now that her dominance is not a sustainable behavior for success. Her use of her influence behavior is important to building her team even though, to the outsider, the team is successful the way it is now.

Kathy's Leadership Team's DISC Profile

The DISC wheels shown in Figures 3.8 and 3.9 are from Kathy's leadership team. The team's natural wheel (Figure 3.8) is relatively balanced with an overall orientation toward strong leadership behaviors. Four of the seven team members are in the leadership areas of conductor, persuader, and promoter. The adapted wheel (Figure 3.9), however, tells a different story. The superintendent is the only one who stays in her role as a leader. The compliance scores of the entire team move up dramatically, moving their adapted stars to the implementor and the analyzer quadrants. The one coordinator is the executive secretary, which makes sense for her position.

The pressure on compliance and implementation has moved to each of the senior leadership team members. This pressure has resulted in each team member focusing on his or her department to make sure that everything is done well and that all compliance issues are handled correctly. Each team member is focused on his or her own

CASE STUDY *(continued)*

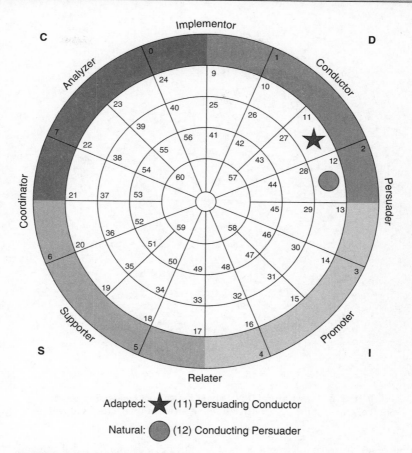

Adapted: ★ (11) Persuading Conductor

Natural: ● (12) Conducting Persuader

FIGURE 3.7 **Kathy's DISC Wheel**
Source: Copyright © 2012 Target Training International, Ltd. Used with permission.

silo, not the whole school system. The only person focused on the whole school system and how all initiatives tie together to accomplish system goals is the superintendent.

As noted earlier, this silo approach creates major vulnerability for the school system. The work that is needed for this leadership team is to delegate implementation and compliance to their managers and staff. This would allow the senior leadership team to join the superintendent in advancing the overall goals of the school system. These need to be interdependent goals that rely on departments working together.

Kathy and the Values Inventory

Kathy's Values inventory provides motivation for her to take on this new challenge. Her high theoretical score provides motivation to finding the best way to improve student achievement. She analyzes the data on students' performance and is relentless to determine the root cause for why some students are not achieving at the highest level. Her social value also motivates her to make a difference in students' lives. However, the realization that some people are not motivated by the same values is intriguing to her. It was pointed out to her that people on

(continued)

CASE STUDY *(continued)*

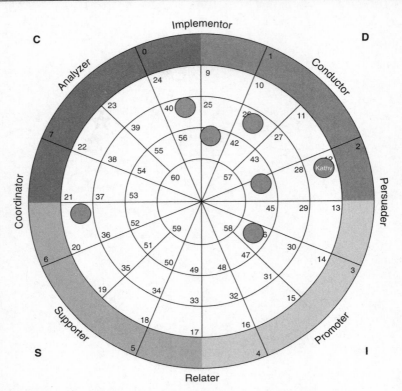

FIGURE 3.8   **The Natural DISC Wheel for Kathy's Leadership Team**
Source: Copyright © 2012 Target Training International, Ltd. Used with permission.

the finance committee for the town might not be motivated by her passion for kids. If a finance committee person were high on utilitarian value and low on social value, that person could see her passionate pleading for resources as a smoke screen for hiding poor fiscal management. In fact, the more she tries to persuade that person to see things her way, the more his or her skepticism and resistance could increase. Instead, her approach with this utilitarian person would be to answer the fiscal questions with clear data that are direct and transparent without the emotion. This more credible approach for the finance committee member will get better results than the usual approach of appealing to his or her love for kids and the need to educate the future leaders of our society.

Kathy's values won't let her just ignore this data, and she realizes that she must work on changing her approach and act on building an HPT that is committed to continuous improvement. She cares about both short- and long-term student success. She understands the importance of leadership and the responsibility that comes with the job. She will move forward carefully with this new approach to building a team. This commitment to change is why she is the type of leader we need in education today.

Kathy's Values Bar Chart

Kathy's Values inventory indicates three high areas (see Figure 3.10). Her highest value is social, meaning that she is driven to make a difference for students and families in her community. Her second highest area is individualistic, which relates to her motivation to use her power to make a difference for kids. The third highest area

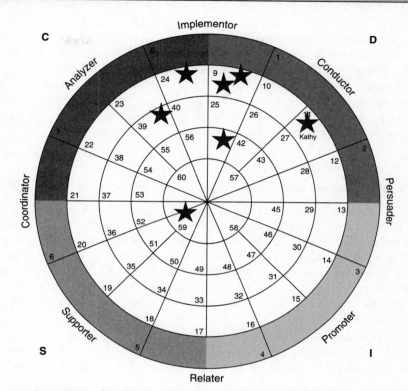

FIGURE 3.9   Kathy's Leadership Team's Adapted DISC Wheel
Source: Copyright © 2012 Target Training International, Ltd. Used with permission.

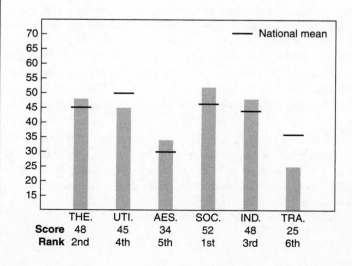

	THE.	UTI.	AES.	SOC.	IND.	TRA.
Score	48	45	34	52	48	25
Rank	2nd	4th	5th	1st	3rd	6th

FIGURE 3.10   Kathy's Values Inventory Bar Chart *Source:* Copyright © 2012 Target Training International, Ltd. Used with permission.

(continued)

is theoretical, which means that she is dedicated to finding root causes for problems with students who are not achieving to their potential. She is very committed to data and deep analysis to determine goals and strategies. Her aesthetic value is also above the average, but not as high as the other previous values. This accounts for her desire to make people comfortable and to provide a positive physical environment for staff and students.

Kathy's lowest scores are utilitarian and traditional. The utilitarian score indicates that she is not motivated by money or return on investment. This does not mean that she would not manage funds well for her district; it means that the money is not as motivating as the social value. This is common among most educational leaders. As mentioned previously, this could cause issues for finance committee members.

Kathy and the Seven Competencies

Kathy matches the competencies we have developed from our data on high-performing leaders.

1. *Challenges the status quo.* Kathy is very focused on goals and outcomes. She views laws, regulations, and mandates within the context of her goals. This means she focuses on the goals first and then determines how the requirements and compliance tasks help her with the goals. If she believes they do match, then the implementation should be rigorous. If they do not, she will determine how she can meet the minimal requirements in a manner that takes less time and does not derail what she and her staff believe is important for students to achieve at their highest levels. Her focus is on a positive, motivating environment, not a punitive environment of discussing failures. She rarely focuses on maintaining the status quo because it is against her basic fabric of always getting better.

2. *Builds trust through clear communications and expectations.* Kathy is a master communicator. She is very strong, organized, and passionate about her focus on students. Her staff trusts her because she consistently follows through. Although politics and other barriers can try to derail her, they never stop her from her goals.

3. *Creates a commonly owned plan for success.* Kathy has a plan with her board and leadership team to improve student achievement. The goals and outcomes she expects are clear throughout the school system. However, Kathy would benefit from an overall strategic plan for her entire district. This would help break down some of the silos involving the different functions at the senior level. The overall plan could be marketed to her community. If Kathy had such a plan, it would be interesting to see what resources she could bring into the school system.

4. *Focuses on team over self.* Kathy is a strong leader who is the ultimate team player. Her great confidence and security allow her to praise others and put her staff in the limelight for the public to see their abilities. Kathy has one problem: The silos of her senior team are blocking them from becoming an HPT. She would like to build a stronger team at the senior level but is concerned that the tensions between departments could break down relationships and adversely affect the great results the district achieves. She does know that not addressing this team issue could have consequences, especially if she ever left. She is hoping that success will ultimately heal all wounds and that her leadership and the great pride and results in the school system will ultimately overcome some of the team concerns at the senior level.

5. *Has a high sense of urgency for change and sustainable results in improving student achievement.* Her sense of urgency is her greatest strength. She has an amazing quality of understanding an issue and committing to quick implementation to get results. Whereas many educational leaders would develop a process for decisions, Kathy is quick and decisive. Her ability to build a positive culture of trust and still make many difficult decisions quickly without input shows her amazing leadership qualities. This high sense of urgency permeates the entire culture of the school system. People return calls immediately, follow through on tasks on time, and always have a great customer service attitude.

6. *Commitment to continuous improvement.* Kathy is a model for continuous improvement. The first time the author met Kathy after she completed her leadership inventories, she took out a piece of paper and asked what she could do to improve as a leader. This openness and commitment to improvement is unique. To ask someone you have never met for feedback on how to improve as a leader shows her security and desire to do the best job she can for all her students. Kathy is relentless in finding professional development opportunities for all her staff, whether it is from educational organizations or the private sector.

7. *Builds networks and partnerships.* Kathy is excellent at this competency. She forms partnerships with universities, consulting firms, other school districts, and businesses to help her district succeed. Her ability to network outside her district is exceptional. She delegates leadership to her senior administrators and focuses her time externally and on supporting them in their jobs. When the fiscal issues became very difficult in her state, she was confident that she would regain their funding through her ability to rally the community behind her district's goals. Once again she was successful in this endeavor. She speaks at conferences and pulls together her colleagues on key issues in a passionate and quietly forceful manner. One goal she has this year is to help other districts succeed in her surrounding area.

Action Plan for Improvement

Kathy's next challenge is to mold the leadership team into a high-performance team. You may think that they could not improve. However, since Kathy is always focused on continuous improvement, she will never stop the learning and development process. Her team is very strong but has become somewhat silo oriented and counts on her alone to look at the entire school system.

This silo approach leaves their success as a district vulnerable. If Kathy left or a couple of key leaders found other jobs, the district could lose its edge. The district must develop more leaders from within and learn how to use each other as resources for meeting system goals. Kathy has assumed that her top leaders have the same leadership qualities that she has and that they see team development as a key priority for sustainable success.

HPTs see their primary role as focusing on what is best for the whole district and their functional role as secondary. They will help each other succeed and will sacrifice their own gain for another area if that will help the district. The high-performing leaders who have been hired have become functionally driven with a major focus on their areas of responsibility. This focus has been core to their success. However, this narrow focus could become a major problem in the future. Because resources have been strong, the leaders have not been pushed to decrease resources and find new ways to succeed. The future will require compromise, sharing resources between leaders, and more focus on cross-functional common goals.

Each senior leader will need to build leadership capacity in his or her department. These leaders will need to focus on hiring the right people who are team oriented and committed to work with other staff outside of their function. The senior leaders will need to make sure there is a succession plan for all key positions. The superintendent will need to find ways to motivate her senior people to work together on common goals and to build a culture of teams throughout the district.

The Final Story

What can we learn from the case study about Kathy and her high-performing district? Kathy has done everything that is required of her and has gone much further than most districts to be a success. All her data show that everything is great and is a model for others to emulate. However, even Kathy and her team are not perfect. The team has lacked reflection on their work in leading the district. Team members have become so task- and short-term results oriented that they have potentially missed the long-term issues that could dramatically affect their success.

(continued)

Now Kathy must work with her leadership team to help them realize something that is innate to her. Success can be the enemy, and even what looks like perfection may not be what it appears to be. Kathy has the instincts and the profile for success that tells her she must gain support from her school board for this high-performance process. She once again uses her influence behavior to gain commitment from the school board to ask them to complete the leadership inventories and commit to build their board as an HPT. One could say that Kathy is lucky that she is realizing that she has a problem in her district. However, the great leaders get lucky because they are open to change, listen to input both within and outside their school system, and are always looking to be the best.

Kathy, while being a model leader for today's education world, did miss something in her road to success. She believed that if she hired the best and created the conditions for success it would be sustainable. However, she now realizes that other leaders are not like her, and she missed the element of creating an HPT at her senior staff level. Now she has to go back and add this element to her comprehensive and systemic approach to change.

Her challenge is difficult because most status quo leaders would tell her to leave it alone and enjoy her success. However, Kathy is a successful leader and is always open to learning and improvement and will not accept her current success as a reason to stray from her continuous improvement philosophy, which has served her well throughout her career.

Kathy has internalized the secret that many leaders do not want to admit and deal with throughout their career. She knows that following all the best practices in education that the experts tell her to implement and satisfying all her constituents' short-term needs is not enough. She knows that she must constantly use her own values to see the truth and be honest about her success. She knows that the secret of success is within her and her team's control. Even all the accolades and promotions cannot hide the truth about the hard work of sustainable change. Kathy and her team must be able to see beyond the outward signs of success to look honestly at the challenges for both the short and long term. They can enjoy their accomplishments but should never let success blind them from the process of continuous improvement and sustainable change.

Kathy will need to use the data from the inventories to engage her leadership team in the process of building members' skills and the work of a high-performance team to develop teams throughout the school system. Kathy has built something special for her community. When the financial issues finally confront the school district, however, it will be a true test if they can stay together as a team in difficult times.

Reflective Questions

1. How would you rate Kathy on a scale of 1 to 7 on each leadership competency?
2. What are her greatest strengths as a leader?
3. How can she increase the leadership capacity of her leadership team?
4. How can you increase the ability and willingness of teams in your school or district to be self-directed?
5. Should Kathy take on the leadership challenges in this case study even though she is very successful?
6. Are there any challenges in your school or district that you are avoiding that you need to meet head on?
7. Can you identify any discreet initiatives that need to be part of a systemic approach to ensure success?
8. Are there any programs in your district that look good but are not really meeting students' needs or are not getting results?

4

The Reality of Practicing Being a High-Performing Leader

When Theory Meets Real Life, It Is Not Always Pretty

Even leaders who are committed to building high-performance teams can fail if they are not self-aware and able to make the adjustments necessary to handle the myriad of challenges they face on a day-to-day basis. Leaders who become reactive and tend to withdraw under pressure or become too aggressive and autocratic when facing a conflict become ineffective in leading their schools or school systems. No matter what their leadership profile states, if they are self-aware and open to change they will seek assistance and be successful.

High-performance leaders have all had to overcome many challenges on their road to success. They were able to break down barriers and stay on target toward their goals. This chapter will review the following:

- How reality and theory are very different for all leaders and why some do not make the necessary adaptations to succeed
- Why leaders in a variety of situations have faced a reality that challenged their skills and the theories they had learned and were not able to meet the demands
- How leadership styles make a difference when facing practical situations that test the theories of being an effective leader
- Examples that show why some people succeed while others fail

To begin, it is important to note that there is a variety of leadership tools and constructs that can help the leader under pressure deal with the reality that is threatening their success. Some of these tools are internal and personal to the leader, whereas others are resources to help mitigate the pressure and increase the prospect of productive problem solving. Each tool requires a high degree of self-awareness and openness to look honestly and critically at one's own behavior. To be self-aware, one needs a certain amount of confidence and self-esteem to be able to believe that self-improvement is part of becoming an excellent leader.

EMOTIONAL INTELLIGENCE

One personal and internal leadership construct involves Daniel Goleman's work on emotional intelligence (Goleman, 1996). *Emotional intelligence* is defined as how we handle ourselves and each other. Goleman has done extensive research that demonstrates how a leader with a high emotional quotient (EQ) is far more successful than a leader with excellent technical skills and a high IQ, but low emotional intelligence. Goleman proposes five factors that can be used to measure someone's EQ:

1. Self-awareness
2. Self-control
3. Motivation
4. Empathy
5. Social networking

Self-awareness is the cornerstone for becoming a high-performance leader, as indicated in the data presented in this text. The leaders who know themselves and understand their effect on others are most effective. The self-control aspect of EQ, which involves the ability of a person to self-regulate his or her behavior, relates to the judging and perception aspects of the MBTI. The perception score indicates great creativity, openness to change, and the ability to go beyond the barriers that are presented to a leader that can restrict his or her success. However, the judging person, who might be less creative and open to change, will tend to exhibit higher self-control. The perception person must learn how to control his or her desires to break out of restrictive situations and pursue options that are often not understood or supported by others. The boundaries that could be crossed by the perception person can cause conflict for the judging person. The perception person's ability to solve seemingly insurmountable problems is very important, but the self-control aspect will help build support for creative and often entrepreneurial ideas.

The motivation aspect of EQ is very important to success. When a leader is facing extraordinary challenges, the ability to stay motivated regarding one's stated goals is essential. In the data used for this text, the leaders who are more extroverted, influential, and dominant tend to be the most motivated under extreme pressure. The individual value score in the Values inventory can also be an indicator of the desire to lead and stay strong in the face of harsh reality. Other styles can exhibit motivation but might tend to withdraw first before venturing out in the arena where the conflict is paramount.

Empathy is a key aspect of high emotional intelligence. Goleman shows research on how empathetic people can read emotional cues and relate well to others' feelings. The feeling score in the MBTI can be an indication of an empathetic style. The data in this text on successful turnaround leaders indicates a thinking style as more conducive to success. It has been clear that the leaders who can face harsh personal criticism and stay true to their beliefs and the plan for success are more effective in the short term. The influence DISC behavior has proven to deal with some aspects of empathy, as indicated in the behavior of influence to empower others and coach and form teams. The caution for the ENTJ and the dominant person is that empathy skills must be developed. If the empathy is absent, Goleman is correct that it could erode the success that the leader has built. If people feel disrespected or ignored, this can become a barrier to success for any leader.

The final aspect of EQ is the social networking behavior. The high EQ person is always building relationships and alliances with others to advance goals. Clearly, the extroverted and influencing styles and behaviors closely relate to this aspect of emotional intelligence. Goleman's research supports that the person who is awkward in the ability to build relationships and connect to people in the external world of work have a more difficult time being successful. In this text it is noted that the extrovert is able to garner more support for change much more quickly than the introvert. The introvert can be social and network, but it is draining and he or she tends to withdraw under pressure of conflict and the need for high energy.

An example of dealing with emotional intelligence and the MBTI inventory involves a principal in a suburban community in the Midwest. The principal was very successful in raising awareness and focus on increasing test scores on student achievement. However, the faculty felt very disconnected and criticized by the principal. In fact, the faculty became so frustrated with the principal they sent a letter with a vote of no confidence to the superintendent. The principal was approached by the superintendent with the letter, and the principal immediately became very defensive. She stated that the school was successful and that student achievement had increased dramatically. She believed that the faculty was complaining because she forced them to pay attention to student data for the first time and that they had to work harder than in the past.

The superintendent stated that while he recognized that the test data was very positive, the principal needed to gain support from her faculty. The principal was provided with a coach to help her deal with this challenge. She was an ISTJ in the MBTI, and she struggled with the concept of empathy in the emotional intelligence framework. After a few sessions, she decided that it was time to make a change in her life. She had always been introverted and was very comfortable with data. She finally realized that although she was trying to help teachers become more successful, her ability to connect to them as people was minimal.

She practiced having conversations with faculty members individually and told them that her goal was to become more personable and spend more time understanding who they were and their concerns. She admitted that this was difficult for her but she wanted to try and asked for their help.

Over a 3-month period she started to win people over. She involved faculty in her presentations and decreased her focus on the data. There were six faculty members who led the effort to obtain the letter of no confidence. The principal met with each person individually to work on improving their relationship.

At the end of the 3 months, the superintendent decided to interview the six faculty members. To his surprise, they unanimously supported the principal. With the new data, the superintendent offered the principal a new 3-year contract.

It is clear that high emotional intelligence is a key to success for leaders in both the public and private sector. The EQ research supports many of the premises about leadership noted in this text. It is not enough to be technically skilled as a leader if you do not have a high emotional intelligence quotient. The five factors noted by Goleman demonstrate that what many people call *soft skills* have a significant effect on a leader's ability to achieve results. Even with high emotional intelligence and the profile of a high-performance leader, there are other tools that can help deal with the realities that can derail the best leaders.

THE TRUST CYCLE

One tool involves understanding how a person builds trust with individuals and groups. The trust cycle outlined in Figure 4.1 is a very valuable tool to use with groups that are beginning to exhibit conflict and the loss of trust. The basis of the trust cycle is that people trust someone they find to be predictable. Even Democrats and Republicans have been able to work together when the trust is evident, which can produce consensus and positive results. This was illustrated during Senator Ted Kennedy's funeral, broadcast on most TV stations around the country and in many parts of the world. Orrin Hatch, a very conservative senator from Utah, told stories about his beloved friend Ted Kennedy. Hatch noted that they never saw any situation in the same way because of their different belief systems. However, they understood and respected each other and knew exactly where the other person was on every issue. They were predictable to each other and respectful even in their disagreements. They trusted each other and were able to propose many bipartisan bills to help the country on critical domestic and international issues. The trust cycle begins with communications (see Figure 4.1). One must clearly communicate his or her idea or point of view to constituents. The second area is shared understanding, which is where most leaders and groups lose trust. As noted throughout this text, people have very different styles of problem solving. They also may have different values that can polarize them on any given issue. Ensuring that what you have communicated is understood by the recipient is critical to building trust. Most leaders skip this step in their rush to number five, which is the assumption of teamwork. The assumption that what is communicated is understood, and that people can now work as a team to implement the new program or idea, is often a factor in derailing a leader's initiative. Many people do not want to take the time to make sure that people understand what has been communicated. They also hesitate to check for shared understanding because they believe that if people do not agree they will sabotage the process of moving ahead. Leaders often don't understand that if trust is built properly then even disagreement will not prevent progress. However, not paying attention to step two will result in wasted time because misunderstandings and conflicts will occur at later stages in the project.

Once the communications have occurred and there is a shared understanding, the dialog can move to shared expectations. At this stage, trust is built on a clear sense of predictable behavior. If this phase is missed people will still predict behavior, but the predictions tend to be inaccurate and negative based on a lack of clear expectations. This will cause more mistrust for people based on perceived actions.

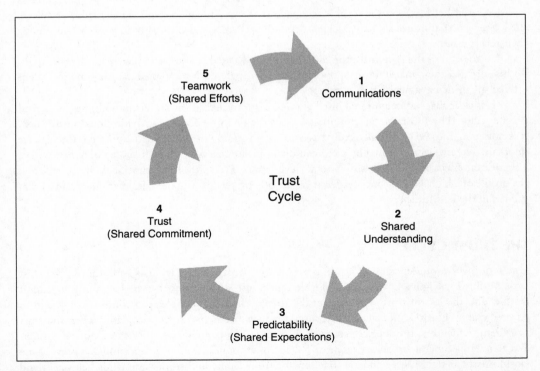

FIGURE 4.1 **The Trust Cycle**
Source: Based on the work of Dr. Jerry Stinnett.

Step four, the shared commitment phase, involves the distribution of responsibility and accountability to complete tasks or assignments. When commitment is established, people can count on each other to get the work done to complete the task. The commitment is strong at this point because trust is building on a sound base of understanding and expectations that are clear to all parties.

The final stage of trust, teamwork, is reached based on a team's goals developed in a safe and trusting environment. A team cannot be formed simply by throwing people into a room and giving them a project. The realities presented in this chapter become insurmountable when the trust is absent and people talk behind each other's backs and work against the goal for personal reasons. The challenges that are outlined in this chapter are difficult enough, but may be insurmountable if there is a lack of trust.

CONFLICT RESOLUTION

An additional skill that is key to dealing with the realities that thwart leaders is conflict resolution. A leader needs to build skills in dealing with conflict. The high-performance leaders deal with conflict directly and confidently and have the emotional intelligence, team building, and negotiation skills necessary for to solve problems.

Figure 4.2 is a helpful construct for dealing with conflict in teams and with outside constituencies. The premise of this design is that many potential conflicts occur every day that can be devastating and defeat the best plans for success. When the conflict occurs at the broad end of the triangle (issues 1, 2, 3, 4, and 5), there are more options than at the narrow end of the

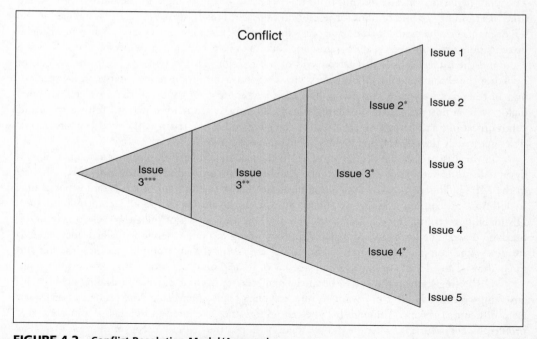

FIGURE 4.2   Conflict Resolution Model/Approach
Source: Based on a 2000 presentation by Charles Baker, Former Chief Executive Officer of Harvard Pilgrim Health Care.

triangle (issue 3***). When an issue is dealt with early (either when all five are identified or in the second panel that includes issue 2*, 3*, and 4*), the conflict is at a low level and can be more easily controlled. When one lets a conflict go unchecked (3**), it tends to grow and moves to the narrow end of the triangle. The issue can become very complicated and potentially almost impossible to control. When the conflict is at a stage in the narrow end, the options are limited for solving the problem.

Why do we let conflicts grow? We are often too busy and tend to deal with the most immediate issue. Leaders and teams tend to ignore issues and hope they will resolve themselves. This method very rarely works. The small initial issues that are ignored ultimately become the major crises, and people wonder how they become so devastating.

This is where a leader needs the team for help. An individual can only manage a few conflicts. However, a team can manage and monitor many conflicts. If a team deals with a conflict at its early stage, it can usually be easily resolved or it can be monitored and stopped from escalating. The options for solutions are many at the large end of the triangle shown in Figure 4.2, but the options are minimal at the narrow end when the problems are most acute.

Ignoring or minimizing problems is the symptom and the cause of most crises. A team should always have a list of the problems at the earliest stages and make sure they deal with them immediately. This method will save a huge amount of time and resources and prevent the problems from becoming the crises that destroy the credibility of the leader and the team.

An example of this occurred in a federal government team of six people. The senior manager ignored early signs of unrest on the team, minimized complaints, and held up decisions because he believed that they were too short-term oriented. The signs of major issues then began to occur. Each time there was a complaint or conflict, it was relatively ignored and not taken seriously. The team behavior was fast moving from the large end of the triangle to the narrow end, where time was running out and options for resolution were few. Finally, three grievances were filed on the senior manager, a harassment complaint was submitted to human resources, and an attorney general investigation was launched on a programmatic issue. All this occurred in a six-person team. Now the team and the leader were at the narrow end of the triangle. The meeting to begin the process of resolving these concerns finally occurred. However, now the union representative, a lawyer, and human resources were asked to attend. The trust was completely gone and the prospects for open dialog were almost impossible. Although many attempts were made to try to restore trust and communications and bring the team back to the large end of the triangle, the recovery was impossible. Ultimately the senior manager lost his job and was reassigned.

In this case we see the combination of trust, conflict, and style all playing a role in creating a dysfunctional team that self-destructed. The leader was very introverted (I) and highly perceptive (P) in the MBTI. This resulted in a lack of communication with the team on goals and expectations. In addition, his communications were often unclear and confusing to a more technical linear staff. His inability to communicate clearly resulted in the second aspect of the trust cycle continuously breaking down. The formation of a shared understanding was rarely developed. The leader was also steadiness and compliance oriented in the DISC. He assumed that people were doing the job and rarely showed any dominant or influencing behavior to help motivate people toward common goals.

His feeling style on the MBTI became a major factor in his avoidance of dealing openly with emerging conflict. He did not want to hurt anyone's feelings and therefore tended to shy away from difficult situations. Although his poor communications resulted in his lack of awareness that problems were occurring, when he did see them he hoped they would disappear on their own. The conflict model (Figure 4.2) became a great graphic to show how avoiding problems until they reach the narrow end of the triangle creates a perfect storm of dysfunctional behavior that is hard to resolve.

Leaders believe education, technical skills, and experience will carry them through the challenges. Although their background and experience was probably the reason they were hired, the ability to understand themselves and use the resources, techniques, and tools of building trust and support are more important for success.

Most educational theories are presented without regard to the situation or culture that the leader will face. Although it is important to possess certain characteristics that make one a better leader, it is even more critical to understand how different leaders cope with the challenges that could derail the attainment of established goals. The realities that leaders confront vary greatly from system to system. This chapter will show how certain leadership styles are able to adjust and overcome the challenges that seem so overwhelming. Although the list of realities that can be encountered seems endless, this chapter will outline some of the most prevalent ones that often derail leaders.

POLITICS

The theories in education that outline the characteristics of leadership rarely account for politics. Even Jim Collins, author of the book *Good to Great,* stated in a presentation at Boston University that there was one elusive factor in the nonprofit, education, and government sectors that seemed to affect results that he could not quantify. This factor was politics, and he could not figure out how it affected organizations that attempted to move from good to great. To the audience of several thousand public sector leaders, this little factor in industry was enormous (Collins, 2001).

In education, a principal can do all the things that he or she learned in training to be a strong instructional leader, but still fail for not understanding and dealing effectively with the politics of the school, school system, and the community. Most leaders will say that they should not have to deal with politics and that doing the right things for kids should over-shadow political issues. These educators are right, but the reality is that if you do not learn about how to deal with politics you will fail at some point in your career. The author of this text was fortunate that a senior administrator pulled him aside early in his career and said, "You have all the right skills to make a major impact on education. However, you know very little about politics." He then stated that he was an expert on politics and would teach the author the skills needed to manage the politics that could derail his career. The administrator was right that the politics of a large urban district were immense and complex, and the author was not prepared for the challenges he would meet. These political challenges related to certain administrators aligning with people they thought would get promotions and making sure that they derailed other people who could be competition. The politics were subtle, and to the naive and inexperienced manager they could have gone undetected.

The lessons that the author of this text learned were very powerful and served him well in his 30 years of working with over 700 organizations. None of these lessons were in a book, a class, or a training program, but they were equally important to his success as a leader. In turn, they are presented here because they are important for all leaders.

What does it mean when someone states that you must deal with the politics? *Politics* often means that there is history behind an issue that involves the relationships of people from the past or a related circumstance. A principal may not realize that her new program is promoting a person who has a negative past with another highly influential member of the school community. Therefore, certain members of the community will not agree with the new initiative because it will help a person they do not want to support. The principal's new program could be doomed and she does not know why. Therefore, it is important for leaders to think and act politically (Heifetz & Linsky, 2002).

Another principal who is trying to hold teachers accountable may not realize that one of his teachers is related to a selectman or a city council member. That political reality might result in a visit from the superintendent, who tells the principal to reduce the pressure on that teacher. Another subtle but important message for that person's career has been delivered.

By ignoring the politics, a leader will be missing key elements that will affect change. The principal must have a leadership style that can understand and manage politics. Certain MBTI styles have no patience for politics. For example, the ISTJ believes that people should focus on the task not the people, and the right answer should prevail. Unfortunately, the right answer often is overshadowed by personal agendas and the egos of people involved. The ISTJ profile leader gets very frustrated and either quits his or her job or ignores the politics to his or her peril.

The characteristics of a person who can manage politics include the following:

- Listening skills are critical for understanding political issues. The ability to listen to others and determine the real issues before proceeding will prevent a leader from walking into a landmine he or she does not know exists.
- Networking is very important because a leader must have a variety of relationships with people to find out the perceptions of change before proceeding. A leader must use a network to find out about personal agendas or history before acting on a plan for change.
- The leader must be able to proceed cautiously and ensure that information presented as fact has at least two sources for verification. People will mislead others to help their agenda. A leader needs to use a network to check out the facts before proceeding. Be careful, but don't be paranoid, is a good motto.

Understanding politics does not mean you have to give special treatment to people with political connections. It does mean that once you understand the political implications, you need to factor in steps to manage the politics. For example, a superintendent recently believed he could not remove a secretary from her job because her family was very powerful in the community. Although the family was well-respected and influential, he could remove the secretary. The knowledge he had was helpful to know in order to discuss this change with the school committee chairperson before he could proceed. Although it was his decision and he did not need the permission of the school committee to execute it, the advance notice allowed the school committee to manage any political fallout from his decision.

A new superintendent in a small suburban district has been very successful in several districts over a long career, but she underestimated the politics of this new community. Someone she was supporting publically had spoken negatively about one of her school committee members during a difficult and hard-fought campaign, and it almost derailed her career. This superintendent did not do her homework and develop a network of contacts in this new community. Instead, she proceeded with her new initiatives without regard to the history and politics of her new community. Her previous superintendency was in an urban district and this new district was a wealthy suburban community. In the urban district, the politics were more out in the open and clearly understood by most people. In the suburban district, the politics were more subtle and only understood by community members with a long history of political awareness and experience.`

The superintendent's ENTJ profile is the profile of a strong leader. However, her overconfidence, which can be a characteristic of this style, and her desire to make her imprint on her new community almost derailed her career. Politics and culture can trump the best leaders' intent and positive ideas for change. The superintendent spent much of her first 4 months in her new location building strong relationships within the community. She was hired to rebuild the trust within the community, which had lost confidence in the school system over the last few years. She proceeded on her own to build this new relationship with the community by being visible and transparent. However, the superintendent did not create a plan with her leadership team and the school committee. The leadership team and the school committee was her best resource for learning about the politics. Her strong directive style, which would serve her well in developing a new vision for the school system that she believed would obtain support from the municipal leaders and community, became a liability due to her inability to factor in the politics of the community.

Her DISC style of high dominance, influence, and compliance also created a problem. She needed to spend more time on the influence behavior, which, while still high, decreased from her natural to her adaptive behavior. If she had spent more time on the influencing behaviors before switching to the dominant, she would have been more effective. Her adaptive style of dominance and compliance and low steadiness (fast change) resulted in her getting out in front of the school committee and moving too fast to manage the politics for change in the community. Her high compliance style also presented a problem. She knew how to be an effective superintendent in her urban district. Therefore, she proceeded from the rules and framework of the role of superintendent based on her past experience. She never looked at what she should do differently in this new situation to be effective. The school committee in her previous district was very political in trying to find jobs for friends in the district. In the new community, the politics had more subtle, and the expectations of the superintendent to work in partnership with the school committee had always been understood in the past. This experienced superintendent with a positive profile for success almost failed dismally because she ignored the culture and expectations of the new community.

All leadership profiles must be self-aware and never become overconfident. Leaders must never assume they understand their standing with the staff and key constituents. Leaders must have a network of people who will tell them the truth, even if it is unpleasant. All leaders must build teams and networks both within the school system and in the community. Politics can become a reality that will test any leader's skills. This superintendent was fortunate that she had built strong relationships in the community in a short time; this provided some capital and leverage for her school committee to work with her on the necessary adjustments she would need to make to be effective.

Another superintendent assumed his first leadership role in a suburban district. The district performed well academically, but had lost several overrides in a row, which put pressure on the resources needed to maintain a quality school district. This superintendent faced a similar situation as the previous one. He needed to gain support from the community and increase transparency. This superintendent spent an enormous amount of time learning about the community. He moved to the community and made a commitment to support its values rather than propose any significant change. He began to build a network in the business community, local community-based agencies, and the municipal government. With a strong background in financial management, he spent a significant amount of time explaining the budget to a variety of people. He went more slowly than the other superintendent and kept his leadership team and school committee informed about his actions. He also faced skepticism from his school committee and the leadership team. The skepticism involved his lack of experience in instructional matters and his lack of time on internal issues in the district.

Over the first year, all his time in the community paid off when the school system won its first override in many years. The superintendent understood the politics of his community and brought all constituents into his plan. In addition, he began to use his credibility to build a fundraising effort to support technology and his success began to attract the best staff. Now the test scores are rising in every category and the community supports his initiatives with increased funding. The trust is restored and he has a strong school committee and leadership team on board.

This superintendent has an ESTP profile. The extrovert style is again critical for communication and networking. The sensing style is helpful in dealing with the current culture before setting goals for the future. The sensing style also helped him focus on the current situation rather than future goals. People had time to get to know him and he had time to form alliances to support his plan for the future. This allowed him to build support from his leadership team and the school committee. The thinking style allowed him to put a logical plan together and not be derailed by skeptics and personal criticism. His perception style, which can be a challenge in some cases due to the lack of a clear, focused plan for success, helped him in this situation. He was creative and open to change. Therefore, he did not have clear plan to move ahead and was able to build his plan based on the ideas of the community.

His DISC style became a plus for him when it could have caused him great problems. He is naturally dominant and influence is his second highest score. He was able to hold back his dominant style and use his influence behavior to build his network before he moved ahead confidently. If he became too dominant early on, this would have caused a problem for his community because they would have believed he was trying to bring about change too fast. This successful story shows again how self-awareness and team building are critical for success no matter what profile you have as a leader.

Politics will always be a factor in school leadership. Dealing with people who are driven by self-interests rather than the common good seems to be an integral part of educational culture. The politics of virtue envisioned by our founding fathers have unfortunately been subjugated by self-interest, deal-making, and compromise for individual gain. A leader must understand and cultivate his or her staff to the understanding that what is rewarded gets done and what people value and believe gets done too. The commitment to developing a value-based team culture will ultimately mitigate the negative effects of the self-interest politics of school today (Sergiovanni, 1995).

UNIONS

Although it must be acknowledged that the impact of unions in education is changing, most states still have a strong union environment. In those states, the attitudes and skills to manage the union relationship are key factors for success. The political nature of unions requires a clear strategy for educational leaders to deliver on the promises of improvement in student achievement.

This is the second reality that can derail leaders, and it is not outlined in leadership theory books. Knowing how to work effectively with unions and bring them in to support your efforts for change is critical for all leaders in every sector. Once again, most leaders complain about unions as blocking success and only caring about the status quo. The unions in education have been a target of policymakers and the media as standing in the way of improvement efforts. They have become a major target for attack, especially with growing budget deficits. With all this rhetoric, the unions have built up defenses to fight change and to make sure that the membership is not disrespected. Although money and salaries are the main battle, the union fight has expanded to most aspects of change. The compliance leaders build a case against the unions and try to battle for concessions at the bargaining table. The reality is that if leaders want to be successful in education today they must have effective strategies for dealing with unions.

To be effective with unions, our highly influential leaders in the DISC often have the best success. They try to understand the union's point of view and develop strong relationships of trust with the union leadership throughout the year. They do not wait until negotiations to build the case for change. The influence style allows the leader to build a sense of teamwork with the union on common goals. In asking many union leaders over the years why they bring out the contract as the key item for all discussions for change, most agree that the contract is used as the bible when the relationships are broken and trust has deteriorated (Guggenheim, 2010).

In books such as *Getting to Yes* (Ury & Fisher, 1991) it is shown that the adversarial approach to bargaining is often not successful. The win–win approach, which is best used by the influence style in the DISC, is used in many school systems. The win–win approach is an inquiry-based decision-making model based on discussions that allows all parties to ask questions for information without judgment. This dialog builds a body of information that is essential for compromise. The advocacy model of determining your position and hiding information that could be used against you builds mistrust and tends to cause long, drawn-out, and painful negotiations. Table 4.1 explains the characteristics of inquiry- and advocacy-based discussions.

Although this table is entitled "Two Approaches to Decision Making," it outlines a method of discussion and problem solving that is highly effective in contentious situations. This table shows the characteristics of advocacy and inquiry in relation to several key aspects of negotiations. The inquiry-based conversation is effective in several decision-making situations besides contract negotiations. Leadership teams often use this method to discuss budget problems, curriculum issues, special education challenges, and a myriad of other key issues facing a school system. The method allows people to listen and understand other team members' points of view. The advocacy method tends to create an atmosphere in which greater understanding is not developed. This is often true because people are building the case for a viewpoint and trying to discredit the other points of disagreement. If leaders can maintain inquiry-based relationships with the union leadership, they can solve problems together without escalating self-interest, advocacy-based exchanges.

An example of this team approach in working with the union occurred in a middle school in a suburban area. The school was extremely high performing, but was considered not to be "kid friendly" by many parents. This meant that the teachers did not relate well to the students and parents in a personal manner. Everything was about academic success, and the teachers believed they were the experts and parents did not feel welcomed to express opinions and concerns. The parents did not believe the students were having any fun, and there was a concern that parents would be reticent to express any personal concerns with teachers and administrators for fear of retribution. Although many of the parents were from professional roles in the business world and were very appreciative of the high test scores, they wanted the children to enjoy their experience in school.

TABLE 4.1   Two Approaches to Decision Making

	Advocacy	Inquiry
Concept of decision making	A contest	Collaborative problem solving
Purpose of discussion	Persuasion and lobbying	Testing and evaluation
Participants' role	Spokespeople	Critical thinkers
Patterns of behavior	Strive to persuade others Defend your position Downplay weaknesses	Present balanced arguments Remain open to alternatives Accept constructive criticism
Minority views	Discouraged or dismissed	Cultivated and valued
Outcome	Winners and losers	Collective ownership

Source: Based on Garvin, David, and Roberto, Michael. (2001, Oct. 15). What you don't know about making decisions. *Harvard Business Review, 79*(8).

The principal, who was an INTJ in the MBTI and high steadiness and compliant in the DISC, was inclined to ignore the parents' concerns and stay with his current strategy due to the academic success. Those with INTJ styles can appear arrogant and aloof to people who do not get to know them at a personal level. The union leadership was in the principal's school and was constantly pressuring him for more involvement in decision making and always bringing up the contract as a barrier to his efforts. His natural tendency was to complain about his misfortune to have the union leadership in his school and avoid conflict by staying with the status quo.

However, the principal's ability to avoid conflict and keep his current practices changed when the superintendent told him he needed to deal with the parents' and the union leadership's concerns. Through the assistance of a consultant, he formed a school culture team to take on these concerns. The consultant coached him initially, against his will, to add the union leader to the team of teachers and administrators on the school culture team. Through the work of developing a high-performance team, the school culture team worked with the principal to build a plan for success to gain the support of the parents and still support the teachers' strong efforts to educate the student body to the highest of standards. One area of focus for the school plan became the social and emotional health of the students. In a middle school, the transition issues for students and parents were often greater than in elementary and high school.

The strategy that was developed was to divide all the teachers and administrators and have them spend 12 minutes a day discussing social and emotional issues with small groups of students. This would allow students to develop relationships with the teachers, and it helped the teachers gain confidence that they had resources to use for the student's personal issues that caused problems for them at home and at school. In one of the meetings, the consultant talked about training the teachers to work with students for the 12-minute periods. The union leader immediately objected and stated that if there were training, she would have to grieve this effort because of the terms of the teachers' contracts and the extra preparation needed for her teachers. The principal again immediately showed regret for involving the union leadership and felt blocked by the prospect of another grievance. However, this time the team effort of involving the union leadership paid off. The union leader further stated that if they called the training "orientation," she could support the effort and would not put in a grievance. The union leader felt that she was part of the team and wanted the new program to move ahead, but still needed to do her job in representing the teachers. She proposed a win–win strategy to move ahead. The consultant and the principal supported the union leader and began to plan the orientation for teachers. The team turned a corner that day, and the principal finally believed he could be successful. The superintendent praised the work of the principal and the school culture team and stated they could be a model for other schools.

The principal, who had long-standing problems with the parents and the union, had learned a valuable lesson. His style of avoiding conflict and his cautious approach (his DISC results showing steadiness and compliance) that tended to maintain the status quo would have held back his progress. Now he was able to build a plan for his entire school with union support and move his vision ahead for the school without any grievances.

RURAL, SUBURBAN, AND URBAN COMMUNITIES

Although the skills, abilities, and attitudes of leaders to manage politics and union relationships is important to advance the work of improving student achievement, the reality of the community surrounding the school is also a factor that needs to be considered for success. The community resources, values, and expectations shape the work of leaders on a day-to-day basis. Facing the reality of a community that demands the best or one that is satisfied with the status quo or has low expectations for the students presents a different challenge to a leader.

Whether you are a leader in a rural, suburban, or urban school system, each presents different challenges. However, do these challenges require different types of leaders? The practicality of leading in each area is very different. However, strong leaders who are self-aware and build teams can be successful in all three venues without regard to their background and experience. As outlined earlier, the superintendent that switched from an urban district to a highly demanding suburban district almost failed because she was overconfident and did not adapt her approach to the culture of the new community. Once she began to adapt her style, she was able to make more progress. Understanding the culture of the community is key when looking at your leadership style and determining how to best adapt to the new setting.

A rural district has a very different reality than a suburban or urban district. The leaders in a rural district end up fulfilling many roles and do not have the staff that larger districts have. The leader often must cover many miles to visit schools and connect to several communities. The difficulty of covering several communities with different cultures is especially acute in regional or county districts. The problems of rural and suburban districts can seem to be mundane to larger urban districts, but they can be just as challenging and cannot be taken lightly. For example, when speaking to a group of principals about spending their time on strategic issues not just operational ones, the author was confronted by a rural principal about playground concerns. The author assumed that the playground was not a strategic issue but found out that this assumption was in error. The principal stated that main street in the town went through the middle of the playground and presented major safety concerns. To this principal, the playground was a major strategic issue.

An example of the differences for an urban district can be found in a scenario in which an underperforming high school of 3,000 students was focusing on literacy to increase student achievement in its very diverse population. The school leadership was being directed by central administration to focus their work on instructional issues at each level and not to be sidetracked by other concerns. However, the day before they had to present their plan to improve literacy to the central office, there was a riot involving 750 students. Reality does sidetrack instructional work. The teachers and the administrators were not able to just move on and ignore the reality of the effects of the riot. Although in an urban district it could be a riot and in a rural district it could be a playground safety issue, each leader must deal with reality and find a way to move ahead on instructional goals.

The urban situation seems so overwhelming and impossible to overcome. It is true that providing leadership in an urban district takes amazing strength and commitment. However, suburban and rural leaders often state that the urban communities get all the resources, while they have to do all the same functions with very little staff and no money. Regardless of the differences in the troubles they face, effective leaders in each setting often have the same characteristics that make them successful. They are successful because they want to be leaders in these communities. They care about the kids and want to make a difference. This is verified in the Values inventory with high scores in social and individualistic areas. The social aspect means that the leader wants to make a difference for students' lives, and the individualistic indicates that the leader wants the power to make long-term change for the kids. In all these settings, the successful leaders are self-aware and know and can speak comfortably about their strengths and weaknesses. The second aspect of all the leaders is they build teams to support their styles and build capacity for change and improvement.

One superintendent in a small suburban district of 1,200 students had a leadership team of three. The county provided other key administration roles such as curriculum, instruction, and special education. The superintendent became so involved in dealing with day-to-day issues and never having time to reflect that she stopped meeting with her team. This superintendent became overwhelmed with her reality and neglected to look at her style and realize that she must lead in the same way as a leader would act in a larger district. It was even more important for her to form a team and bring in county resources and other potential partners to support her plans.

In each case outlined, the profiles of the leaders are different. None of the examples have the profile that we have found to be the most effective in turnaround situations. However, in each case the leaders who have struggled with challenges and the reality of their situations have several factors in common.

- These leaders were not self-aware about their leadership style and how to adapt to the situation they were confronting.
- The leaders' attitudes were negative and they used challenges as excuses for negative performance.
- They withdrew into their own realities and did not reach out to key groups and individuals who could help them.
- They did not form high-performance teams, no matter how many staff members were in their school or district.
- They did not spend time learning about the cultures of their communities to develop strategies for change.

STRESS AND PERSONAL ISSUES

Leaders' education and experience in previous roles allow them to watch others deal with realities that arise in education, but once they are in the leadership chair the experience is quite different. No one can tell another person about how he or she will handle the stress of the leadership position. It is noted that you can watch the president of the United States age through the weight of his responsibilities. The superintendent and the principal are not in roles that are like the president of the United States, but the pressure and strain of caring for many students' lives and keeping the often diverse constituents satisfied takes a toll on all educational leaders.

This major reality can derail even the best leaders as stress and personal problems distract them from the work. Many people who seek leadership roles believe that they must always be strong and never let their personal problems spill over into their work life. Aspiring leaders hear the message that they must not show any vulnerability or weaknesses to their staff in order to build confidence for the times when people need support. The most effective leaders have personal lives and do not try to appear superhuman. They let people know when they are having difficulties and they communicate to people at both a personal and a staff level. It is true that leaders need to show an executive presence in how they look and act to inspire others to follow their directions. It is also true that effective leaders do not let their personal issues permeate the office. However, their ability to balance personal and professional issues reduces their stress and keeps them motivated to lead their organizations. The stress of the leader's job can become overwhelming, and it is a necessity for the leader to seek sanctuary and get away from the stress to gain strength for the challenges ahead (Heifetz & Linsky, 2002).

Keeping one's personal life so private that the stress builds up does have a negative effect on the work. There was one leadership team in the nonprofit world that was having trouble following through on their goals. When the consultant asked what was going on and whether other personal issues were getting in the way, each member of the team admitted to taking psychotropic drugs to control their stress. This admission was critical to the team's development, allowing them to prioritize time and stress management. In another case, the CEO of a nonprofit was showing signs of extreme anger. When the consultant asked what was causing this anger, he admitted that the original parents of his adopted child were trying to take his daughter away after 8 years. It was important for this CEO to talk to his leadership team about this personal problem. The team members wondered what they had done to cause his anger and were relieved that they were not the cause. The team then became very supportive of the CEO, and each member stepped up on issues that would allow the CEO to have more time to deal with his personal challenges.

The DISC inventory has been very helpful in dealing with extreme stress issues with specific team members. If a member's scores are all over the 50-point energy line, a special e-mail warning message is sent to the administrator of the DISC inventory. This message indicates that a person who has completed the inventory may be striving to be an overachiever and thus basing answers on what an individual goal may be instead of an actual behavioral pattern. The report encourages the administrator to help monitor the person's stress levels and allow him or her to retake the DISC once the person achieves balance. This message is rare, but it has occurred more frequently in urban schools. When the consultant has approached the people who have received this message, the members have agreed that their stress has become a problem in their daily lives. High-stress individuals reported greater instances of personal and physical health problems based on the stress of the job. In some cases, a member is new to a team and is thus trying to overachieve in order to impress. Other instances involve those who are perfectionists and thus do not set realistic goals for success. All the people with warning messages on the DISC stated that they were having trouble sleeping at night and were very irritable at work. DISC assessments are an excellent way to monitor and help high-stress individuals on one's team.

One case of high stress involved an information technology (IT) person in a suburban district. Her natural behavior on the DISC was dominant and the other scores were relatively low. She indicated to her superintendent that she wanted to drive certain needed changes in the school system but was having difficulty gaining support. The school staff was not always cooperative and she believed that everyone wanted so much support she had to do much of the work herself. The consultant brought in to assess the concern asked the IT person if she were willing to talk to the team about their situation. The IT person seemed relieved to no longer have to hold in her concerns and to be able to talk about her stress. The team and the superintendent were very supportive. The superintendent agreed to help her adjust her job responsibilities and coach her on her time management and prioritization. The IT person is much more effective on the job now and a lot less stressed. The reality of her situation became clear through the DISC, and the superintendent and the team demonstrated that all functions performed by team members are the team's responsibility and no one individual has to do all the work himself or herself.

Many challenges and problems facing leaders could derail them from their goals. The realities of the job are very different than the theories that are presented in one's education or in most training programs for aspiring leaders. Once a leader is on the job, the people he or she deals with are real, not case studies. School committees can and will fire or embarrass the superintendent. The media will publish articles that will put pressure on the school committee and cause problems in the school system. The principal can be undermined and look ineffective because of the mishandling of an issue that had political implications.

Leaders today in education are supposed to be instructional leaders. It is unrealistic to expect leaders to focus on instructional practices and ignore their personal lives. This text is not just about being a more effective leader. A leader must be secure in himself or herself in order to build and use the talents of the leadership team to support strengths and complement weaknesses. The team environment allows the leader to receive help on issues and the needed support to allow the leader to maintain his or her role as the strategic leader of the school or school system. The leader who tries to do too much alone becomes overwhelmed and begins to make mistakes. The leader who believes that he or she must always show strength becomes stressed in his or her personal life and begins to show weaknesses in key aspects of the job.

A high-performance team takes the pressure off the leader. The team can meet on their own to solve problems and each team member can support his or her colleagues through difficult times. The leader in a high-performance environment has time to reflect and think strategically and put time into the aspects of the job that have the highest leverage for change and success.

The key to stress issues is to be able to talk about them and not be afraid to seek help. A consultant asked a group of superintendents once how many evenings a week they are out. Most of them said 4 nights a week. The consultant then asked if their communities are satisfied with how much they are out in the public at events, meetings, and so forth. The superintendents said their communities wanted more and were not satisfied. The consultant's response was that each superintendent should only go out 2 nights a week and should spend more time with his or her family. The consultant also said that the more they are out, the more people will ask them to attend their events. The consultant continued that if you tell people you have a family and that you are trying to model the values that your school system stands for, the community will understand. Manage the stress and be open, and people will respect your values and strength in leadership.

ELEMENTARY, MIDDLE, AND HIGH SCHOOLS

It is clear that each type of community, whether rural, urban, or suburban, presents different challenges. Are the same leadership qualities successful in each level of schooling, as was proposed in the last section regarding different types of communities? Does each level of schooling require a unique set of skills, abilities, experience, and attitude for a leader?

Many educators believe that the skills and abilities needed are very different for each level of educational leadership. There is a belief, or even a perceived reality, that a principal is either an elementary, middle, or high school type. Many say that teachers teach children in elementary school, but high school teachers teach subjects. The middle school, which is key to transition between elementary and high school, can often determine the success of a school system. The middle school therefore has a very distinctive culture of its own. Are there certain profiles that are compatible with the level in a school system?

Teachers often gravitate toward the level of student that they are most comfortable teaching. This same tendency for teachers often carries over to principals as they move through their career. Based on the author's experience conducting district superintendent searches, it is important for superintendents to show the search committee that they have experience at all three levels. This type of knowledge assures a search committee that the candidate has direct experience facing the issues that an elementary, middle, or high school sees on a daily basis. Most administrators, however, do not have experience at all three levels. Many of these administrators are very successful at the level that they do not have direct experience in, despite what the search committee believes is critical for success.

There are many examples of administrators who have switched between levels and have failed, and situations in which people have switched and have succeeded. One example is a 10-year high school principal in an urban district who had been an elementary principal earlier in his career. He moved to a suburban elementary school that had major morale problems. The very entitled faculty had a history of resisting accountability. The previous principal tried to bring in discipline and accountability and was not successful. This new principal was more laid back and tried to build relationships with faculty. However, his high school experience of having a staff to help him complete many of the responsibilities caused him to become overwhelmed and left him spending most of his time in his office. He was an ESTJ and was very engaging in his first impression. However, under pressure he resorted to a dominant style of directing tasks. The parents and the teachers saw him as an administrator with no clear vision for the school. He responded negatively to parents' involvement in many of the school issues, which he did not see in his previous high school setting.

He became very negative about his job, the demanding teachers, and the community, and ended up leaving and becoming a high school principal again.

Does this example show that some people are meant to be in either elementary, middle, or high school settings? This principal was certainly more comfortable in the urban high school. If he had exhibited strong leader skills, however, could he have been successful in the elementary school? The answer is yes. If he was self-aware he would have spent more time learning about and respecting the culture of the community. He could have formed a leadership team to prevent being overwhelmed with the tasks he was used to delegating in a high school. He could have been aware of his leadership profile, which had a proclivity to focus on more day-to-day operational tasks. He could have worked with a leadership team of administrators and teachers to develop a vision and strategic plan for the school.

It is important for education to develop administrators who can be successful at all three levels. The fact that most school systems do not function as systems is a concern for education today. Elementary, middle, and high schools are often seen as different worlds that do not connect. However, the school system is supposed to provide a seamless education for students as they move through the levels to graduation. If we maintain separate cultures and silos, our leaders will gravitate to the level they feel is most comfortable. If we help leaders understand that they are part of one K–12 (or preK–12) system, we will enhance the education for students and the experiences for families by having leaders who understand all levels and can make the transitions seamless. Focusing on the transitions for student and parents would enhance the academic, social, and emotional success of the students. The parents often struggle with the transitions as well. If more effort were placed on understanding and planning for transitions, there would be more programs to help parents adjust. The struggle for parents can result in frustration, which can be taken out on their children and even the school system.

One example of a superintendent that focused on creating a true K–12 school system is in a suburban district. She worked for 2 years on forming an HPT. The team supported each other and began to see her role and her focus on the system first and each level second. One exercise the superintendent provided for her team was prior to the budget process. She asked each team member to visit all schools and departments. The host school or department would show the visitor around the school and explain the goals and the challenges to providing the best education for all students. The host was not allowed to advocate for support and could only focus on the facts and answer questions based on the inquiry method.

At first the leadership team thought this exercise was a waste of energy and that they could not afford the time to complete the task. The superintendent reinforced the importance of their functioning as a part of an entire school system not as advocates for their own level. This was a key operating principle for the HPT. Once all the visits were completed, the light went on in each member that the success of everyone was key to the success of the school or department. They began to understand that if one person failed they all failed, and that the functions of a school system are interdependent. The budget process was difficult, but they felt successful as a team through supporting all departments' needs. If leaders become high-performance leaders, the level does not matter.

The superintendent was an INTJ and was dominant and compliant in the DISC inventory. These characteristics do not lend themselves to the exercise previously outlined. She was also a "high school person" by experience. However, her commitment to being a self-aware, reflective leader who developed high-performance teams allowed her to take on a difficult reality and adapt her leadership style.

The next two realities often derail superintendents more than principals. If one asked superintendents to name the major issues that trouble them, budget cuts that will cause them to lay off key teachers and staff and the challenges of working for their school board would be their likely answers.

BUDGET

The constant budget constraints facing school systems today are major factors that derail a leader from reaching the goals that are required for success. Most educational leaders spend an enormous amount of time complaining about budget cuts and how it is impossible to do the job with dwindling resources. One former superintendent told the author that he should not have to worry about budgets because he was hired to be an instructional leader. That superintendent left his district in a huge deficit with the town appointing an overseeing committee to straighten out the budget crisis. Most superintendents believe that they cannot succeed because of budget problems and are waiting for the financial situation to improve. If we step back and look at all sectors, it is clear that the days of budget surpluses and freedom to spend without criticism are gone. Even the private sector is now open to public scrutiny about spending and budget controls.

Effective leaders adapt their leadership in order to succeed under budget constraints. Leaders who succumb to the philosophy that they cannot achieve excellence during times of financial difficulty are doomed to fail. One superintendent of a moderately sized urban school district is always saying she has no money and staff to meet the basic needs of her school system. Her mayor and community are always talking about how she must survive with the funds she has and not ask for more money. She has accepted this passive leadership role and maintains the status quo and does not take any risks. She does not present a vision for success or try to rally the community and other potential partners around any strategy for excellence. She does what the school committee says and avoids all conflicts to survive. She states that this is the only strategy she can adopt to stay in her job.

Her style is an ISTJ and she shows steadiness and compliance characteristics in the DISC. She keeps her head down to stay out of trouble and is a true maintenance leader. Recently, her school committee evaluated her performance. She was rated poorly in almost every aspect of her performance as a superintendent. This evaluation was then printed on the front page of the newspaper. The superintendent is not changing her behavior, and she blames the politics of the school committee for her evaluation. Clearly, keeping her head down and avoiding conflict is not working. Even though all the realities she sees tell her to withdraw and not lead, the outward signs are misleading. If she adapted her style toward an ENTJ confident leader that worked with her leadership team to present a plan for success, would she receive a better evaluation? If she confidently engaged the mayor and the school committee in a team effort to build a community plan for success for the schools, would she gain more financial support? If she were entrepreneurial with partnerships with industry leaders to change the image of the community and the schools, would she bring in new resources? We do not know if this would work in this community. The only clear knowledge we have is that lack of leadership and allowing barriers to become excuses for poor performance has never resulted in success.

A leader of a collaborative of 13 communities focusing on shared services for special education did not let budget cuts derail his success. He developed an aggressive plan to raise money from the community and the parents and expand to new strategic partnerships. His board of superintendents was very concerned with his leadership style and believed he would fail and embarrass the collaborative and the superintendents. Three superintendents agreed to attend a fundraising event that was being held at the height of the economic crisis, and they were shocked when they walked into the ballroom of a local hotel and saw 750 people in attendance. There were political leaders, members of the media, local businesspeople, and almost all of the parents of the students in the collaborative. The event raised over $100,000 and gained fabulous press for the effectiveness of the programs in the collaborative. The same executive director also leveraged the event to conduct a capital campaign to buy a new building, rather than using inadequate spaces in the schools. Did the board learn about effective leadership from this leader's success? The leader retired and the board replaced him with typical steadiness compliance, introverted style that will probably bring the collaborative back to its days of struggling with staying solvent.

Why did this board miss this amazing learning experience? Once again, the profile of effective high-performing leaders is not understood in education. The board hadn't realized that the collaborative needed a high-performing leader to continue the work the former leader had begun. This will prove to be an unfortunate decision unless the new leader works to become a high-performing leader.

Budget concerns were troubling to Kathy in the case study in Chapter 3. However, Kathy did not wait until the budget fell apart before she acted. She formed a team of people from both within and outside the school system to look at entrepreneurial efforts to raise money before the problem occurred. There is no doubt that Kathy will be successful as her colleagues spend their time complaining about the budget and wishing they had the budgets from the past.

The budget concerns in districts are exacerbated by the fact that most educational leaders score rather low in the utilitarian category of the Values inventory. This indicates a low value toward return on investment. This can be explained by the fact that most people in education enter the field because they want to make a difference in the lives of children, not earn a lot of money. The social score is very high on most educators' Values inventory results. Because most leaders move up the ranks from teachers to principals to central administrators to superintendents, we are likely to have very few utilitarian leaders.

An example of a utilitarian leader who came from industry into education in a suburban community had very mixed results. This new superintendent had been a school committee member and volunteered to be an assistant superintendent for $1 for one year to get experience. He attended a highly prestigious superintendent training program funded by a foundation and most of the faculty was from industry. This superintendent was an INTJ and was dominant and compliant in the DISC. He was high in the theoretical, utilitarian, and individualistic areas of the Values inventory. He believed that if he used his extensive experience as a very successful corporate CEO, his Ivy League MBA, and his ability to manage finances, he would be very successful.

His financial skills became apparent immediately as he was able to straighten out long-standing financial problems in the schools. The town leaders were very impressed and were his greatest supporters. The school committee, which had taken a chance on an alternative candidate, was also very pleased. The internal leadership team and teachers were very skeptical. That skepticism turned to anger when he began to hold people accountable for their behavior and results on student achievement. Poor performers began to lose their jobs and the performance of the district began to increase. He did his homework on student achievement issues in the district and redirected the budget to the key areas that needed focus for sustainable results. He even invested in his best people with coaching support and began to work on developing a high-performance leadership team. He brought in entrepreneurial programs involving students from overseas to add diversity and new revenue.

These results sound great! What went wrong? Politics became a major factor in the budget process. Too many leaders underestimate the aspects of the budget process that do not involve numbers. The effect of politics and dealing with change can derail the best budget process. In this situation, politics and too much change created several groups that would not support this leader when problems occurred. He also was not prepared for the education culture, which spoke about the desire for change and improvement and fiscal controls, but was not willing to do what it would take to get these results. He eventually resigned from his position and began a consulting business in education which has been very successful.

Did the school system learn from this situation? The answer is no! They hired a very popular person from the inside who had an instructional background, was very cautious with change (high steadiness and compliance), had a low utilitarian value, and was an ENFJ. The safe hire would presumably calm down the system and keep the status quo. Unfortunately, this strategy does not work today. Within a few months the school system was in a major fiscal crisis and layoffs were imminent. Now the success that was built by the superintendent who moved too quickly and was not a true educator was lost by a more traditional instructional leader. Hopefully this new, very capable leader can turn things around fiscally to move the system ahead.

SCHOOL BOARDS

The other reality that causes many sleepless nights for superintendents is the relationship they have with their school boards. This is becoming the number one concern of superintendents throughout the country. Boards are often cited as the reason that superintendents lose their jobs or do not succeed in their goals. They are rarely cited as effective leadership bodies that help a school system succeed. They are seen by many superintendents as the bastions of politics, special agendas, and ego driven self-absorbed citizens trying to exert power. If you attended a school board association meeting you would hear a different story. They see themselves as concerned citizens trying to improve their districts, represent people in the community who are disenfranchised, manage community resources, and make a difference for kids (Kowalski, 2006, p. 126).

How can there be such a schism of perception of a leadership body in schools? The principal or superintendent comes into a new school system with so much promise and is hired to make needed change. The board publically supports the hiring. Where does this love fest break down? The effective superintendent understands that the school committee is his or her boss, and he or she must develop a strong relationship with each member and a sense of teamwork with the school board. The typical superintendent comes in with the attitude that "I am the boss and they need to set policy and stay out of my day to day work." The struggle for power often begins within months of the hiring of the superintendent. The principal feels he or she is hired to run the school and the school committee is the superintendent's problem.

The examples of superintendents who have battled with school committees and have lost are too numerous to outline here. The superintendents with power profiles in the MBTI and the DISC and individualistic values in the Values inventory tend to show who is in charge and outline roles and responsibilities of the school board members and tell them they must stay in their lane. This power profile rarely works. In fact, this approach by superintendents often promotes people to run for school committees with specific agendas to challenge the superintendent.

One example of a superintendent who tried to use power with his school committee and was losing ground and then switched his style is from a suburban east coast community. Jim is an ESTJ and shows natural dominance and influence in his DISC. He came into a district in which the school committee drove out four superintendents in 7 years. He began his tenure as a strong, dominant superintendent. He respected the school committee but made it clear that they were not going to cross into his area of running the school system.

This strategy worked for about a year. However, people began to run for the school committee because they believed he had too much power and that the board was a rubber stamp for his initiatives. He was a very competent superintendent and was spending much of his time trying to put discipline into a school system that was very individualistically oriented. This superintendent is a high-performance leader who is always studying how to be more effective. He spends time attending conferences outside education to increase his network of ideas and people resources. His compliance score on the DISC was increasing for the first year in his effort to bring the system of independents together as one group and one school system.

His self-awareness was an asset when he realized that his dominant style was not working with the school committee. There was dissention within the committee and some struggling with his style by one or two members. He moved quickly to focus on team building using his natural influence style. He committed to high-performance team building with his leadership team and school committee. Now his school committee understands how important it is to be a team and works with a consultant three times per year to further its development as a team and to incorporate new members into this team approach. The superintendent now has the perfect situation any leader would want involving his school committee. The school committee continues to work on its own issues as a developing team and he does not need to attend the workshops. The school committee has adopted the high-performance principles, completed the MBTI as a team, worked on open and honest communication, and set goals and operating principles for school committee meetings. The committee members are confident that if they have issues with the superintendent they can speak directly to him and he will listen and find a win–win solution to their problem.

Another superintendent followed a colleague who viewed the school committee as a barrier. The new superintendent has now developed a strong sense of team within her committee. The previous superintendent complained that the school committee was always critical and never did any real work. This superintendent's contract was not renewed by the school committee. The new superintendent, who is committed to building HPTs, has presented a very different attitude to the school committee. She sees them as part of her team and has explained to her leadership team that she wants them to work on building a new relationship with the committee. The leadership team is very angry with the school committee as a result of a difficult budget season the two previous years. The new superintendent has committed to ongoing team development work with the school committee and the leadership team. She has modeled her behavior by looking at her style of leadership and how she must adapt to the community. Her challenge is for both groups to change and begin to develop trust and commitment for the hard work ahead. The school committee members who were critical of the previous superintendent and began micromanaging are now assuming broader leadership roles in the community and supporting the superintendent. The superintendent never had to tell them to stay in their own role or lane. She modeled teamwork and trust and built positive relationships that have resulted in people respecting her role.

In looking back at over 30 years of coaching leaders and helping them build high-performing teams, there is a pattern worth noting about those who struggle and those who succeed. The leaders who have focused on building HPTs in which each individual commits to the hard, arduous work of improvement have spent 3 to 5 years in the process. These leaders in education, town government, human services, and industry were all introverts. They worked in-depth to build their teams based on honest and open communication, enabled their team members to support each other for the good of the organization, and supported everyone's professional development. The length of time is significant to do this work and the introvert is more likely to commit to the depth of this effort.

Each of these leaders was able to demonstrate measurable success. Many of the members of each team have moved on to higher leadership roles. There is, however, one concern that has occurred in each of the situations. The leaders finished their tenure with major problems and in some cases lost their positions. The introvert style that served these leaders well ultimately caused them insurmountable problems. Each leader became too internally focused. The educator spent very little time with teachers and the community and lost their support during tough financial times. The town manager did not develop relationships with key community leaders who resented his power and used their political capital to undermine his initiatives. The board became tired of the CEO's combative style in the human service agency and fired her suddenly. All these leaders worked on their areas of improvement but ultimately were not able to sustain success.

This text has been presenting a profile of the effective leader, which is different than the profile of the best leaders who have developed high-performance teams. Why is there a discrepancy between high-performing leaders and people who have focused on developing high-performing teams? The message that is learned from this discrepancy is to maintain balance and to make sure that the leadership you provide is equal in its focus both internally and externally. The extroverts find it easier to work on the external and the introverts often become internally focused. Leaders can do both, but must be very careful to not lose their balance or they will eventually fail. We must be careful that the movement for internal focus on instructional leadership does not neglect the messages from this chapter. If it does, the success might occur in the short term but the leaders will not be able to sustain gains over the long term because they will have neglected many of the external challenges.

The following case study involves a superintendent who has faced many of the challenges outlined in this chapter and is on the verge of failure. He needs to make major changes in his leadership style and behavior to be successful in a district that has had a parade of superintendents over the years that left without success. This superintendent needs to break away from the desire to conform to the requirements of federal and state government mandates, as well as those from his school board, and chart his own course for success. He must realize that if he does everything that he is being told to do, it might not lead to success. At the same time, the barriers of politics that have plagued the community for years and that cause him countless sleepless nights cannot deter him from his values and goals. He must be courageous and adopt a new attitude and role to lead his district or he will become one more casualty of a community that cannot break out of its history of poor performance in the schools.

CASE STUDY

ROBERT

Overview

Robert is a superintendent who is a very popular, affable person who gets along with everybody. He was hired to take over a highly political, low performing urban district. The previous two superintendents were driven out by the politics on the school board and the poor results of the school system. Robert was hired because he had a vision for success for the school system and an ability to build positive relationships with everyone across political party lines. The school system had a victim mentality, in which all groups believed they would never succeed because of the past and had no hope for change in the future. The school board was aware that the test scores were the lowest in the state. Instead of committing to improvement plans, they spent most of the time disputing the accuracy of the state and federal tests. There were three types of board members. One group was tied to the teachers and supported them to the extreme no matter what the results displayed. A second group was using the school board as a stepping stone for their political careers. This group enjoyed promising favors to friends and supported issues that would advance their personal status. The third group actually lived and worked in the community and wanted the education to improve. They wanted to stop the jokes about their community and hoped to give back to their citizens. The 12-member school board was led by the mayor, who had a clear political agenda to save money and cut government expenses and waste.

The community wondered how long this new friendly and bright superintendent would last. He came into the district with hope for everyone to work together to provide an excellent education for all students. Then reality hit and he became part of the long history of politics and poor performance for the school system. He built relationships with all the key people but was not courageous enough to deal with the conflict that had ruled the community for many years. His principals acted as if their schools were on islands and did not have to be part of the whole school system. The schools had their own cultures and tried to avoid being aligned with the school system and the politics.

The superintendent tried to raise system-wide standards for curriculum and instruction and professional development. He tried to work on strategic planning and team building with the school board and his leadership team. He built strong relationships with the chamber of commerce, municipal government, and community agencies. The financial constraints were always an issue for sustaining any positive initiatives for change.

The community hoped that this new superintendent would be promising for the school system. However, the hope began to disappear. The state department of education tried to support the district and the superintendent, but did not have the authority to change any of the conditions in the district to bring about significant change. The district has been able to hire talented people but has also lost qualified staff who believed the conditions would never change. The superintendent has not been able to build and sustain a leadership team to lead the district to improving student achievement.

The culture of a school or school system can completely overcome the best leaders. These leaders often underestimate the power of a culture to overcome their efforts and make them part of the culture they are trying to change. This superintendent continually believes he cannot run the school system because the mayor is micromanaging. He continually states that the principals are not accountable and do whatever they want. This very friendly and affable man with the positive attitude has become jaded and negative and is now part of the culture.

He has been coached to look at his leadership style and work on building on his strengths and attending to his weaknesses. He started to work with his leadership team to build a plan for success and sustain their efforts despite the politics and the history of failure in their schools.

Robert and the MBTI

Robert's MBTI provides data that describe the challenges to his leadership (see Figures 4.3 and 4.4). His high perception style could be very positive because of his creativity and ability to solve problems. He likes challenges and tends to not let the past hold him back from the opportunities of tomorrow. He can be strategic (intuitive), and his extrovert and feeling style has helped him develop relationships with all groups. However, now that he is working as a coordinator and not leading, his MBTI style is becoming a liability. The feeling style can cause emotional paralysis and make him withdraw from people because he fears disappointing them. He takes criticism too personally and avoids conflict. The pattern of the MBTI with the DISC would be avoidance of conflict and more withdrawal behind the scenes. The stress will increase and begin to affect him by causing mood swings that will further affect his leadership.

The MBTI team profile (Figure 4.5) shows an extroverted team that is very capable with strong leadership for connecting to principals and the community. There is a good balance on the intuitive and sensing grid, indicating that the balance for short- and long-term planning is strong.

The balance on the superintendent's leadership team is also strong for the thinking and feeling and the judging and perceiving scales (Figure 4.6). This team could be an HPT and help the superintendent lead the district if there were a commitment from the superintendent of 1 to 2 years of hard, focused work on leadership and team development. Unfortunately, the high score in the MBTI perception makes it difficult for the superintendent to choose a plan and stay the course.

(continued)

CASE STUDY *(continued)*

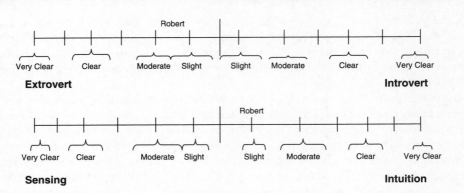

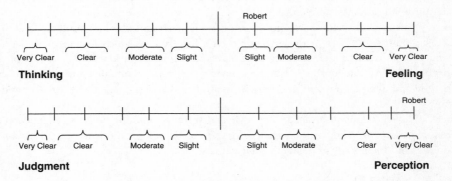

FIGURE 4.3   Robert's Scores on the Extrovert/Introvert Scale and Sensing/Intuitive Scale

FIGURE 4.4   Robert's Scores on the Thinking/Feeling Scale and the Judging/Perceiving Scale

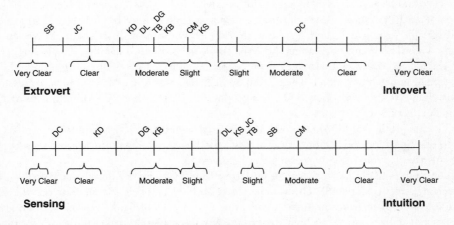

FIGURE 4.5   The E/I and S/N Scores for Robert's Leadership Team

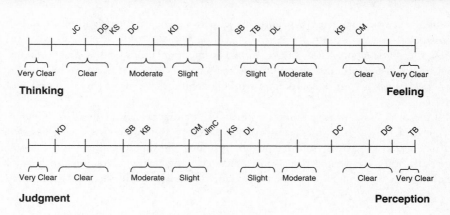

FIGURE 4.6   The T/F and J/P Scores for Robert's Leadership Team

Robert and the DISC

Robert's DISC bar chart is shown in Figure 4.7. He is naturally high in influence and just over the line in dominance and steadiness. His compliance score is relatively low. He will naturally build relationships and coach and support his team. He tends to trust his team about compliance issues and would not be a micromanager.

His adapted style tells a different story. His compliance score rises by 44 points. His steadiness score is also increasing, meaning that he is trying to slow things down to get people involved in decisions and to set up systems. He is increasing his cautious behavior and believes he is moving too fast. His influence score decreases but is still high. He is still spending time on relationships but less than he would like to. The major concern is his

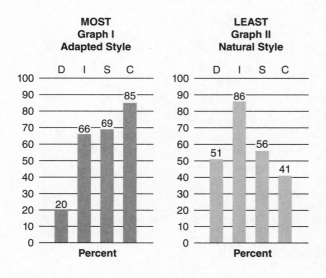

FIGURE 4.7   Robert's **DISC Bar Chart**   *Source:* Copyright © 2012 Target Training International, Ltd. Used with permission.

CASE STUDY *(continued)*

decrease in dominance by 31 points. He is losing his sense of urgency and trying to please all parties instead of acting decisively.

In the DISC wheel (see Figure 4.8) he moves from a promoter to a coordinator. The promoter style was very positive when he began the job making promises to the school system and the community of raising student achievement. Now he has become a coordinator working behind the scenes trying to please everyone and not leading the system.

Figures 4.9 and 4.10 show his team's DISC wheels. The natural behavior wheel has only one person in the dominant or persuader areas that would tend to drive change with a high sense of urgency, which is desperately needed in the district. There are three people including the superintendent in the promoter category. This behavior is helpful to leadership but not oriented to driving change more quickly. The only leader with a high sense of urgency for change is the athletic director. The adapted wheel depicts the dramatic problem in

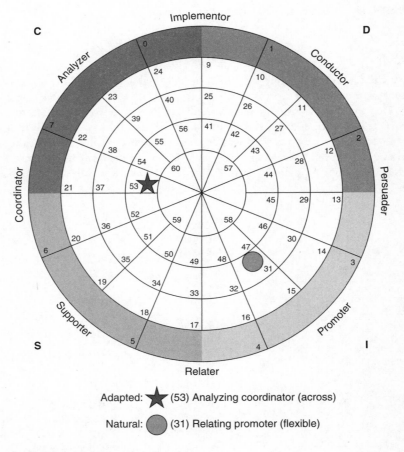

Adapted: ★ (53) Analyzing coordinator (across)

Natural: ● (31) Relating promoter (flexible)

FIGURE 4.8   Robert's DISC Wheel
Source: Copyright © 2012 Target Training International, Ltd. Used with permission.

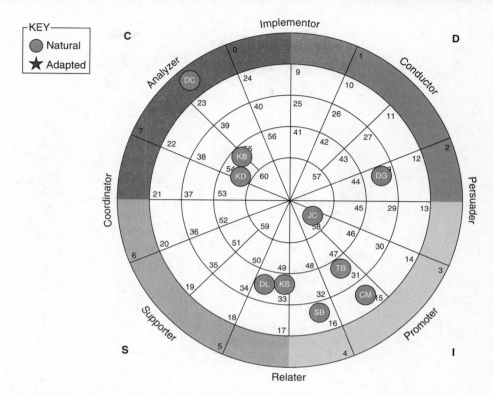

FIGURE 4.9   The Natural DISC Wheel for Robert's Team
Source: Copyright © 2012 Target Training International, Ltd. Used with permission.

the district. No one is in the dominant and persuader areas providing the leadership behavior needed to move the system ahead in this politically paralyzing community. The athletic director becomes unplaceable and too stressed to provide leadership. This is a team that desperately needs new leaders and a plan to increase their urgency for change.

Robert and the Values Inventory

Robert's Values inventory results (Figure 4.11) show that he cares greatly about his students and wants to lead the district to success. He has traditional values about how people should act and respect each other, which are not prevalent in the community. His values are core to his style and could be a motivator for him to regain his leadership role.

Robert and the Seven Competencies

Robert has some of the competencies for success. However, there are a few that need serious work for him to be a high-performing leader.

(continued)

CASE STUDY *(continued)*

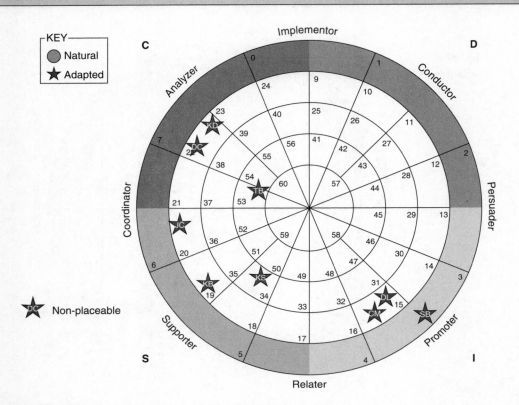

FIGURE 4.10   **The Adapted DISC Wheel for Robert's Team**
Source: Copyright © 2012 Target Training International, Ltd. Used with permission.

FIGURE 4.11   Robert's Values
Inventory Bar Chart   *Source:*
Copyright © 2012 Target Training
International, Ltd. Used with
permission.

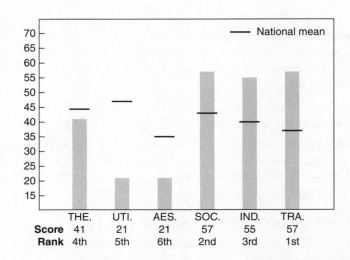

	THE.	UTI.	AES.	SOC.	IND.	TRA.
Score	41	21	21	57	55	57
Rank	4th	5th	6th	2nd	3rd	1st

1. *Challenges the status quo.* Robert is strong in his leadership style and his beliefs about doing what it takes for his school system to be successful. He is innovative and visionary and his tendency is to chart his own path for success and not worry about challenging convention. However, he is having a difficult time dealing with his school board, which challenges all of his ideas with their personal agendas. This pressure results in Robert being inconsistent with his goals and plans. There are some areas where he stays true to his beliefs and challenges the norms and practices of the district, and in other areas he maintains the status quo. Unfortunately, in a low-performing district, staying with the practices that do not work can completely derail any progress. For example, keeping incompetent people in jobs because of political pressure is not a luxury that an underperforming district can afford.

2. *Builds trust through clear communications and expectations.* Robert has the skills to present his vision clearly. However, he is often hesitant and worries about the politics or offending people when he presents his ideas. This results in unclear and inconsistent messages to staff and the public. People tend to trust him personally because he is a very warm and caring person. However, this lack of clarity in direction is hurting his ability to improve his school district's performance. He does not set clear expectations or stay focused on the results. He is very indecisive and tends to start and stop initiatives. He usually says that the politics and the money are the reasons he has to change direction. This seems like a convenient excuse, not the words of clarity and decisiveness needed in a high-performing leader.

3. *Creates a commonly owned plan for success.* Robert has not been able to create one plan for success that is owned by all constituents. He tends to allow and support plans for initiatives based on funding and politics. This has resulted in a fractured school system. Recently, he did work on one plan for success with his leadership team and the principals. This effort was received very positively by all parties. The school board was not part of this process. This was a conscious decision due to the likelihood that they would derail the effort. The question remains whether Robert can stay focused on implementing the plan. If he waivers and succumbs to politics again this will be a major blow to his district. He has used a lot of his personal capital and support to pull people together around this new plan. The principals were beginning to see the benefit of being a school system and not separate islands. Unfortunately, if he loses his focus again, it will be almost impossible for him to recover.

4. *Focuses on team over self.* Robert's belief system is very team oriented. His ego does not get in the way of his work in building a team environment. This personality trait and his willingness to publically admit his weaknesses are great strengths. However, he cannot stay with the team building process consistently. If he did, his team could accomplish great results. The team needs him to be the external person in the system dealing with the school board and the public. The team can and is better suited to run the internal system. His style in the DISC as a promoter makes him a great ambassador for the system. The leadership team is more focused and detail oriented and under his overall direction is capable of disciplined implementation.

5. *Has a high sense of urgency for change and sustainable results in improving student achievement.* Robert has a high sense of urgency for change. However, his style of leadership does not allow him to implement plans that get clear results. His ability to learn how to stay focused on change efforts and not become derailed by politics, money, and his own indecisive style will allow him to achieve results that the students in the district need now.

6. *Commits to continuous improvement for self.* Robert is open to feedback and wants to improve. However, once again, he cannot stay with any change and improvement effort long enough to achieve results. He believes that his team would benefit from the same effort and has helped them take the first few steps to learning about their leadership profiles. Will he be able to stay committed to this process? History says no.

(continued)

7. *Builds external networks and partnerships.* This competency is Robert's greatest strength. He is very extroverted and is able to develop relationships and potential partnerships with many people and organizations. If he commits to being the external person in the system this skill can result in major support from political groups and businesses that need the school system to be successful. Currently, Robert once again is inconsistent on his implementation. He starts a partnership and then may get criticism from his school board and withdraws. His ability in this competency is a great asset to the school system if it can be actualized.

Action Plan for Improvement

Robert and his leadership team are at a crucial point. The superintendent must show the courage to lead his district and realize he cannot please everybody. He must not fall into the political landmines that have destroyed all his predecessors. He must use his influence style to form key alliances that will support a plan for success. He needs to commit to building a strong high-performance leadership team that develops a strategic plan for the next 3 years. He needs to form a new partnership with the mayor that is built on respect of his role and his support for the community, and not be intimated by the politics. He must be able to lead and risk losing his job for promising the community high student achievement and respectful dialog. He needs a cadre of support systems around him that can bring expertise into his community along with the state playing a leadership role in support of his plan. The superintendent needs to stop using excuses about money, politics, poor principals who work in silos, and a community who lacks a desire to be great. He must be strong and show them the way without excuses. If he loses his job over staying with his values and building alliances for success, then the job could not be done and the community will deteriorate for another 20 to 30 years until the state finds a way to take over. If Robert develops a professional plan for himself and stays committed to his own improvement, he will have many offers to be a superintendent in his state and throughout the country.

Will this happen? Looking at what is happening in so many communities trapped in poor performance in education, it looks unlikely. However, Robert is driven by his values of caring for students and families and an undying belief that all kids can and will learn. He is beginning to build a new strategy for success.

He has delegated the leadership of his district on an operational basis to his leadership team. He has pulled all the principals and assistant principals together to build a unified spirit for success that uses the high-performance principles. He has supported every leader to complete the leadership inventories and to build high-performance leadership teams in their schools and departments.

Robert has worked with a consultant to build one consolidated plan for success for the district. There will be no separate plans generated by special interest groups pulling the district into disparate directions.

The Final Story

Robert is putting most of his effort into working with the school board and the community to sell his consolidated plan and to build a positive culture of teamwork. He realizes that the external part of his job is full time and will require all his skills and abilities. He will resume his role as a promoter in the DISC inventory and persuade all constituencies that the districts can break out of the politics and work together for the common good of the students' goals and dreams.

This superintendent is trying to make changes in his leadership style to get out in front and lead, rather than withdrawing into the background and reacting and letting the system deteriorate over the remaining years of his tenure. Time will tell whether Robert can resist the temptations to succumb to political pressure and the stress of the job. He is energized now and is driven to succeed. Let's hope he stays the course.

Reflective Questions

1. What could Robert do to increase his success as a leader?
2. If he took a stronger role as a leader, what would be his risks?
3. How could Robert mitigate some of his risks to increase his results?
4. What have you learned about how reality and risk affect you as a leader?
5. How could you avoid the trap of letting the realities of the job control you?

5

Beginning the Hard Work of Improving Your Leadership

When Do I Start to Take Control of a Runaway Train?

Now that we know what the profile is for a successful leader, we should understand that being a high-performance leader is hard work and cannot be done alone. All leaders need strong high-performance teams around them to succeed. We also know that all the theories on leadership do not teach us how to overcome reality when it hits us on a day-to-day basis. There are so many issues that can and often do derail leaders who, on paper, have all the skills and competencies to be effective. The statistics on superintendent turnover show the mean tenure is between 5 and 6 years, and the continuous transitions to new leaders in education are commonplace and very disruptive (Glass & Franceschini, 2006). Each time a leader changes, there is a learning period for staff to become familiar with the new leader's style and for the new leader to assess the staff and the new community. This transition time often results in good people leaving due to the stress caused by change. Whether the change of leaders is successful or not, each transition takes time and costs in student performance. During this time, momentum is lost and progress is halted. Although a new leader can be very positive and can achieve great success, it is more productive to maintain leadership for a long enough period of time to develop and implement a plan to improve a school or district.

There are many leaders who want to make a difference in a school or school district and make an impact over time. However, because they do not understand how to lead a change process by building a plan and constructing strategy for long-term improvement, they become turn-key leaders. These leaders do not consider the time needed to build a sustainable change and improvement strategy. By the time change occurs, these leaders have left the district. Many leaders talk about results, but if they are not around to ensure successful implementation, they never fulfill their goals. These leaders who come and go quickly blame their school committees, the budget, the politics, and the teachers who will not change. These leaders need to look at themselves before they blame others. Knowing how to create and implement change is what the work of improving education for kids is all about. This chapter will help all leaders stay long enough to reap the fruits of their labor. The talent and commitment to stay in a school or in a district takes skill and self-awareness.

When assuming a position of leadership, educators begin with excitement, hopes, and dreams. They begin their tenures believing that their impact on students will be dramatic and the personal and professional rewards will be substantial. However, they may soon find that they have taken over a runaway train that they must quickly stabilize to achieve the best goals for students. This chapter will outline the process of taking over a leadership role, reviewing your leadership style, and adjusting to all the challenges that will confront you to move the train down the track to sustainable success.

DON'T TRY TO CHANGE THINGS TOO FAST

Each leader comes into a new job believing that he or she can make a difference quickly. That leader is hired for his or her passion and skills that meet needs based on the problems of the past. Often the leader is told when he or she is hired that more communication with the community, an increased focus on fiscal management, or an improved relationship with the teachers is needed. Although these messages are often true, they can be very distracting to the new leader. If a new leader takes this direction from the school board, he or she assumes things will be off to a great start. However, by taking others' assessment of the problems at face value, he or she will be walking into a landmine. The search process is designed to hire the best leader for the problems that are facing the school or school system. Because the focus is on finding a leader who will quickly fix the problems, little effort is put into the long-term issues that create the situation, and the person hired is only dealing with symptoms and not real issues.

Therefore, new leaders must step back and conduct their own assessments of the issues. An entry plan is advisable (Jentz, 1982) to begin a more thorough and deliberate analysis of the issues that the leader will face, both in the short and long term. The leader should identify all the constituents whose support will be needed and develop key questions. The constituents' responses are very important to make sure that all perspectives are considered. The leader then summarizes all the themes and presents them to the school board in a public session to launch his plan for effective entry into the school system and the community. The leader should include his or her leadership profile and how it will impact the entry plan and the issues the school or school system faces both in the short and long term.

The leader also needs to find out all the concerns and issues that were considered during the hiring process. The leader is usually hired based on the results of community focus groups and a leadership profile that was developed by the community. However, this profile is not provided to the new leader. This information is very important and needs to be reviewed by the new leader. Identifying issues that emerged during the hiring process will help the new leader avoid mistakes. For example, a new superintendent was hired because of his ability to work with the community. However, the school committee was concerned that if too much information was shared with the community, the town leaders would use it in a negative manner. If the new superintendent had made all information transparent to help build a positive relationship with the community, he would have immediately caused a problem with the school committee.

KNOW YOURSELF AND WHAT CAN DERAIL YOU

Once the new leader conducts an entry plan and reviews the data and information collected during the search process, a new plan to move ahead can be developed. New leaders must now stop and look at themselves and understand their leadership styles, behaviors, and values before proceeding. They also must know and understand their leadership team and their strengths and weaknesses. This self-awareness can prevent this runaway train from becoming a train wreck.

A new principal was hired to lead a school that had four principals over the last 5 years. This principal was hired for her vision and passion for education and extensive experience in professional development on a state-wide and national level. The school was not focused and lacked follow-through due to the lack of skills of the previous leaders. The teachers were very talented, but they were frustrated by the constant change in principals and the top-down initiatives from the central office.

The principal came in with great energy and commitment to overcome the concerns of the superintendent and the faculty. Initially, the plan to move ahead on key instructional issues was received positively. Suddenly, however, the principal realized she was leading a runaway train. The faculty didn't want any more changes or new ideas. They had had enough and wanted stability and status quo. Although the principal knew about the instability in leadership, she did not realize how sensitive and resistant the faculty members were to change.

The principal was an ENTP and showed high dominance and low steadiness on the DISC. The principal's highest value was theoretical. Therefore, this principal was a naturally strong leader who would be great at initiating and driving change, making quick improvements, and using data to analyze student achievement. If the principal used all her natural skills and experience it would threaten the faculty and create a negative environment and culture at the school.

The hiring of a very skilled leader by a superintendent without a strong entry plan, including coaching to help adapt one's style, is often a formula for failure. An entry plan typically includes a full analysis of the issues that are current in a school and the opportunity for the new leader to talk to a range of people from all constituencies that are core to a school's direction and operations. Once all data is gathered and analyzed, the new leader shares the information and his or her analysis and understanding of the needs of the new school with all constituents. The importance of making sure that everyone is on the same page regarding the needs and steps for improvement allows the leader to obtain the support needed to move ahead with improvement efforts. It is suggested that we add the elements of self-awareness of leadership style to this process to help the new leader understand how his or her profile either matches the needs or could be a problem in making needed improvements.

This new principal had to adapt her style immediately to the culture of the school. The dominant behavior needed to be decreased significantly, and a team environment needed to be developed using her influencing behavior on the DISC. The principal brought the leadership team together and set up a process to engage the faculty. The faculty was asked about their concerns and listed items that spanned several pages. These issues were a culmination of all the years of turnover and frustration the faculty had experienced. The principal and the leadership team realized that they must deal with this list in partnership with the faculty to begin to develop a new team culture.

The school is now stabilizing. However, if the principal had proceeded with her natural style of dealing with the issues at the school, the runaway train would have probably crashed, resulting in her being fired or resigning.

CAN YOU REALLY CHANGE YOUR MAJOR WEAKNESSES?

Fundamental behavioral change takes major commitment and strength of character. It is easy to say you want to change, then make attempts that fall short, and blame others for your failures. The key to changing one's behavior is to be able to receive and use critical feedback for improvement. Being open to critical feedback is very difficult. Each of us wants to believe that we have the ability to be effective leaders. Leaders often hear criticism and defend their behaviors or disregard the messages as incorrect. Leaders also may discount the messages because they believe the messenger is not credible. We all want to hear praise and are motivated by positive feedback.

The journey to real behavioral change starts with the openness and honesty to understand and accept your strengths and weaknesses. It is not helpful to refute the data of the leadership inventories, a 360 evaluation, or your boss's feedback. Telling someone that his or her observations or concerns about your behavior or performance are wrong will not work. When a person has the courage and commitment to provide critical feedback, the last response that person wants to hear is defensiveness, denial, attacks on their character, or disregard for his or her point of view. The typical response from a person receiving these reactions is frustration, anger, withdrawal, and resignation that you will never change. Very rarely does a defensive reaction to critical feedback leave a positive impression. To really commit to fundamental change and improvement, one must be able to hear all feedback as positive and constructive. A leadership team developed a principle for high performance that states, "listen and accept all feedback; at least 99% is productive."

It must be noted that how one delivers feedback is critical to how it will be received. If one has the skills to deliver feedback in a manner that is not personal and attacking, the chances of success increase dramatically. However, it is more important that the receiver be open to hearing and understanding feedback, even if the message is delivered poorly. Feedback is data for you to use in developing a strategy for improvement. People who can accept constructive criticism are often viewed positively by colleagues, subordinates, and outside constituents.

It is important to remember that when someone is being critical, it is not about whether he or she is right. It is more about why that person reacts to you or your behavior in a manner that is nonproductive. You may have very positive intent, but if someone perceives it in a negative manner, you may need to change your delivery. You might be thinking that some people are the problem and it has nothing to do with you. That may be true; however, their feedback can be helpful in providing data on how to deal with others that may appear irrational to you.

One principal lost control of his runaway train by not being able to fully integrate the feedback from his staff. This principal was very innovative and technologically savvy. He came in to a school that had replaced three principals in 5 years. He received feedback from the faculty to listen first and not to try to change things too quickly. Although he believed he was listening, he tried to add new technologies to instruction right way. The teachers and the union complained vigorously that they were overwhelmed and asked him to slow down. He kept pushing that the new technology would help with their workload.

The faculty believed that he wasn't listening. He felt he was listening and was helping them with their problem of feeling overwhelmed. The runaway train became derailed when he had a key meeting with the union. He was attempting to demonstrate that he was sensitive to them and heard their message, and would adjust his strategy. He had also been criticized for being late to meetings, showing that he did not care about their time. The meeting was set for one hour and he showed up 25 minutes late. He said he was buying doughnuts for the meeting. This was the straw that broke the camel's back, and the union and the rest of the faculty decided that he was incapable of adjusting to their needs. The principal lost his job soon after that ill-fated meeting. The principal was not able to hear the criticisms and make the needed changes, and was still holding on to the belief that he was right.

What about strength-based approaches that say we need to spend less time on the negative and build on the positives? The positives are important, and they are a major part of building a plan for success. However, even in strength-based approaches (Rath, 2007), the major weaknesses need to be addressed. It is also true that strength can become a weakness.

An example involves a principal who is driven to get results quickly and tends to work every weekend. She e-mails her staff on the weekend and expects them to be driven in the same way by working weekends. She gets frustrated and believes they do not care about the kids as much as she does because they do not respond to her on the weekend or read her e-mails in order to discuss the issues on Monday morning. The principal has lost the support of her staff, who feels that there are no boundaries or respect for their personal lives.

To make fundamental change there must be an incentive. People are motivated by a goal or a fear. A person finally changes his or her diet after the heart attack. In the same way, a leader may not become motivated to improve until after he or she is fired. A leader can see other colleagues failing or dissatisfied with their work and become motivated to not be like them.

Positive goals are often motivators. The teacher leader that wants to become a principal has a clear direction in mind. Even for career goals it is important for people to know more about themselves and their styles, behaviors, and values. If they explore these personal leadership issues now, they will have a deeper understanding of why they want to move up in the leadership ranks.

Some people are motivated by a desire for continuous improvement. They are never satisfied with their current situation and always want to improve. Thomas Edison once stated, "Show me a satisfied man and I will show you a failure." Those who are very motivated to improve must be comfortable learning from failure. Failure or setbacks are another source of data. Ask yourself, "if I was so prepared and my goals and intent was right, then why did this fail?" Prevent yourself from blaming others and really be honest with yourself about your role in the failure.

The simple answer to whether you can really change a major weakness is yes. It takes hard work and commitment to learn and to be honest with yourself. Major weaknesses tend to be issues that need attention over long periods to change. This is where your team can help. They can provide both positive and negative feedback to you on your improvement efforts.

A principal that was late to meetings and continually sent reports in late always used the excuse of not having enough staff or being too busy. The principal, with the help of a coach, made a major paradigm shift to being on time. The coach said that being on time is not a matter of trying to improve from 50% to 60% over the next year. The coach said that either you are on time or not, and you have to decide whether you want to be an on-time or late person in life. It was 100% or don't even try.

This shocking revelation was monumental to the principal. She had to then determine the attitudes and behavior of an on-time person and what a life like that would be. She realized that on-time people are always early. They do not try to time things to the end, because then problems occur. They do not double book appointments. They prepare in advance and are very disciplined. Her exploration went even further to realizing that being on time was less stressful and more satisfying. This principal was motivated to change to being 100% on time. Her team knew the goal and supported the commitment. This principal has slight setbacks, and she receives honest feedback from her team when they occur. The change has been fundamental and, while not 100%, her punctuality is at least 95%. Although she is proud of her work on improving, she is still driven to the 100% figure as the only measure of success.

FIND TRAINING FOR SKILL DEFICITS

Although it is important to work on self-development, there are also areas of improvement that involve skill, training, and support. The focus of most educational training and support today is on instructional leadership. Increasing your skills in classroom observations, data analysis, and how to increase rigor and relevance in curriculum and instruction are all important skills for educational leaders.

All the focus cannot be on instruction and assessment. The role of the leader is broader in scope as a principal, a central administrator, or a superintendent. For example, superintendents and principals are not encouraged to improve their financial management skills to the equivalent of comparable positions in other sectors such as health care. The superintendent is often told to focus on instruction and hire a good business manager. Although having a good business manager is important, the focus is potentially harmful to that superintendent. If the superintendent has a greater understanding of financial planning and management, he or she would realize that a chief financial officer is needed, not just a business manager. The superintendent would be able to speak more fluently about financial management in a finance committee meeting or to corporate leaders in the community.

Strategic planning, marketing, forming strategic partnerships, customer service, project management, building HPTs, and other areas are very important for educational leaders. Most educational leaders would say they have no time or reason to increase their skills in these areas. However, if they built leadership capacity in their districts, built leadership teams, and increased teacher instructional leadership, they would have more time for these areas that will have an impact on success.

Another skill that is completely ignored in education is fundraising. Educators have become dependent on local, state, and federal dollars for their success, but these dollars have been decreasing every year. In the nonprofit world, leaders understand that fundraising is critical to their success. Superintendents and principals that increase these skills will have an advantage in both job searches and in the ability to help their districts find alternative sources of funding. The superintendent in this chapter's case study raised $1 million from an individual donor for science education.

COACHING IS A KEY ELEMENT FOR SUCCESS

Unfortunately, many educational leaders believe having a coach is a sign of weakness. Some school boards and superintendents believe that if they are paying a fair salary and the person was hired for their skills, abilities, and background, they should not need a coach. Others say we do not have the money to coach people. Mentoring is much more popular and accepted in education. Mentors are generally other educational leaders who use their experience to advise new leaders on specific matters such as how to give an opening day speech, handling teacher negotiations, and so forth.

Coaching or executive coaching is much more accepted in industry, health care, government, and the nonprofit world (Coutu & Kauffman, 2009). People in these other fields realize that the stress, pressure, and the complexity of their positions warrant having someone to talk to who can help them sort through the issues and determine a strategy for success. A coach does not have to be from one's field of expertise. It is helpful if the individual has an understanding of education, even though the role is not to give advice. The person also does not have to be a certified coach (Reeves, 2007) to help an educational leader look at his or her personal leadership style and gain insights into behavior. The in-depth analysis of issues and the person is part of the coaching experience.

Coaches work with educational leaders to help them see themselves in an honest and direct manner. A coach puts a "mirror" up for the leader to really see his or her behavior in an unadulterated manner. All leaders need to be able to understand how their behavior affects people. There are a variety of tools that can help the leaders gain an honest assessment of their behavior and effectiveness. Of course, the leader's evaluation is a tool for understanding effectiveness; unfortunately, most evaluation processes are not clear, measurable, or useful for the person in developing a plan for improvement. School boards are so influenced by politics, special interest groups, and their own lack of knowledge of the leader's job that their feedback is important but not comprehensive. Principals receive evaluations from a superintendent, but often lack ongoing honest feedback to gain deeper understanding of the areas for improvement.

Therefore, a process of self-assessment is often more helpful for a leader. This process would include leadership inventories such as the ones discussed in this text. In addition, a 360 development process is extremely helpful. Having a group of people above you, people who report to you, and colleagues provide feedback on a range of questions involving your leadership and management skills can provide data that can make a difference in your ability to be effective. A 720 review (which uses the same process as a 360 review but also includes external viewpoints) can also be helpful by adding customers to the feedback group. However, the 720 is rarely used in education. The 720 could include people from the chamber of commerce, municipal leadership for the superintendent, or parents or community organizations for the principals.

Once a coach has the data from your inventories, a 360 review, and from your own self-assessment on the 360, a real conversation can begin to occur about your effectiveness. A 360 can often point out that a person may be very effective managing with his or her boss, but could have problems with his or her staff. It is hard to keep all groups satisfied at the same time. Therefore, the 360 can give you a snapshot of your effectiveness at a point that could be reviewed in 6 months to a year for progress to be measured.

The coach's job is to point out inconsistencies in the data or clear patterns for your reaction. One governmental leader in a high-level position had been very successful in moving up the ladder. Her technical skills, intelligence, work ethic, and presentation skills were superior. However, her interpersonal skills were becoming a problem. The leader intimidated others both below her and her colleagues. The coach was able to show the leader her successes and the ratings and comments from the people who were intimidated. Right away the leader wanted to know the identity of the people who made negative comments. This behavior demonstrated the intimidation behavior the coach was trying to explain to her.

Once the leader was able to calm down, listen, and understand how her behavior affected others, she could begin the process of understanding why she acted in this intimidating manner. She was able to point out that she always had to fight hard for issues in her family and as a woman in a male-dominated technical field. She had also grown up in New York and was very used to a more combative, engaging climate at work and at home. However, now she was not in New York and her ability, intelligence, and position gave her the ability and choice not to fight in the same way. She could coach others and build their skills to fight their own battles. Her DISC score was 100 on the dominant and 86 on the influence, and she was low steadiness and low compliance in a government position in which most leaders have the opposite DISC score. She will need to lower her dominance score and rely more on the influence behaviors to build the leadership capacity in her organization.

The coach has to be direct and effectively confront his client's behavior. The coach must have the courage to challenge and then support the client's growth process. The coach must be willing to lose the client's business if necessary, and ensure he is not just supportive to keep the money. The power of the coach is that he will risk the contract to do what is necessary help the client in the growth and development process.

BUILDING LEADERSHIP CAPACITY

Once a leader is well underway in the process of self-development, he or she must begin the process of building the leadership capacity of the district or school. The key to a leader's success is to have strong people around to help complement his or her skills. Every leader needs to identify who the current and potential leaders are in the school or district. In education, we often wait for leaders to take the initiative and manage their own careers. We need to shift the role of our leaders to explicitly seek out potential and begin to provide opportunities, coaching, and support for leadership. Too many potential leaders do not want to assume traditional leadership roles in education. They see the roles of principal, central administration, and superintendent as too political and difficult and not appreciated by school committees or the general public. Teachers are often satisfied staying teachers and avoiding all the challenges of higher leadership roles.

A key strategy for education is to maximize opportunities for teacher leadership. Providing assignments and projects for teachers to lead other teachers is a key for education to build capacity for change. Superintendents and principals need to balance their roles as instructional leaders by developing instructional leadership in the teacher ranks. When teachers emerge as leaders, they have immediate respect and credibility with their colleagues. The unions also become more supportive of teachers in leadership roles.

A master teacher can be very effective in providing constructive feedback with a new young teacher and even a more experienced colleague. The power of a colleague can be even more effective than the principal in changing behavior. Education must become flexible in creating time and opportunity for teachers to lead.

The ability for a leader to move power and influence closer to the point of service has been the definition of efforts to increase school-based management. However, efforts to increase school-based management have faded in education. The increased pressure on a more centralized effort to improve school achievement through high-stakes testing seems to have a negative impact on school-based management. Moreover, leaders who recognize that they need a highly motivated and talented teaching staff to increase student achievement tend to flourish in the effort to build leadership capacity.

Another key reason for focusing on building leadership capacity is to take the pressure off administrators. If an administrator can feel confident delegating to staff who have the skills to lead a project, the administrator will have more time to pursue other initiatives that are important to the district or school. The principal can work with parents, the community, and other key groups and coach their teachers to lead, which will expand their effectiveness both within and outside of their building.

HOW TO BUILD YOUR LEADERSHIP TEAM TO INCREASE CAPACITY

The ability to build leadership capacity is increased exponentially by building a high-performance leadership team. When team members become focused on common goals for a school or school system and learn how to support each other and hold each other accountable, the capacity for achievement increases. The principal does not have to manage and hold everyone accountable. Team members take initiative and reach out to others without having to wait for the principal to approve each next step.

A school leadership team consists mostly of teachers but can include other leaders in the school. Parents, community and business leaders, central office personnel, and municipal personnel can all be part of the team. Many states have passed legislation to develop school councils to be leadership teams for schools. However, as many new efforts to improve education have come and gone, the roles of these school advisory councils have faded. Because change is driven from the federal and state government and not from sound methods to develop effective organizations, high-priority initiatives get displaced with new fashionable efforts. School councils have been effective with high-performing principals. Most principals spend much of their time complying with legislation instead of understanding and nurturing the team concept in their schools. New superintendents come in and displace the priorities of the previous superintendent.

Professional learning communities (PLC) have become the new terminology for teams in schools. PLCs have become a goal in many districts throughout the country. However, if the principal is a dominant top-down leader, a PLC will become ineffective. PLCs should not be the goal; they are a means to improve student achievement. If PLCs become the new initiative to change education, they will fade out once again as a new answer is presented that displaces their efforts. It is important for the leader to be clear about the role and the expectations for a PLC. The ENTJ style cited in several case studies tends to be explicit, set a broad and measurable goal, and support the development of a clear plan for action with timelines and outcomes. PLCs that are clear about their role and the plan of action have a higher degree of success. The influence behavior in the DISC is very important for PLCs. A group of faculty reviewing data is not a team. PLCs need the coaching and support of the principal to become a high-performing team that can make a difference in student achievement.

Parent–teacher organizations (PTOs) have lasted throughout all the change efforts, but they play very different roles in communities. Some PTOs are influential on policy and direction in schools and school systems (The Wallace Foundation, 2010). Other PTOs deal only with operational support or fundraising for classroom activities.

A common organizational issue for a leader in a school or school system is to form a leadership team. Developing subteams or groups that take on specific roles is fine, as long as they tie back to the overall strategic plan for the school or school district. Many urban districts are plagued by too many teams or groups that are not integrated into common goals. Recently, a low-performing district created leadership teams at the school and school district levels, but there were 10 other teams formed based on grants, community involvement, technology, a new vocational school, and specific issues such as bullying that were not tied or integrated into school and district plans. Each group took time and resources away from each other to pursue their goals. In an already financially strapped district, these separate groups were part of the problem, not part of the solution. To help this school system focus, the consultant helped develop one consolidated plan, pulling separate, discreet projects into one document. Three goals were developed for the district to act as the umbrella for all the improvement efforts. The leadership team oversaw the plans for the three goals. One goal involved improving student achievement, goal two dealt with people and financial resources inside and outside the district, and the third goal involved space and redistricting efforts. Three committees were formed with central office personnel and principals to work on these three goals. The progress on the goals was to be reviewed during system wide meetings four times per year. The status of the three goals was to be reported during school board meetings on a regular basis to help focus the school board.

No new committees were formed that would work outside of these three goals. The school system looked at data and measurement for success and began the process of moving leadership development and capacity to the schools and teacher leaders. The superintendent worked externally on selling the plan to the community and finding resources to support the goals. This underperforming district is now focused and streamlined in its effort to improve. They will not let all the distractions and initiatives pull them away from their plan. The district is supporting teams that are becoming HPTs at both a district and a school level.

MANAGING UP AND DEALING WITH THE SCHOOL BOARD AND COMMUNITY LEADERS

The message today is to focus on instructional leadership and enhance the rigor of the curriculum to improve student achievement. Although improving student achievement is the core focus for all schools and school systems, a leader must be able to manage up, across, and outside the school and school system. To manage up, a principal must work effectively with the central office, the superintendent, and the school committee. A superintendent is managing up effectively if he or she has a strong partnership with the school board. To manage across, the educational leader needs to connect well with his or her colleagues. If the leader is too competitive or noncollaborative with colleagues, it can cause a problem. For example, two high school principals in one district needed to make sure that there was consistency in their curriculum to meet district goals. If they did not want to work together due to a desire to be number one, that would prevent them from taking the time to meet to discuss aligning the curriculum.

A superintendent's colleagues are other superintendents or municipal leaders. Business and community leaders could also be seen as colleagues. There is an unspoken code of conduct among superintendents that allows them to be colleagues. Superintendents expect their colleagues to support and not compete with them. This unspoken code often relates to recruiting or "stealing" administrators from each other. One superintendent violated this code by recruiting a business manager from a neighboring district without calling the superintendent in that district. The concerned superintendent believed that it was a professional courtesy to inform another superintendent of the fact that his or her administrator was a candidate for a key role in the school system. In fact, the issue of whether another colleague should recruit was a major concern.

To manage across, administrators need to develop positive relationships with other community leaders, the chamber of commerce, and industry leaders. For the superintendent, the relationship with the town manager, the mayor, or the CEO of a local corporation might be critical. The principal must be able to work effectively with community leaders, the president of the PTO, and community leaders.

Why are all these relationships so important? A principal could be a very effective instructional leader but engage in antagonistic relationships with parents and lose his or her job. A superintendent can have great support from his or her staff but become the enemy of key community leaders and end up in a political situation that aligns a school committee member against the superintendent on an issue that can also cost the latter his or her job.

Managing relationships with people and organizational leaders who are not directly related to the work of improving instruction allows a leader to use a network of contacts to support the district's budget, provide advice on a key political or community issue, and build alliances for a controversial initiative. Being a school system and community leader provides a base of influence that can be critical to an educational leader's career.

One principal was known to be very innovative and a risk taker in his community. He continually tried new, unconventional ideas to help students achieve. He was known for going his own way on many educational initiatives and not staying true to the school system programs. This principal could have been seen as a maverick and risked losing his job at several points in his career. However, this principal was extremely adept at forming community relationships of influence and gaining a broad base of support that protected him from any superintendent or school board. He spent a lot of time getting to know all the parents, community leaders, and any potential resources that could help his school. He tried to develop relationships with community resources that could enhance the educational experience for his students. One of the parents in the community was involved in the Thunderbird aerial shows that draw large crowds in communities throughout the country. Through his networking, the principal took advantage of the Thunderbird show happening in at the local airfield and arranged to have the Thunderbird pilots—who are very well trained in aviation science and have a wealth of knowledge—come to his school to become a part of a science class and discuss aviation. The kids were amazed that the pilots arrived at the school and came into their classrooms. The relevance and excitement in the school was amazing. As a result of this sort of successful school event, the principal's test scores were always high and his colleagues were very jealous of the special attention he received. Newspaper reporters showed up to cover events in the school, and the publicity for the principal was extensive.

Was this principal a team player? He began his career as a person who wanted to be a member of the team. However, because the superintendent and the central office became intolerant of his antics, he found a way to manage up and across in a manner that made him untouchable. If the leadership in the school system was more open to innovation and worked with this principal to help his colleagues, would this entrepreneurial spirit help other schools? We will never know if this principal would have been a team player if he had had more support. However, his methods of gaining political support allowed him, his teachers, and his school to excel.

Managing relationships with other groups or your boss requires the influence behavior noted in the DISC. The extrovert style in the MBTI is beneficial because it helps one communicate with people so there are no surprises. The ability to move outside your own world to help others usually has a great return. The superintendent who helps the town manager gain support for the police department budget usually benefits from the town manager supporting the school department budget or the surprise extra costs in the special education budget that were not anticipated. The ability to influence results without direct power is essential for leaders in education. However, these skills are often seen as political and nonsubstantive in educational circles. Building networks of resources are seen as outside of the work of an educational leader and a potential distraction from the core work of a school system.

Superintendents who spend time working with their state or national associations can be seen as self-serving and trying to help their individual careers. School committee members often count the number of days the superintendent is outside the school system and use this data against him or her in a public evaluation. It is imperative for an educational leader to inform and educate people on the benefit of this external networking. Educators can enlist industry leaders or other community leaders to support the idea that their time spent networking is of benefit to the school system. In other sectors external networking is a key activity of senior leadership and is recognized and rewarded.

Managing up requires an understanding of the issues facing the person above you in the hierarchy. A principal once felt frustrated that the superintendent kept cancelling her meetings for other issues that constantly seemed to emerge at the last second. She believed the superintendent did not care or want to understand her issues in the school. Her coach helped her see that focusing on the issues that her superintendent believed were important and determining how she could contribute to her goals would change the importance of the meetings for the superintendent. The principal spent time understanding her boss's job and challenges and found ways to help. The cancellations decreased dramatically and the superintendent began to become more interested in the events of the school. The principal's relationship with the superintendent improved and she received a new 3-year contract with a raise.

The following is a case study of a superintendent who embraced the concepts of this book and the key learning noted in this chapter. He has a strong leadership profile but has been able to identify and begin working on the areas of his profile that need improvement to become a great leader.

CASE STUDY

RON

Overview

Ron is the superintendent of an urban district in the Southeast. He has just completed his first year within this large district, which has both suburban and urban populations that have underachieved in relationship to the resources that are available for the school system. The previous superintendent had a strong urban background and training to be a leader for urban education and had received training in a prestigious superintendent training program. Although the previous leader had a strong educational vision, leadership presence, and the courage to drive change, she lacked the interpersonal skills and community building attributes to create a culture for sustainable change and success.

Ron was hired for his vision, similar passion for education as the previous superintendent, and his ability to communicate and build a community of support for the education system. Ron had experience in both urban education and in a high-performing suburban district. His desire to commit to this new community was high and focused on making the school system a national model. His standards for himself were high and easily transferable to the people around him.

Ron has a variety of data and information to assess his strengths and areas for improvement as a high-performing leader. His evaluations by the school committee have been very positive, noting the amazing accomplishments that have occurred in the school system in a short time. The one area noted for improvement was to be more open to different points of view stated by the school committee. Being open to school committee involvement has been difficult for Ron due to the committee's proclivity to become over-involved in operations outside of its role. His 360 degree assessment has noted that he is respected by his colleagues, and those who report to him feel he is very knowledgeable of what it will take to improve the school system. His principals did note that they felt there was too much pressure for fast change and improvement.

Ron and the MBTI

As Ron uses the variety of feedback points to work on understanding his own leadership style and behaviors, it is important for him to use the perspective that the leadership inventories add to his profile. Ron's MBTI style is an ENFJ (see Figures 5.1 and 5.2). He understands that becoming a great leader starts with looking at himself and developing the strength and confidence to build a strong team around him that can make sustainable change. His leadership inventories have identified two major areas of focus for improvement. His feeling score presents great benefits but also major challenges to his success. His passion and ability to empathize with others is a great strength. However, the feeling score indicates a problem with taking criticism too personally and a potential desire to form personal connections with people who can be uncomfortable with their stricter boundary profiles. This does not mean inappropriate relationships. It does mean that Ron is more comfortable discussing personal issues with people who may be uncomfortable with that style. The emotion of a feeling person combined with his extroverted style can present an intensity to others that is hard to manage.

His MBTI score of being a very high extrovert and intuitive person matches the position very well. However, the extrovert style can interrupt others and create a feeling that everything is all about him. This is a coaching issue for Ron to work on. His high conceptual style could be difficult for sensing types to understand. Ron needs to work on how to communicate and support high-sensing staff. The high judging score allows Ron to make plans that are results oriented. However, the high judging style can also prevent Ron from being open to change and may make him appear too rigid to perceiving styles.

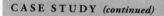

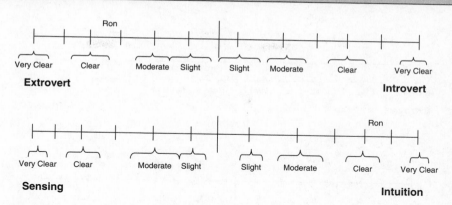

FIGURE 5.1   Ron's Scores on the Extrovert/Introvert Scale and Sensing/Intuitive Scale

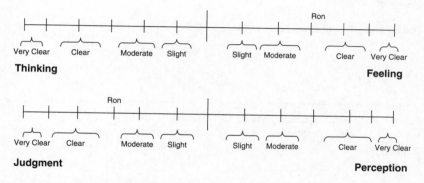

FIGURE 5.2   Ron's Scores on the Thinking/Feeling Scale and the Judging/Perceiving Scale

The ENFJ style can be great for leaders if they work on controlling some of the negative aspects for the feeling profile and work on communicating to other styles more effectively. The ENFJ person is initially trusting, but when the person is disappointed and let down he or she can write off people for a long time. Such a person can be highly judgmental of others.

Ron's leadership team is relatively balanced on the MBTI (see Figures 5.3 and 5.4). The only area out of balance is the judging style. This means the team could develop a plan and want to stick to it no matter what others outside want. This happened on an issue on the team, and it resulted in great concern and stress for the superintendent, the leadership team, and the school board. The school board ultimately decided to support the changes to a policy and plan from the community. The leadership team must be more flexible in the future to prevent this from happening again. In addition, the team must understand that changing a plan is not a failure, but rather success in gaining buy-in from all constituencies. As a plan is discussed it is clear that there are different perspectives that all have some value. The act of negotiation and compromise is the way to build support for a plan or a budget. When the final plan is developed it may look very different than the one developed by the leadership team. This is an indicator of success because the support of policymakers is critical to making progress. Although the compromise budget or plan may be of great concern to the school department people, it must be clear that the policymakers are the ultimate decision makers. The school department people must implement

(continued)

CASE STUDY *(continued)*

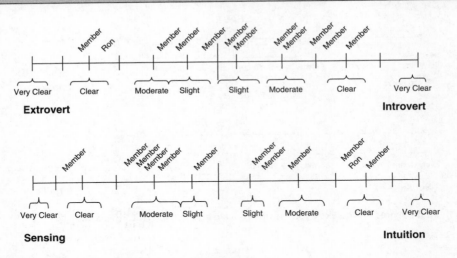

FIGURE 5.3   The E/I and S/N Scores for Ron's Leadership Team

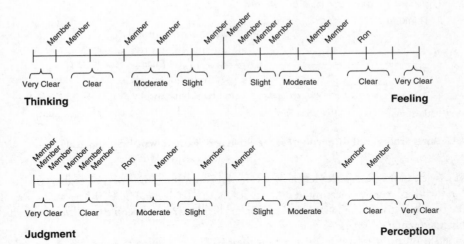

FIGURE 5.4   The T/F and J/P Scores for Ron's Leadership Team

the plan that is voted on by policymakers. The obligation is to support the plan and do the best job possible to make it work. It is still important for school officials to gather data on how aspects of the plan were not successful for future planning and budget discussions.

Ron and the DISC

Ron is a natural high influencing and compliant person in the DISC (see Figure 5.5). Based on the data in this text, he has two areas that are different from the typical high-performing leader. The dominant score is low and the compliance score is high. It should be noted that the influencing score needs to be higher than the

CASE STUDY *(continued)*

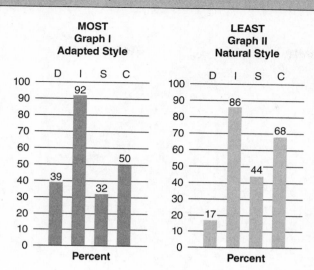

FIGURE 5.5 Ron's DISC Bar Chart *Source:* Copyright © 2012 Target Training International, Ltd. Used with permission.

dominance score to ensure that the drive for change is team oriented and committed to building leadership capacity for sustainable change. The secondary high dominance allows the leader to make the tough decisions when needed to get quick results. His high compliance score on the DISC combined with his judging score on the MBTI can show up as rigidity and control to people with different styles.

Ron is very high in his influencing score on the natural bar chart and even increases his score in the adapted chart. His compliance score is high but decreases in his adapted style. This shows the results of his delegation and trust for other staff. His steadiness is below the line in the natural and decreases in the adapted. This shows his fast paced movement for change. He will need to slow down slightly to build leadership capacity. His dominance score is low naturally but has increased significantly. This shows the adaptation to his role as a superintendent and his urgency to drive results. This will need to be decreased slightly to allow other people to build their leadership. However, the rise in his adapted score does make sense for the role. Ron's DISC wheel (see Figure 5.6) notes that he is very adaptable at this point in his career, which will help the coaching process for change. He needs to move more strongly into the persuasive area for success.

Ron and the Values Inventory

The Values inventory also provides Ron with data to use in creating his professional development plan. The values score allows Ron to formulate a plan that meets his values and therefore can be sustainable. Ron's high scores are social, individual, and traditional (see Figure 5.7). His high social score is common for educational leaders. The desire to make a difference in students' lives is the major motivation for why people become educational leaders. The individual score shows that Ron wants to have power to make change for improving students' lives. The traditional score is important for Ron's professional development plan. His high score indicates a high set of values and personal and professional ethics that defines who he is. Although the goal is not to change this value system, it presents certain challenges. Ron is a person of high integrity who expects loyalty. If he believes that the person is not loyal to him the person can become invisible and Ron can no longer work with that individual. That value combined with the self-regulation and feeling issues can result in quick judgment about people, which may be problematic and hard to reverse.

(continued)

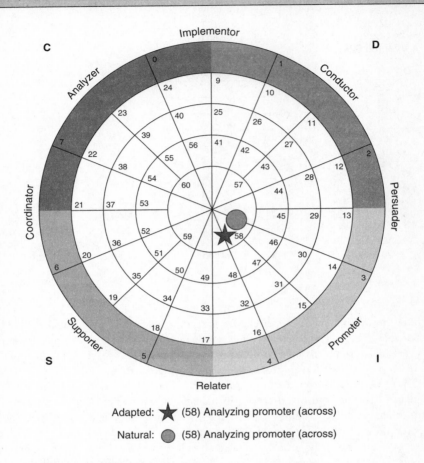

Adapted: ★ (58) Analyzing promoter (across)

Natural: ● (58) Analyzing promoter (across)

FIGURE 5.6 **Ron's DISC Wheel**
Source: Copyright © 2012 Target Training International, Ltd.
Used with permission.

Ron and the Seven Competencies

Ron is a very high achiever and is driven to success. He is strong at most of the seven leadership competencies.

1. *Challenges the status quo.* He is willing to challenge the status quo if the results are best for students. However, he is concerned about following rules and regulations set by the state for fear of punitive action by the government.

2. *Builds trust through clear communications and expectations.* His communications are relatively clear and his expectations are explicit for his team. The only concern is that at times he can be very general and conceptual, and more concrete and sequential members of his team can struggle with his lack of specifics when introducing an idea. He is concerned and is dedicated to building a high-trust environment through consistent messages and expectations.

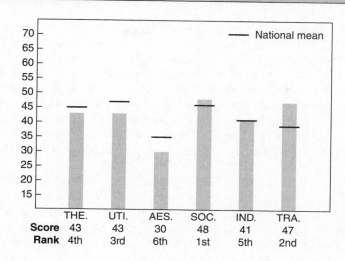

	THE.	UTI.	AES.	SOC.	IND.	TRA.
Score	43	43	30	48	41	47
Rank	4th	3rd	6th	1st	5th	2nd

FIGURE 5.7 Ron's Values Inventory Bar Chart *Source:* Copyright © 2012 Target Training International, Ltd. Used with permission.

3. *Creates a commonly owned plan for success.* He has developed goals with his leadership team and the school committee. These first year goals will form a basis for a plan. This plan needs to be strategic and set for a period of 3 years. The plan should involve the community to help build trust beyond the school walls.

4. *Focuses on team over self.* Ron is very focused on team over self. Some people believe he is more focused on himself and that perception needs to be a focus of his work in building a team. Ron is committed to the long-term, hard work of building a team.

5. *Has a high sense of urgency for change and sustainable results in improving student achievement.* This is one of his major strengths. His profiles and his assessments consistently score high in style and behaviors that show a sense of urgency for results. This sense of urgency is a positive for his school committee but is part of the reason his principals feel overwhelmed by pressure to change quickly.

6. *Commits to continuous improvement for self.* The sixth competency of continuous improvement is key to his potential for high performance. He is willing and committed to improving every day and is open to critical feedback. He wants to be the best for his students, his staff, and himself. He spends time working with his coach on improvement strategies and has a range of colleagues that he looks to for feedback on areas for improvement.

7. *Builds external networks and partnerships.* The last competency of building networks and partnerships is a potential area of strength. However, putting time into partnerships has not been part of his development to this point. He has built a strong network of colleagues that he could utilize for potential partnerships. He needs to broaden his network outside of education and find ways of building relationships with other leaders that can result in new ventures to help his school system. His skills for building partnerships are excellent. These include his strategic thinking, interpersonal skills, strong follow-through, and focus on results. However, his high expectations often put him in a position of feeling disappointed by people and organizations that could be important business relationships. He needs to work on being more patient with people who do not meet all his expectations.

As Ron uses the variety of feedback points to understand his own leadership style and behaviors, it is important for him to use the perspective that the leadership inventories add to his profile. Based on the data in this

(continued)

text, he needs to work on controlling his feelings and emotions, fully utilize his ability to influence others, and reduce his focus on details and compliance.

Ron has one advantage that most superintendents do not have. He is fully committed to learning and developing his leadership skills to be a great leader. Ego and confidence are key to effective leadership, but the ability to honestly engage in introspection for self-improvement is a rare quality. Ron is focused on all areas of emotional intelligence (Goleman, 1996). His self-awareness is acute and developing, and his social networking abilities are a strength. His empathy is a true positive factor that helps him build lasting relationships. The motivation factor of emotional intelligence has never been a problem for Ron since he is internally driven to succeed. His major area of work for improvement is self-regulation, but he is committed to doing whatever it takes to manage this area of improvement effectively.

Action Plan for Improvement

Understanding Ron's first-year challenges set a context for his action plan. Ron had a very challenging first year as a superintendent. In his first week, the high school principal took another job. Not only is it difficult to lose a high school principal in your first week, but it was also the goal of the school system to stabilize the high school leadership after several years of major turnover. Ron could have just tried to survive his first year and take on very little in relation to goals and improvements. However, the school board hired him because of his great passion and set a high bar for improvement. Ron's leadership style is not a coasting style. His excitement about finally being a superintendent after several attempts that resulted in being a finalist but not getting hired is very high, and he is grateful to the community that has hired him.

Ron hired another principal and is fully committed to his success. Ron was trusting of the new principal right from the beginning. However, once that principal began to express dissatisfaction with Ron to the school board chairperson, the trust went to zero. His values on loyalty presented a difficult dilemma of how to support and coach the principal. Ron also had to look at how he could work with the chairperson of the school board if he could not trust her. In addition, the fear and paranoia increased when Ron became concerned whether keeping the principal was more important to the school board than keeping and supporting him. The goal of stabilizing the high school leadership was a strong goal when Ron began his tenure.

In addition, some of Ron's team was having a major problem with the concept of being a high-performance team. It was difficult confronting Ron on his leadership style, even though he encouraged feedback. There were several issues that were affecting the members' ability to become a high-performance team. These were some of their questions:

- Is he too intense and is the fear of his value of loyalty presenting a risk not worth taking?
- If I am too critical to the superintendent, is there going to be retribution?
- Should we just accept each other and not talk about our weaknesses?

These questions were showing that each member was uncomfortable and did not feel safe talking about his or her weaknesses.

Ron made it clear that he expected each member to work on his or her leadership style and to create a high-performance team in his or her department or school. This resulted in one member, the business manager, resisting this performance expectation in the business office that had experienced poor morale and difficult working conditions for staff. The business manager was focused on the numbers and results, not the morale of his staff. His results on the finances were very high and, to him, warranted ignoring the people issues on his staff. Ron stated that the people and the technical results were both important and the business manager needed to work with a coach to improve the morale of his staff and to build an HPT. In addition, the superintendent went much further and only offered a 1-year contract with no raise to the business manager, even though his technical results were high. This gave a strong message to the business manager that the expectations were clear and not about to change. The superintendent also stated that a 3-year contract and a raise would be offered once he genuinely engaged in the HPT work with his team.

Ron, while having the support of his school board, struggled all throughout the year. The school board demanded excellence from him and set up a long list of goals and outcomes for success and tied the goals to his salary. This merit pay concept has been a major struggle to establish in education and is rare in its implementation with superintendents and school boards. The concept of pay being tied to the measurable accomplishment of goals has not been embraced across education (Lunnenburg & Orstein, 2012). Ron embraced the goals and outcomes because he was highly motivated and demanded success from himself and was willing to set up expectations for school department personnel.

Setting up such high expectations had a major downside for the entire system. Ron, with his impulse control issues and high compliance and passionate commitment for results, was the wrong person to set up this system. The goals were too ambitious without the development of a clear set of operating principles for success that could make them more reasonable to achieve. Ron, who by profile is very intense and demanding, now had been tied to a very demanding school board through goals and a merit pay system. This resulted in too many demands and created too much intensity in the school system that almost paralyzed the administrators and caused several strong administrators to want to leave.

There was no realistic picture of how to create effective change that would be sustainable. The intensity coupled with several crises that came up throughout the year increased the stress for the leaders. The stress associated with their leadership position created a feeling that being a leader in the district could seem almost impossible. Everyone was just trying to survive and keep his or her head above water. The district began to see quick results, but at a cost to staff that would make the short-term gains not seem to be sustainable.

Ron, in his commitment to team development, set up a process of working with the school board on a plan to structure goals and demands differently for his second year. Ron's openness to bringing in the school board into his work on school system management will reduce the stress and serve him well in the long run. He will create a true partnership with the board for sustainable success. However, the downside of the school board potentially moving outside of its role into internal management was becoming a problem and presenting too many demands that were impossible to achieve. Ron, using his influencing style, will work out a new process of goal setting that will hopefully work for all constituents.

Ron realizes the hard work ahead to be a great leader. He is relentless in his caring about students and his own self-development. He is also singular in his focus on developing a community of learners in the school system and the formation of high-performance teams to obtain high results for students and families in the community. Ron knows this work is not short term with an end date for completion, but rather a lifetime endeavor that will warrant a full-time commitment.

Ron also knows that he will get a lot of resistance to his commitment to forming HPTs. The formation of an HPT seems great on paper, but when it means looking openly at your weaknesses in front of other people, most people become very uncomfortable. Ron is willing and committed to model this behavior to his leadership team and the school board, and he realizes that it will take time for others to follow.

This effort of team building and self-improvement is being extended to the school board. Ron wants to partner with the school board in leading the district. He will face criticism from his colleagues and his team that he should keep the board out of the internal issues of the district. Ron has watched his colleagues try to control their school boards and keep them in their place. Many of these superintendents have lost their job trying to control their boards. He knows this road of teamwork will be difficult and the school board will probably continue to try to micromanage (Strauss, 2011). He is committed to building trust and a strong relationship of respect that will allow the board to hold each of its members accountable for the role he or she needs to play in

(continued)

policy and direction, and avoid the temptation to micromanage. He has been able to get a commitment from the school board to begin working on its team and partnership with the superintendent. Instead of trying to control the school board members, he is helping them understand how their requests and involvement in the internal workings of the system have a negative impact on their goals for the school system.

As Ron extricates himself from the internal management and builds the capacity of his leaders to work across the system to implement their individual and collective goals, Ron can become more of a CEO. He can put more energy into the external work of building partnerships to help the school system take on the major issues. The issues relating to finances and increasing the rigor for academic achievement are major undertakings for the school system to be great. He is working more with municipal leaders on issues such as economic development of the city. He is forming international partnerships with school districts to expose his people to the global challenges ahead for students. Ron is exploring a partnership with a mayor in a nearby city to expand offerings in the high school with added resources gained by educating more kids. He is working with technology companies on partnerships to enhance the district's ability to individualize learning. Ron also spends time helping young professionals improve their careers, providing them with opportunities he has had during his career.

As a true CEO, Ron is working on his skills to be a leader in any sector, not just education. This involves improving his financial management skills to become less dependent on his business manager. Ron understands that his leadership presence and knowledge of a broad base of leadership issues increases the credibility of the school system and his influence on motivating an entire community to excellence.

Ron could withdraw and be an internal instructional leader for his school system. His internal drive for success and insatiable ability to learn does not allow him to settle for what other people say he should do based on their narrow goals. Ron is in this work for the long run. He is not trying to build his career to move to a bigger or better district for more prestige.

Ron also knows that his goals and dreams can fall apart quickly. He knows that if he cannot control his impulsive behavior and insecurities, he could lose everything he has worked for in his career. He treasures his opportunity to make a difference and will not let it slip through his fingers. He will not join his colleagues who have lost their jobs and blame everyone else for his problems. He knows there are no excuses and his success is in his own hands. Ron has the courage to become a great leader in a time when it is easier to just survive and count the days to retirement and receiving one's pension.

The following are the professional development goals of the superintendent that will drive his plan for success:

1. To build on his strengths as a leader and build a high-performance culture both within the district and community
2. To develop an HPT and support the school board team development
3. To coach and support his leadership team to build HPTs within their departments and their schools
4. To enhance his skills in self-regulation to allow other people to engage with him in a high-performance manner
5. To slow down change in order to build other people's capacity to drive change
6. To decrease time on compliance behaviors by delegating them to other team members
7. To increase time in being more visible in the schools, the community, and the broader external world as he develops partnerships and networks to better serve his district
8. To form external strategic partnerships to enable the district to sustain improvement strategies for improvement
9. To increase his financial planning and management skills

CASE STUDY *(continued)*

Ron is looking at freeing up time to engage with other leaders in education, government, and the private sector to increase his network. He will use his knowledge and background in instruction and curriculum to ensure that the district has the best talent in key positions and that the work is focused on making a difference for students. Ron will work on his coaching skills, which are natural and can be very important to his goal of building leadership capacity in the district.

The leadership inventories have identified two major areas of focus for improvement. His first challenge is to manage his intensity with others. His second challenge is to control his emotions and to make decisions in a manner that is less impulsive. His profile indicates a desire to please people and to meet their professional needs. He will need to rely more on his own ability and judgment and make decisions that meet the needs of students with less focus on meeting the needs of all the adults. Of course he will need to seek the counsel of a variety of people when necessary to manage the politics of a situation.

Ron's professional development plan begins with his work on self-improvement. He is working with a coach on understanding why he is impulsive, intense, and often overpersonalizes issues. He is not embarrassed or fearful that people will think he is weak because he has hired a coach for himself and his team. He is open to criticism for asking for help. He also is confident that strong leaders need a coach to help them effectively lead their organizations. He will continue to work with his coach to understand and explore the patterns in his life at earlier stages that have formed his current behaviors. As he gains insight on these behavioral patterns and past messages of either insecurities or negative critics, he will begin the process of redirecting his responses to more productive behavior. He will need to slow down and be patient and realize that when he is more measured and calm he is more effective. His ability to handle the press and respond in a crisis situation is very calm and thoughtful. Now he has to bring that set of behaviors into his day-to-day life.

As Ron continues to work on his self-improvement plan he needs to shift his attention to developing his leadership team. He has worked with a coach and team facilitator to help the team understand what it means to be an HPT. Now he is modeling the self-improvement process that he wants each member of the team to engage in. He will then coach them to build their leadership teams in their schools and departments.

He knows that it is easier for them to talk about his improvements than to focus on themselves, so he will continue to encourage them to help him be a better leader as they begin the hard work of understanding their strengths and weaknesses and open up to their teams to improve.

As Ron works on his professional development plan he will need to continually adjust to the pressures of being a superintendent in a very demanding district. His self-awareness and commitment to the success of all students will serve him well in staying focused on his values and beliefs.

The Final Story

In conclusion, Ron is working to build a real leadership team that includes the principals, the central office, and the school board. In addition, he has built a strong relationship with the teachers union leadership, which rounds out the governance that is needed to build a high-performance organization and a school district that is a true system. Ron knows that there are days when the teamwork and his leadership approach are working smoothly and the prospects of success are amazing. However, there are also many days that this fragile and unique leadership approach of bringing everyone together as a team seems impossible. He is working on controlling his emotional reaction to those mood swings to keep the progress steady. Will most superintendents do the difficult personal work that Ron has undertaken? Unfortunately, the answer is probably no. Ron and his system will reap the benefits of this commitment for years to come. Even if Ron left the district at some point, the people will understand what they could lose if they went back to a district that has fractured leadership and silos for schools.

Reflective Questions

1. What did you learn from Ron's case that can help you as a leader?
2. What change do you need to make to improve yourself?
3. How will you work with your staff and your supervisor or board on making fundamental change and improvement?
4. What feedback or critical data have you or your team received over the years that you may have ignored or not taken seriously?
5. Are there any issues that your team believes it can't discuss but that need to be put on the table for discussion?
6. How do you or your team improve your ability to handle critical feedback?

6

Hiring the Right Leaders Who Will Get Results

Stop the Insanity: Now It Is Time for a New Hiring Process

The age old adage is that the definition of insanity is doing the same thing over and over again and expecting a different result. This is what we are doing with the hiring process in education when the stakes are too high for results and the ability to recover from failure is too difficult. The hiring process in education has stayed the same for many years and has not adjusted to the world around us.

Although this text is about how to become a high-performing leader and how to build your skills and behavior to focus on a broader organizational role beyond instructional leadership, the ability to hire the right people is a key factor for success. Understanding the competencies that are needed for a position and recruitment or development of internal talent is a better use of your time than to put all your focus on the evaluation of poor performers.

Some readers might feel this chapter is for the human resources people in your district. Although this may be helpful for human resource people, it is even more important for educational leaders to understand the issues and practices outlined in this chapter. The highest-performing leaders in education own the hiring process and use human resource people as a resource. The ability to find the right person for a teaching position or a leader for school change might be the most important decision you make to improve student achievement.

Another reason the hiring process needs to change is that to improve results in a school and school system a leader must change the culture of how people act on a daily basis. Hiring the right people is a key element of culture change that cannot be delegated to an HR person. The leader can receive assistance of the HR people, but the leader must know what competencies are needed to develop a culture of success.

The former CEO of IBM speaks about how the company was a leader in the technology field for many years and then suffered a huge decline in business. When asked about what products, strategies, or new technologies allowed him to lead a turnaround when so many similar companies failed, he states that it was all about changing the culture (Menn & Silverstein, 2002). Educational change is also about changing a culture and focusing on hiring and developing the right people. IBM had to change from an internal culture to an external culture that listened and adjusted internally based on customer needs. Leaders in education face the same challenge of changing culture and it starts with the hiring process.

Hiring the people you need for a new culture starts with looking at recruiting, reward systems, professional development needs, roles and responsibilities of employees, and the development of a team-oriented culture. This focus on talent management is critical for education, especially under the pressures of urgency and accountability for results.

Based on the author's experience in working with a variety of human resource departments, most sectors, such as industry, health care, and nonprofits, have changed the hiring process dramatically. In education, change is very slow and we often stay with the same traditional methods even if they do not work. We are in a time in which there is a high sense of urgency for results and there is more accountability than ever before. However, the hiring process in education today is too slow and process oriented, with not enough focus on results.

We are hiring people who are compliant and process oriented who want to slow down the pace of change, when the demands are for fast change and clear results. We are hiring the wrong people over and over again and we keep the hiring process the same. One major educational leader said we are not hiring the wrong people and the hiring process is not flawed. He then stated that our process is fine for hiring the people we have tended to look for to lead our schools and districts. He continues by stating that our problem is that we are looking for the wrong skills and competencies in leaders. If we change what we look for we would need to change the hiring process. What he essentially means is that people will not change the hiring process because it seems successful. If we realized that we are hiring the wrong people, we would be more open to changing the hiring process.

Our current approach in education to improve performance is to improve the evaluation tool for teachers and administrators. Unfortunately, the evaluation tool is too late in the process for finding the best people to lead and participate in significant change. Instead of focusing on the evaluation tool, we need to invest our time and resources on the front end of the process by identifying what skills and competencies we need and designing a process to find the best. Then we need to support and develop the talent we hire. This approach will prevent the need for all the focus to be on evaluation. Evaluation is important, but it will take less time and reduce costs in turnover from poor hiring decisions if the investment and focus is on improving the front end of the hiring process.

There is a need to change the hiring process now. There is a long list of flaws so numerous that it would take a whole book to explain all of the problems and why the process needs to change. The reason this list is so long is due to the fact that the traditional practices do not match the needs of today's educational systems. Some of the flaws in the current process are the following:

- Too much stakeholder involvement in defining the competencies of the leaders
- Too much time forming search committees and deliberating about candidates
- Too many steps in the process
- Getting derailed by single negative comments or small problems with candidates stated by special interest groups
- Lack of definition of short- and long-term needs of the school or school system
- Lack of recruitment and too much focus on advertisement as a source of the best candidates
- Poor interviewing process
- Too much dependence on written references
- Too much control by search committees
- Too much emphasis on following the details of the process with a lack of focus on results
- School committees and superintendents delegating too much control over decision making
- Too much passivity in search firms
- Superintendents and school committees trying to save money by doing the process themselves

- Not using the well-established leadership assessments used in hiring in most sectors
- Open meeting laws curtailing the effectiveness of finding the best talent
- Ineffective use of site visits
- Lack of succession planning
- Too much focus on evaluation and the back end of the process

As Jim Collins stated in *Good to Great* (2001), we must hire the right people and get them in the right seat on the bus. The current process can actually prevent hiring the right people and putting them in the right position.

It is time to completely revamp the hiring process for school districts and bring it into the 21st century. Retrofitting the current process will not work. A new process for hiring will be proposed in this chapter with the understanding that there is a difference in hiring from the private sector based on public sector laws and practices. The process cannot be the same as in the private sector. However, we must bring the process as close as possible to an effort that will result in hiring the best people. Education cannot afford to be ineffective in hiring the best leaders when the stakes for results are so high.

USING PROFESSIONAL TALENT MANAGEMENT OR EXISTING HUMAN RESOURCES PERSONNEL

Having the best teachers and leaders in school districts is critical to success. Therefore, it does not make sense to put so little credence in the importance of this human resources position. A strong HR person can save money for a district by preventing grievances and discrimination charges, and can help make sure that the right people are hired for key positions. Having the best talent is paramount to success.

The focus in educational reform is to put more funds into the teaching and learning process and professional development. Although this is the core focus to improve student achievement, we must be careful that we are leaving funds to improve the hiring process for teachers and administrators. The Wallace Foundation (2010) noted in its recent study on turnarounds that the number one factor for improving schools is to hire the best teachers. The second factor was to hire a strong leader. Both of these factors assume that there is a strong, comprehensive HR function in school districts.

Unfortunately, the human resource function is very weak in most districts. If there is a professionally trained HR person, he or she is usually overwhelmed and lacks the staff necessary to be effective in all aspects of the hiring process. The HR function requires knowledge of laws and regulations involved in the hiring process. There is much legality in ensuring that affirmative action laws are being followed and that all proper documentation is complete for any disciplinary or firing actions. In addition, a strong HR person can plan for staffing changes, find creative ways to pay for key staff positions, develop a training program for administrators, and handle employee relations problems.

The HR person needs to be well-versed in how to define job responsibilities. This is more than just making sure that there is a job description for a position. A strong HR person understands that a position needs to have a well-developed idea of the competencies that a successful person will be able to accomplish in a specific job.

Too many districts do not have a highly trained professional HR position. In some smaller districts the basic personnel functions are filled by clerical people in the superintendent's or finance office. If the district has a person in human resources, he or she is often self-trained or a person who has failed as a principal or in some other central office position who is reassigned to fulfill contract specifications. Although some districts do have qualified HR people, the importance of this function is underestimated in education nationally.

If a district cannot afford a position, it should hire a consultant to help with these functions. In some cases, districts can share HR services or obtain them through a collaborative. A collaborative would involve several districts sharing services. These services are usually in relation to special education or areas such as combined purchasing (to obtain better pricing through bulk services) to save money. If a collaborative were assisting districts in the search process for teachers and administrators, the districts could be more effective in their recruitment efforts and reference checking, and the search would be less costly in terms of advertising.

The amount of money that it costs to hire people or remove inadequate staff is significant (Blake, 2006). Instead of hiring a professional to do this work, we try to implement state and national HR practices like new teacher evaluation processes. A district should develop its own employee hiring and development programs and not rely on the state and federal government to dictate HR practices. If we had strong HR and talent management systems, we would not need to have the state and federal government become involved in the functions of HR in schools.

Although union issues are difficult to manage in districts and may need state and national policy to alleviate restrictions on best practices, the teacher evaluation process is better handled within a district. It is important that motivation and development are emphasized over punitive evaluation efforts to ensure that teachers are effective in improving student achievement.

WHAT ARE THE BEST PRACTICES IN HIRING THAT WE NEED TO ADOPT NOW?

Hiring the best people is critical to improving student achievement. There are several strategies for hiring and development that need to be brought into the educational process. Figure 6.1 shows the steps of a *talent management system*, which is the terminology used in the private sector.

For many years, the term *personnel* was used to describe this function in education. In the past, the term *personnel* was more limited and did not include some of the more advanced functions of both HR offices and talent management departments. Director of personnel or personnel coordinator is a common title for the person in a school system who handles grievances and filing reports on staffing required by the state or federal government. The position is basically transactional in nature, meaning that it is paperwork and compliance oriented. The field of personnel has changed to being called human resources, which can mean that there are more direct functions beyond the paperwork dealing with employee relations, staffing plans, discrimination complaints, and so forth. If a school system has people in these positions, their backgrounds are usually clerical or midlevel office positions.

In industry and fields such as health care, human resources have developed into higher-level positions in terms of their skills and functions. The new field of talent management has emerged due

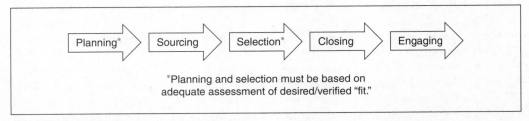

FIGURE 6.1   **Steps of a Talent Management System**
Source: Based on the work of Peter Jones of Future Management Systems.

to the critical importance and competition for talented people in key positions. The idea of hiring the best and making every effort to keep talent has become critical in the private and public sectors.

Education is in the same position, and needs to establish talent management systems. It is amazing what a great teacher, administrator, principal, and superintendent can do in any district to improve results. The best school systems know how important it is to have the best staff. Therefore, the time has come for school systems to adopt these practices from other sectors to meet their very challenging goals.

STEPS FOR ESTABLISHING A TALENT MANAGEMENT SYSTEM

The following five steps are outlined in Figure 6.1 and should be followed by a school system to establish a talent management process that will improve the hiring of the best people for key positions in the district.

Planning

The first step of talent management is planning. This involves looking at the demographics of staff and determining when people might retire, which positions have a shrinking pool of qualified candidates, and matching the needs for staffing with the goals for the school system. If a school system started from scratch today, hiring people for the obvious positions would still be the priority. However, the need for staff on data analysis and management would be very important and should be considered a priority for hiring.

Sourcing

The second step is sourcing. This means determining all the potential avenues for finding the best staff. Although advertising is important, it is the least effective way to get the best people. Recruitment is the number one method for finding talented people. This could be accomplished using a recruiter or using a network of resources that are respected in the education field to find the best people. One was to expand the sourcing process is through listservs, which are used in many states. Another method is to contact talented staff in the role you are looking for and ask for their recommendations for potential candidates. The best leaders are usually able to identify and recognize talent. They know what it takes to be successful and they can usually identify people who have similar skills and talents that they know are needed. Other sourcing methods are looking for well-respected aspiring leaders programs, looking for people who have worked for well-respected leaders in other school systems, or contacting people who provide coaching or mentoring to leaders.

Many districts struggle to find diverse candidates for their pool for leadership positions. There is significant competition for the best people from diverse cultures. Recently, this author participated in an aspiring superintendent program for the Alliance for Latino Administrators and Superintendents (ALAS). The 15 people who were selected for this program are all exceptional leaders and the training program is exemplary. All the leaders were administered DISC assessments, which were then used to rate them on Kirtman's Seven Competencies for School Leadership. Most had the profile of leadership that is needed in turning around schools and districts. This program is a jewel for the recruitment of leaders for school districts. Another aspect of recruiting diverse people is to ensure that a process is developed in the district to help them become part of the leadership team. People are often recruited to bring in new ideas and perspectives, but when they arrive they are supposed to fit into the culture that already exists. It is important that the team within the district spends time working on building their skills and behaviors in relation to valuing diversity. This is a strategic issue that is often not receiving enough focus in districts and schools.

Another concern in education is that we are excluding younger, less experienced people for leadership roles. The current and past culture in education was based on certain assumptions of the progression of experience a person needs to move on to higher levels of leadership. One must teach for a certain number of years, be a principal, be a central office administrator, and then after 15 to 20 years (or more) the person can become a superintendent. However, the world has changed and younger people with less experience are leading major organizations. Although experience is important, strong leadership skills and abilities enable people to assume leadership roles at much younger ages. Therefore, the sourcing process needs to be open to looking at people earlier in their careers for potential high-level roles in a school or school system.

Selection

The next step is selection, which involves finding people who fit the school system in terms of their skills, abilities, cultures, and life match. In a talent management program, people learn that we can hire the best and it does not always mean at the highest salary. Because education is mission-driven more than some private sector organizations, there are other factors that attract people to a district, such as the reputation of a superintendent or a school committee, the number of support people for a particular position, the location, the type of community, and the opportunities for professional development. People will give up a higher salary for other areas that they believe are of more value.

Closing

The closing step is the actual hiring. This includes factors such as the salary, benefits, working conditions, professional development opportunities, and succession planning. The actual negotiations of a salary and benefit package need to be handled skillfully to get the best people. School systems who do not handle this effectively often lose the best candidates. This can fail due to a take it or leave it salary offer that states there is no more money available, which leaves the candidate feeling devalued. Another poor practice is dragging negotiations on too long with no response to questions for days or weeks. The skilled negotiator makes sure that the candidate is respected throughout the entire process. This does not mean that the district has to meet the salary demands. If a positive negotiation is maintained, the person will be excited about assuming his or her new leadership role.

Engaging

The final step is engaging the new leader. The leader must be very positively engaged in the new school or school system. We often hire a new teacher and throw him or her into a school with no entry or orientation process. A new principal must be welcomed by the community. The superintendent must take time to bring new staff members into the team environment for the school and the school system.

Too often a new superintendent hires a talented young leader as a principal and does not meet with that person for months because the superintendent is too busy. The person may have chosen the district because of the reputation of the superintendent but now has very little chance to learn from the superintendent. How new hires are treated and engaged affects future recruitment. Education has a small insular network. Both negative and positive information is shared about districts and experiences. A superintendent who is known for treating principals well and mentoring them regularly will attract the best candidates.

Although most school systems will say they do not have the resources to put in a talent management system, they do not realize that they could adopt many of the practices for little cost with great payoff. The cost of turnover is very high in both dollars and results. The cost of not having the best talent results in compromising the results for student achievement.

HIRING PROCESS TIPS THAT MAKE A DIFFERENCE

The following are some basic, minimal-cost practices that should change now in every school system:

1. Use an opening for a position as an opportunity to rethink your structure.
2. Use a competency-based model to determine what you need and to interview candidates.
3. Focus more on recruitment and use of leadership assessments to find the best leaders.
4. Reduce the steps for and the time needed for the process. It is important to move the process faster and prioritize results over process and protect the confidentiality of the candidates.

Although a school system will not be able to completely rethink a position every time a science teacher position opens, there are still opportunities created when a change in personnel occurs. For example, a school system had an opening for a Spanish teacher. The opening occurred just before the beginning of the school year, so the principal's search for a new teacher had a short deadline. Advertisements were the only approach used to hire this new teacher. The fast process resulted in a very small number of candidates. The principal felt it was critical to get a teacher in front of the students for the first day of school, so a teacher with poor credentials was hired and there was no time for reference checking.

In education, there are too many times that a "warm body" is hired rather than looking at other options. This practice must stop! The new Spanish teacher was completely unskilled and not able to provide a proper education for the middle school students. The parents complained about how the students were falling behind. The principal, remaining loyal to the teaching staff, defended the teacher while knowing that the parents were right. The parents hired tutors for their children after school to make sure that they kept up with the curriculum. Many of the kids involved were in the band and could no longer attend the practices due to their time meeting with the tutor. A number of kids dropped out of the band. The principal decided to form a committee to study the problem and report a set of recommendations to the superintendent and the school committee over the next 3 to 6 months to help the band with membership.

A well-known and excellent Spanish teacher was already teaching in the middle school. She was teaching English even though her passion was in teaching Spanish. No one even considered putting her in the Spanish class, firing the new teacher, and finding a new English teacher. When a parent brought up these basic human resource planning strategies, the superintendent said that is not the way things are done in education. However, the superintendent agreed with the proposal by the parent and asked her to present this case to the school committee. The school committee also agreed that the proposal made sense but also stated that this was not a normal practice in education. Even though it made sense to make the changes suggested by the parent, nothing changed.

When a principal leaves, there is an opportunity to determine the skills and competencies to move another principal into the school who could have the right skills for the current needs. The school might need new energy after having a principal for a long period of time or may need leadership on technology based on several new initiatives. A principal in another school might have just the right skills for the leadership of the school. However, the general trend in education is keeping a principal in his or her school rather than moving the person to another school. The ability to move leadership around can be very successful and help turn schools around without looking to the outside for a person who does not know the culture of the district. Because human resource functions are rare in school districts, these HR planning methods are not often used.

A superintendent recently lost someone in a special education clerical position whose salary was $40,000. The superintendent had a human resources background and analyzed the needs of special education before hiring a new person. She did not fall into the trap of just trying to save money and not refilling the position. She realized that the person in this position was responsible for making decisions that were affecting a large number of resources. The clerical person did not have the skills to look at options for meeting children's individual education plans (IEPs) using outside placements (e.g., private schools) that could save money. The superintendent told the school committee she was going to hire a more skilled position at a salary of $80,000 to replace the $40,000 position. This new position, however, could save over $500,000 in special education costs. Luckily, the school committee was smart enough to allow this change in organizational structure.

The next practice that must change in education is how a position is defined. More focus needs to be put on the competencies that are needed to succeed in the positions. Typically educational hiring is based on job descriptions only. Although descriptions are important, it is critical to look at skills, competencies, and qualifications of candidates. A *competency* is defined as the quality of being adequately or well-qualified physically and intellectually to be successful in the job. To be a competent speaker one would need to have the ability to prepare his or her thoughts, organize the thoughts into a clear and coherent presentation, and be able to speak clearly to an audience. In addition, presenting to one or two people can require different competencies than speaking to 200 people. To hire someone to be a highly competent speaker, one must be much more thorough in ascertaining a candidate's ability to present. Instead, we often ask the person whether he or she has experience in presenting to groups of people. If the candidate says yes, we feel satisfied. This answer, however, tells us very little about the person's speaking competencies in relation to the requirements of the job. Too often people who are hired have experience but are not qualified to do the jobs that are needed to get results.

For example, a principal lists on her resume that she worked on a strategic plan for her previous school. She has experience in the strategic planning process, but does she have any strategic planning competencies? A competency could be the ability to develop a vision for a school and communicate it effectively to faculty. This competency is important for performance and just having experience is not a measure of a competency. When interviewing people, a principal can be asked if he or she has experience in strategic planning. If we wanted to test the person's skill, however, we would ask a different question that would demonstrate the skill. For example, the candidate could be asked to articulate a vision for his or her previous school and how it might need to be adjusted for the current position.

The next part of the hiring process that needs to be changed is how we find candidates. There is a real shortage of highly qualified people in many key positions in education. Superintendent and principal positions are very competitive and the pools are getting smaller. A core strategy of aggressive recruitment is required.

To save money, districts put ads in papers and wait for people to respond. The district personnel may also ask their colleagues for recommendations. Their colleagues could be helpful, but they also may want to hold on to the best people for their own district. The flaw in the hiring process for high-demand positions is that many of the typical applicants responding to ads are not the strong people. Many have lost their positions or might be having problems in their district. The best people are recruited and are more likely to be the easier candidates to check on references. The typical candidate responding to an advertisement may not be known by anyone involved in the search process. Such candidates supply written references, which are limited in value. The ability to go beyond the references provided is critical to find the "real story" about the candidate. If those doing the hiring do not know the candidate and have no knowledge of the district the candidate currently works in, it will be difficult to find any references beyond the ones provided.

A district must get professional help with this recruitment and reference checking. If people think of poor performers and how they were hired, they usually track the process to lack of knowledge about the people. It is difficult to find the best people and check out their skills and abilities. One thing the author always remembers is what a professional HR person said to him: "we hire for skills and experience and fire people for who they are." It is also difficult to make sure people match the skills and qualities that are deemed to be critical for success in a particular community. Someone can succeed in one school or community and fail dramatically in a similar position elsewhere.

In other fields outside education it is also hard to find the best people and make sure they fit the new position. One practice not being used in education is the use of the leadership inventories. In industry, health care, and many other public sectors, the inventories discussed in this text and others are used routinely in hiring. It is important to have data and information on a candidate that are not biased by the experience of a colleague or a staff member. Having objective data on style, behaviors, and values can provide information to compare with traditional methods of judging a candidate from an interview and reference checking. The best way to add these tools to your hiring process is to benchmark the position. For example, a district hiring a principal would find a current or past principal who was successful to benchmark the position. The current or past person would take the assessments and a profile of success would be developed. The search consultant would then add this profile to a position or leadership description to begin to look for candidates. The benefit of having the profile of someone who has been successful in a position in the district is that that person was able to successfully adjust to the demands of the position and the culture. If we know the style, behavior, and values that have worked in combination for one person, it can be a predictor of what we need for another person in the same position.

For example, in one district the superintendent wants a high sense of urgency in his leadership positions. He has benchmarked his best principals and has found that on the DISC they are all high influence or dominant, and on the WPI they are high in categories that relate to high sense of urgency such as achievement, adaptability, initiative, independence, innovation, leadership, persistence, social orientation, and stress tolerance. The recruiter can look for people who have demonstrated the ability to create fast change and are results oriented. The inventories can be administered to the candidates to determine whether they are likely to have a high sense of urgency. The inventories are only one aspect of the hiring process. They should be used as only one aspect of the decision making process. The next process that needs to be changed is to decrease the input efforts from all aspects of the community. Traditionally, all inside and outside groups become very involved in the search process for a superintendent and a principal. This involvement is based on the importance of the community's feelings of ownership for the person who is hired.

However, the stakes are too high for results and the competition for the best is too intense to keep this practice intact for the foreseeable future. The superintendent can have a brief input process from parents, community, teachers, and outside groups. This process should be quick and informal for the superintendent to gather input on specific issues. For example, parents could be asked about the level of communication that is currently in the school and what needs to be improved.

The input stage is important to define the needs and goals for the new principal, but not helpful in the hiring process. For example, a search committee recently looking for a new principal in a suburban district stated that they wanted the new principal to have no new goals for 3 years. The teachers in the elementary school felt overwhelmed and placed this restriction on the process. The search committee agreed. Now this search committee believed that they had to deliver three finalists to the superintendent who would commit to not having any new goals for 3 years. This restriction that was accepted by this search committee is not acceptable in today's world of pressure to increase student achievement and results. Superintendents and principals cannot let other people define and restrict their hiring. There is no real need for a search committee for these positions. However, due to the political issues, districts would have a hard time eliminating these search committees. Therefore, it is important to emphasize that they are advisory and understand that their recommendations might not be followed. The superintendent needs to be active in the process while not completely delegating his or her responsibility to the committee.

It is recommended that superintendents always talk to perspective candidates to attract them to their district. The potential candidate must still apply and participate in the same process that other candidates follow. This is where compliance becomes a problem. To make sure the process is pure, we often eliminate the superintendent from the recruitment process. This is a mistake. A strong superintendent is a major selling point for top candidates to apply and should be used effectively in the process.

A superintendent recently recruited a candidate for a key central office curriculum position in her district. To keep the process pure, she was not involved directly in defining the needs and competencies of the position and never told the committee that she had recruited someone to apply. She was high compliance and did not want to go outside the designated process. The search committee eliminated her recruited candidate and brought her three finalists who she believed were well below the quality of the person she had recruited, but she decided to hire one of them. Now this superintendent may have inadvertently set herself up for failure by not making sure that she had a process that would result in hiring the best person for a key role. By being high compliance, she could compromise her ability to get results by not hiring the person she believed matched the needs for the position. She put the process of the screening committee recommending candidates to her over her own judgment of the skills and competencies of the person she believed would be successful in the position. Therefore, it is important to focus more on results than on process. The process, in this case, may not have produced the best results.

Although process is important, it is critical to make sure that following the process does not compromise results. When looking for a superintendent, the search process is often too long and protracted to get the best people. The ability to present well on paper in a resume or cover letter and interview publically are often the main characteristics that result in being hired. Hiring the superintendent can become a popularity contest resulting in the winner having the best interviewing skills. Even though interviewing skills are important, they are only one small indicator for the hiring of the best person to lead an organization.

Sometimes the informal aspects of the search process can actually drive away the best candidates. Often, the school board's reputation can dramatically affect who applies. Media stories about the school board's conflicts and turmoil can cause the best performer to stay away.

Another informal issue that can adversely affect the candidate pool is fear from a candidate that his or her name will become exposed at an early stage. This fear can prevent the best candidates from applying. The reason for the fear is that the candidate's current district will know he or she is looking for a new position. This knowledge could affect the school board and the staff in their belief that the superintendent wants to lead their district. If the superintendent does not get the position, he or she will go back to the current position with some trust issues that could hurt his or her effectiveness.

A third factor that can affect the pool of candidates is the potential of an internal candidate applying for the position. Because the fear of exposure can influence whether a person applies for a position, the prospect of an internal candidate being favored for a position may be too risky for a standing superintendent. The experienced superintendent might fear that if an internal person with fewer qualifications is hired, the experienced superintendent's current district could perceive the experienced superintendent's skills as weaker. Losing a job to a less qualified candidate may make the superintendent not look as strong *and* not seem to be interested in staying in the district. This can result in lack of support for the superintendent if he or she chooses to stay in the district.

The process must be made more confidential within the limits of open-meeting or sunshine laws. In Texas, the government code 552.126 allows the entire process of hiring a superintendent to be confidential. The school board is allowed to present one finalist for approval and protect all other candidates from identity as applicants. The corporate world could never complete the hiring of key positions if the process had to be so public. In most states, we are expecting the best results but are clinging to a process that discourages people to apply for the positions in which they are most needed.

The school board and the superintendent do not have to form search committees. It is common practice to appoint broad-based committees to build support for the new leader. However, there are many special interest people on these committees and the process becomes very political. The committees eliminate candidates for the wrong reasons and promote others because of a special connection to their issues. The process often does not produce someone that really matches the leadership profile they developed. In some cases the leadership profile is so general anyone could match it and the likelihood of success is not clear. If the school board is effective at working as a team and conducts a thorough and objective process, they will often attract the best candidates. In addition, the cohesiveness and teamwork of the school board often become a major advantage in recruiting the best candidates. Superintendents are attracted to school boards that are team oriented and clear about their own role and respectful of the role and function of the superintendent.

WHAT HIRING PROCESS WOULD BE BETTER?

The open meeting laws in the United States should not apply directly to educational hiring processes. In fact, many states have developed laws to protect the confidentiality of semifinalists to improve the candidate pool. The following is a set of recommendations, based on the author's experience conducting more than 100 superintendent searches, to improve the pools of qualified candidates within the confines of the open meeting laws that exist throughout the country.

1. The school board works with a consultant to ensure that the board is a high-performance team and a positive factor for the search. This will prevent conflict within a school board from being a major detraction for the search process.

2. The school board defines the leadership profile with the consultant to ensure that it matches the leadership competencies needed for the superintendent to be successful. In this effort, the board or a consultant would survey people internally and externally for input on the needs that could influence the leadership profile. Interviews with key leaders in the community could be added to the process.

3. There would be a benchmarking process that would identify a successful superintendent who may have been in the community at a previous time or another superintendent that has the qualities that the school system is looking for in their next hire. The results of this benchmarking would be added to the recruitment process and the leadership profile development.

4. The chairperson of the school board would become a key part of the recruitment process. A potential recruit would be able to talk to the chairperson to determine whether he or she is a good fit for the position. This confidential conversation would allow the candidates to determine whether they want to apply. This practice will dramatically increase the pool of potential applicants.

5. An advisory committee would be formed to work with the consultant to screen the candidates. The chairperson of the school board will be an ex officio member of the committee. No additional school board members should be on this committee. The committee would then interview six to eight candidates in a semifinalist confidential interview. The questions would be behavioral in nature and competency based. The process could be completed in 1 month.

6. One candidate will be recommended to the school board. Two or three backup candidates will be held as alternates. The chairperson will be involved in narrowing the semifinalist list to the final recommended candidate. The number one candidate would be interviewed by the school board in public. The leadership assessments would be completed on all potential finalists and extensive references would be sought on the number one candidate. Salary information for all finalists would be obtained by the consultant, and an attempt to make sure that an agreement could be reached will be pursued by the consultant with the number one candidate.

7. If there is a substantial reason to not hire the number one candidate, the number two candidate could be recommended. Although this is not ideal and it looks like the secondary candidate is not as strong, the concept of the right fit for the community or other confidential reasons could be used to explain the move to the next candidate. The advantage of this process is that it will be much faster than the traditional process and will protect confidentiality of the finalists to keep them in the process. The confidentiality will also dramatically increase the pool of qualified people.

8. The school committee can be explicit in telling the community that it is changing the process to bring in a deeper, more qualified field of candidates. The honesty about why this process is better and faster will appeal to the community. The other positive aspect of this effort is the ability to move faster on the best people. If the process moves faster and the confidentiality is protected, the community will support the effort to get the best leader.

9. Once the leader is hired, the school committee chairperson should review the leadership assessments and work with the superintendent on a professional development plan including the formation of a leadership team. This should be done with both new and experienced superintendents. The experienced superintendents may not believe they need to have a formal process to build their leadership team and a team with the school board. However, many experienced superintendents do not realize that their new community is different and that past practices do not always work in new communities. In fact, a number of superintendents have made the fatal mistake of believing they knew what they were doing and did not need a formal team building process in their new community. Another sound practice that is used more in larger districts is to form a transition team of key internal and external people to help the superintendent in the transition process. This may involve an analysis of the key issues that need to change and the traditions that are important to preserve as the change in leadership progresses. These teams advise the new superintendent on how to make sure that the transition is smooth both within the district and in the community.

This new process would increase the pool of qualified candidates significantly. It would allow school boards and superintendents to hire the best people and not have to try to appeal to all of the special interest groups and political pressures. The process could be completed in 3 to 4 months at the most, and would allow a district to compete for the best leaders. The public would be involved in the process in a manner that serves the public good and builds ownership of the new leader.

More important, the process would match the needs of today's educational climate. There are skills and abilities that are needed in our leaders today. We cannot afford to have a process that gets bogged down in politics and compromise. We must hire leaders that can get results and the process has to be designed to that end.

USING KIRTMAN'S SEVEN COMPETENCIES FOR SCHOOL LEADERSHIP IN HIRING

Based on the data compiled for this text and from experience in 300 school districts, the seven competencies should be used in the hiring process for new leaders. Leaders should do the following:

1. *Challenge the status quo.* As stated earlier, the ability to be innovative and not focus as much on compliance activities presented by state, federal, and local policymakers is an important competency for a successful leader. The delegation of compliance is important and the formation of team that focuses on results, not the preservation of the current condition, is very important.

2. *Build trust through clear communications and expectations.* The ability to be clear in one's communications, even during times filled with ambiguity, is critical for a leader today. Clear communications allow leaders to set expectations for all parties in a manner that has shared understanding and ultimate commitment. As stated in Chapter 4, shared understanding and commitment are two steps that are important to building trust. Leaders must develop trust with a number of internal and external constituents.

3. *Create a commonly owned plan for success.* Strong leaders must have plans for success that everyone understands. The question of whether everyone needs to buy into the plan is controversial. The successful leaders outlined in this text have been able to get buy-in for their plans. However, this does not mean that everyone has to agree with all elements of a plan or that if someone does not buy in the plan stops and is not implemented. The influence behavior takes time to gain support from all parties. A strong leader continually works to gain support from all constituents. However, as it has been said many times in this text, results must overshadow process when it comes to improving student achievement.

4. *Focus on team over self.* High-performing leaders do not let their egos get in the way. Leaders must have strong egos and self-confidence, but they must be willing to build real high-performance teams. They must be able to hire people who are smarter and better than them to get the best people for the district. Building a team means a lot of work to gain the trust necessary to get results. If the leaders are impatient and not willing to work at this issue, they will ultimately fail or lose their jobs.

5. *Have a sense of urgency for change and sustainable results in improving student achievement.* The profiles of successful leaders show a high sense of urgency whether they are in high-performing or low-performing districts or schools. They want the best for the students now and do not want to let the adult issues get in the way of helping the students achieve. However, if they are too top-down focused and urgent without building a high-performance team, the change will not be sustainable.

6. *Commit to continuous improvement for self.* The best leaders are those trying to improve every day. They are always learning and are always open to new ideas to improve their practices. The leaders who believe that they have arrived and can coast to their retirement should not be in leadership positions in education today.

7. *Build external networks and partnerships.* This competency is relatively weak and is decreasing in focus in education today. Although the leaders in other fields are forming more partnerships and networks of service, educators are focusing more internally. This is a dangerous trend that could have a major negative impact on education. The best leaders in education have developed networks of support in and outside of education. They must be leaders in their communities, not just educators.

The seventh competency could be applied in education using a talent management system to provide the high-level HR services needed by school systems. A superintendent could work with an outside organization to assess internal talent, develop competencies for key positions that open up over the year, and search for the best people for each position. This could extend to assisting in developing entry plans for leaders and helping them build high-performance teams. Although these functions could be performed better if districts had the internal capabilities, it might be more cost effective to use an outside resource or partner to provide these services. A collaborative could be used to provide these services for multiple districts.

If school boards and superintendents focus on these competencies and align their hiring processes to find people who are true high performers, they will benefit from the results in improving student achievement in their schools and districts.

DEVELOPING PEOPLE FROM WITHIN: SUCCESSION PLANNING

Although the hiring process outlined previously will enhance the pool of quality candidates for leadership positions, it is important to develop talent from within the school district. It is very frustrating for talented people to be passed over for someone outside of the school system. These high-quality people often leave to further their careers and the district loses valuable people. The district should have a process of succession planning for all key positions. This process is important in order to provide motivation for people to be promoted to higher levels in the district. In addition, hiring from within can be very important in preserving institutional memory, maintaining momentum on key district or school initiatives, and creating stability in the face of too much change. If the district has an HR person, he or she would lead the development of the succession planning process.

Key positions would be identified, and a determination would be made about talented people within the district who could emerge and take vacated positions. The district should be continuously looking for people who may be promotable, and they should be explicit in speaking to them about their value to the district.

Typically districts are passive in this process, and people have to make their own opportunities or apply outside the district. This practice results in the most talented people becoming frustrated and often leaving. The highly skilled people will leave first. The cost and time for a search makes the process of succession planning very important. It also sends a message to the talented people that they are valued, which increases their motivation and performance.

A leadership team should discuss the people who are the future talent in their district and make sure they are providing opportunities for their development. These conversations should happen at a leadership level. School systems are reluctant to talk about people in this manner, fearing union repercussions. However, this is not an evaluation process but instead is a development effort. All potential leaders are discussed in order to help them seek opportunities. The performance evaluation is a private process not discussed in this meeting.

It is helpful to look at people in a district-wide context as a part of developing a high-performance organization. It is possible that a new school for a teacher or a new leadership project for an assistant principal might develop his or her skills for future opportunities. In industry, succession planning is a well-established process. Strong companies invest in their people to motivate them to higher performance by helping them determine the process of moving up in role, influence, and salary. This process is needed in school districts. Because school systems are mission driven, the opportunities do not always have to be about more money in relation to assuming higher leadership roles.

The development of a teacher leader track is important for the development of future assistant principals and principals. If we can formally develop a program for aspiring leaders from teachers, we will have more options for filling the roles of assistant principals and principals. A principal in an elementary school may want to learn about the high school for his or her future development. A project at the high school on how to transition students from middle to high school might be of interest to help the potential leader understand the issues in both middle and high school. If the person later becomes an assistant superintendent or a superintendent, he or she will have more knowledge and perspective about the needs of the district.

There are many more examples for internal people becoming principals and superintendents. Unfortunately this isn't usually a planned process with a clear plan for professional development. Sometimes the assistant superintendent is made the superintendent to save money on a search and because the school committee is panicking because the superintendent left suddenly. Although many assistants do become excellent leaders, the process should be more proactive with the formation of well-developed plans to ensure success.

HIRING TO BUILD A TEAM OF LEADERS, NOT JUST A HERO LEADER

Another adjustment needed in the hiring process is that school boards and superintendents need to realize that just hiring a talented leader is not enough. The leader needs to have the support and resources to build a high-performance team to lead the school or school department. Too often the school board does not support funds for coaching or mentoring a new leader or for building a leadership team. The argument is that the school is paying good money for that individual to lead, so why should that leader need help?

This narrow-minded view is misinformed in relation to today's world of leadership in complex organizations. The school system, although it appears simple to some school board or community members, is a very complex organization. The leaders benefit greatly from mentoring, coaching, and support for team development. As budgets are cut, we are asking more and more from our leaders with higher standards for success.

It is not a weakness but strength to hire a coach for a leader. In the corporate and health care worlds it is common practice to hire coaches. A doctor who is now leading a health organization is not looked at as weak when he or she hires a coach. Obviously a position as a leader in a managed care environment requires complex skills and abilities, and the physician leader benefits greatly from a coach to challenge his or her thinking in a direct and supportive manner. Although mentoring does exist in other sectors, it usually is more informal and involves new leaders that are hired. The coaching role is much more common and formalized outside of education. In education, an experienced person in the field being in the mentor role is a more common practice. The outside professional coach is less common but growing in popularity.

We must educate school boards and the community about why coaching is an important investment for educational leaders. Key leaders in other sectors could be brought in to speak to the board about supporting this practice.

The development process needs to begin when the person is hired. The results of the search indicate challenges that the new hire needs to handle. The assessments present strengths and areas for improvement that should be used to begin working with the new superintendent and the leadership team. In addition, it might be important for the new superintendent to increase the diversity on his or her leadership team to match the demographics of the community or to provide new perspectives to the team process. This might mean focusing more on hiring ethnically diverse people for key positions either through recruitment or succession planning.

The chairperson can begin to work with the new superintendent on his or her professional development plan on day one. Even if a new superintendent is experienced, there is still a need for professional development. Ironically, there are many experienced superintendents that move to districts and do not continue to work on their professional development. The school committee may not feel that it is necessary to work on professional development with the superintendent, and problems often emerge without early detection. Then suddenly the experienced superintendent is experiencing major distress, and he or she finds out in an evaluation that there are performance problems.

These shocks to experienced superintendents are occurring more frequently as evaluations are made more public. The experienced superintendent is being criticized by laypeople and is insulted that these people do not understand what he or she is talking about. This breakdown can result in the removal of a superintendent or in one resigning. This would be unnecessary if there were an immediate connection made on professional development when a leader is hired.

Superintendents should follow the same process for their new hires. People are hired for how they fit the community's needs. The factors that made them a strong fit should be reviewed on a periodic basis and be integrated into their professional development plans. For example, a strong high school principal recently left a prestigious district to make a move to another one closer to home. He has four young kids and he needed to be able to decrease his time away from home. Now the principal is being asked to apply for the superintendent position in his new district. He has a desire to be a superintendent but is torn by the prospect of many late meetings and extra hours with the school board that will take him away from his family. He came to the community because it was the right fit for his personal life, but now it may become a problem if he applies for the superintendent position. The school board is not considering the fit issue in its process. However, the high school principal needs to determine whether he could assume the superintendent position and still meet his family commitments. This leader's concerns need to become a part of his professional development plan.

Making sure that each person has a professional development plan is very important. Even an experienced leader who is hired needs to adjust to a new community and culture. The principal needs to develop a leadership team to complement his strengths and compensate for his weaknesses.

HIRING AN INTERIM OR TRANSITIONAL LEADER

It was stated earlier that it is not good practice to hire the best person available if he or she is not right for the position. Just putting in a warm body into a key role is not acceptable. This is an especially bad practice when in many cases there are many qualified interim or transitional leaders who can fill a position until you can find the right person.

Early retirements have left a strong temporary workforce in education. The skills and experience of many retired leaders are far superior to the pool of candidates for the permanent position. Therefore, it should not be necessary to hire someone who is not the right person for the position. It is a good human resources strategy to hire strong retired leaders for transitional leader positions. This can help ensure that the best people are hired for the long term.

If the need is for a short-term leader, a maintenance type of leader could be hired from the retired ranks to fill the position while other candidates are sought. If there is a need for change, a transitional leader could be hired from the retired pool. A transitional leader is a person who can come into a school or district and make needed short-term change. Because this person will not be there for the long term, he or she can often be bolder and take more risks in the change process.

Too many districts, however, have hired retired leaders to keep the school system operating for 6 months to a year and lost an opportunity for change and improvement. In other sectors, the transitional leader role is more well established (Bridges, 2009). A transitional leader can move a district ahead and allow the school board to bring in a new leader after the transition period to build on the changes made by the previous leader. In one urban district, a new transitional superintendent was hired to replace a retiring maintenance type of leader whose goal was to keep the status quo. The transitional superintendent had the competencies and the leadership profile recommended in this text for high performance. She was low steadiness and compliance and high influencing in her DISC. She was also a high extrovert, following the maintenance-oriented leader who was a very high introvert. She has immediately taken on key issues that have languished for over a year in the district and moved them ahead. The district needs a strategic plan and has been cited by the high school accreditation process for lack of direction. The school board did not want to spend the money on this process and tried to get by with the status quo. This new transitional superintendent convinced them that they must have a plan and it would be cost effective to make sure that it happened quickly.

The transitional leader is also taking on performance issues with personnel that the previous person thought were too difficult because of political issues. This desire and clear expectation of excellence is starting to excite people and encourage them that the system can succeed. This transitional leader, who is adept at dealing with politics, is creating a new culture in this district. She is also setting a process in place for improving student achievement with a high sense of urgency. This transitional superintendent is changing the qualities that the school board is looking for in a new superintendent. The board is trying to do its own search to save money, which has resulted in poor leaders who have not been able to improve results. It will be interesting to see whether this transitional leader can help the board realize that it needs to get some help to find the best superintendent.

School boards should be careful about whom they select as a transitional leader. The person usually needs to be extroverted and focused in his or her approach to leading a school or district. The high sense of urgency is usually important for this role. The inventories for leadership should be used to assess the transitional leader's fit with the community and the time frame for change.

The ideas put forth in this chapter will help school boards, superintendents, and principals develop processes for hiring and leadership development that will result in more high-performing leaders in our schools and districts. With a focus on the best leaders who can build leadership teams to get results, school districts can break the mold of trying to hire traditional leaders with an antiquated hiring process.

In the current process, there are many situations in which strong leaders would never apply or get hired by districts. The current process barriers tend to eliminate the best people from applying because of the risks that will occur when their names are public. We are losing the leaders we need who can produce extraordinary results for students, especially in underperforming districts. School boards and educators need to be open to change and must understand that true high-performing leaders can have a variety of backgrounds, experiences, and leadership qualities. If our focus is on leadership competencies for our hiring and we support the leaders with proper mentoring, coaching, and team development assistance, the results will increase.

The following is a case study of a superintendent that was hired through a process that was flexible and followed many of the recommendations made in this chapter. If the traditional process had been used, this high-performing leader would never have been hired.

 CASE STUDY

STACEY

Overview

A school committee in a conservative, suburban community lost the superintendent who had led their district for 8 years. She moved to a high-profile district that was able to pay a significantly higher salary. This district was already high performing in relation to test scores, but the school committee was still demanding increases in student achievement although they were reluctant to add additional funding for the schools.

(continued)

The superintendent who left had been able to do an excellent job in maintaining a strong school system despite the lack of increased funding. She was very focused on the internal planning and implementation of the goals for instruction and human resources and was not overly involved in the community.

When she decided to leave, the school committee engaged a search firm to lead the hiring process to find a new superintendent. The committee scheduled the usual focus groups with teachers, students, parents, community members, and town groups. The focus groups produced input on what each believed were the skills and competencies needed for their new superintendent. The profile included some of the following:

Personal Skill Set

- Highly effective communicator
- Treats people with respect
- Has impeccable integrity
- Collaborative leader
- Able to resolve problems and conflicts
- Confident decision maker
- Student centered

Professional Skill Set

- Builds relationships with the schools and community
- Demonstrates a command of school and municipal finance
- Politically savvy
- Conceptual thinker and planner
- Able to hire and retain top-quality people
- Build educational excellence by improving the educational program

The search firm began to search for candidates for this position. The pool of potential candidates was very thin and searches in other districts were ranging from 15 to 25 candidates per search. The number of high-performing educational leaders on the list of candidates was minimal. There were 12 superintendents in the pool of 35 candidates that applied for the position. The other problem with the pool was that a majority of the candidates were in the last 3 years of their careers. The number of up-and-coming candidates who matched the leadership profile was less than five. The recruiter was able to bring in more candidates than most searches, but the pool of talent was still relatively weak.

The search firm narrowed the candidates to eight semifinalists for interviews. The goal was to have three to four finalists for the school committee to interview. The general expectations of the search committee were to find an instructional leader with a doctorate in education that had solid communications skills and a financial management background. The school committee also wanted the next superintendent to stay for at least 8 years and be a part of the community.

The eight finalists were chosen and interviewed in private sessions in accordance with the laws and guidelines of the state. There were three experienced superintendents, three assistant superintendents, one business manager, and one high school principal. There were no internal candidates.

The search firm recruited five of the eight semifinalists. The search firm was very active in presenting the profiles of the five recruits and any information the firm had gathered on the other three candidates. There was a limit to any reference checking that could be done based on the importance of confidentiality at this point.

The search firm had experience working with school departments in other capacities outside the search process. This experience allowed them to see many candidates in their own districts and to be able to gain information on their effectiveness without breaking confidentiality. This resulted in more information about candidates than was typical at this point of a search.

The three finalists were chosen by the search committee. Two of the three were recruited by the search firm. One was a superintendent later in her career who was a solid candidate. The other was a business manager who was early in his career with great potential.

The school committee was pleased with the three candidates. They believed the three people had variety and strong backgrounds that could be excellent for the community. The one candidate they were concerned about was the 33-year-old business manager, Stacey. He had an MBA and no doctorate. He did not have an instructional background. However, they liked his financial skills and reputation for clear communications.

They interviewed all three candidates publically for an hour and a half. They asked the candidates to spend a day in their district to meet a range of people informally. Comment sheets were given to people who met each candidate to gather their impressions of the potential leadership fit for the district. The school committee also had dinner with each candidate to have some informal time to get to know them personally.

The search firm discouraged the school committee from visiting the candidates' districts. The information reviewed earlier about how this dog and pony show did not usually result in added value and delayed the process was supported by the school committee. The search firm did reference checks on the three finalists and completed the three leadership inventories for each candidate. The search firm found references well beyond the standard references provided by the candidates to make more accurate profiles and determine the fit of each candidate for the district.

The references and results of the inventories showed that Stacey matched most closely with what the school committee and the community were looking for in a new superintendent. The only two mismatches with the profile that had been created was that he did not have "a track record supporting the ability to build educational excellence by improving the educational program." The other mismatch was the ability to show empathy as part of effective communication.

The recruiter spent time talking with the school committee about how a strong high-performance leader can build a team of leaders who can get results for student achievement. The leader did not need to be the educational expert. On the empathy issue, Stacey was very strong in communication skills but would not be as skilled at empathy as some of the other candidates. This did not mean that there would be a lack of respect for people. The leader would fully capitalize on the skills of other members and work on improving their areas that need improvement. Therefore, while empathy was not a strength, his abilities to be self-reflective and to build a team would be high skill areas.

All three finalists' interviews proceeded as the search moved to the final stages. However, Stacey made an almost-fatal mistake in his final interview. He was asked the question that is typical in most superintendent interviews: What is your vision for the school system? He froze in his answer and did not present a response that would meet the minimum standards for a superintendent. The rest of his interview was fine, but the mistake on the vision question resulted in a call from the school committee chairperson to the recruiter.

The school committee believed that this misstep was a sign of his lack of experience and lack of instructional leadership background. At this time, the recruiter went outside of the typical educational search process and proposed an alternative approach for the next steps.

Although it was clear that Stacey had been nervous and—by his own admission—actually overprepared for the interview and made a major mistake, he was still a viable candidate for the position. In other sectors in which the process is not as public, adjustments often occur in the process to get the best person for a position.

(continued)

The recruiter, confident in Stacey's ability and wanting the school committee to have three finalists instead of two, proposed a new step in the process. He suggested that each candidate have an opportunity to meet one-on-one with a series of key leaders in the community. Individuals and key organizations in the community were selected for the interviews. These included the town finance committee, a selectman, the town manager, the teacher's union president, and the parent–teacher organization president. Each finalist had similar one-on-one interviews. This would allow a more in-depth look at an each candidate to determine who was best qualified to lead the district.

Stacey still had a negative evaluation from the public finalist interview that would be factored into the decision. The other two candidates, although they had more experience, did not have the potential that the business manager had for the future. The school committee and the search committee agreed that this adjustment was fair and the process continued.

The results of the one-on-one interview were overwhelmingly in favor of Stacey. His skills, personal qualities, and commitment to the community were very apparent. The school committee unanimously voted for Stacey to become the new superintendent.

The process was adjusted to ensure that the best candidate was chosen for the community. Mistakes happen in these search processes—a typo appears on a resume of a great candidate, a person gets tired at an evening dinner with the school board and shows a lack of energy, or a person from the past says something negative from 10 years earlier in the candidate's career. The process is flawed and needs to be changed.

Stacey and the MBTI

Stacey is an ESTP in the MBTI. His extrovert score equated to the competencies needed for communications and networking with the community. His sensing score will be important in making sure that all plans for improvement were grounded in reality. He will need more focus and support on strategic planning and visioning. His background in finance could account for his high detail score in this area. He is a true thinking person in the MBTI, which means he can be very direct with people. This will make him clear in his expectations but could cause interpersonal issues with people on the feeling side. He is relatively high in the perceiving score. This means he can be very creative in developing and implementing plans. This is unusual for a finance person. However, it probably is a reason why he makes a good superintendent because he can change direction based on the needs of the system.

Stacey and the DISC

Stacey is high dominant and influence and low steadiness and compliance in the DISC. The high dominant and influencing scores make him very decisive as a leader. He can build necessary relationships with key people as well as make the tough decisions. His low score on steadiness indicates that he can move quickly on change and implementation of new ideas. This is a good characteristic for creating change. However, because most people in education are much more deliberate and cautious, it can create problems.

Stacey and the Values Inventory

Stacey has high individual, social, and utilitarian scores in the Values inventory. This means that he likes to have the power to lead and create change in relation to what is best for students, which is his social value. He wants to create change and improvement in a manner in which resources are used effectively, which reflects his utilitarian value. He is unusual in having a high utilitarian score for a superintendent. This is clearly from his previous work as a business manager. This gives his new district an advantage of having a leader who can build a plan for academic and financial success.

Stacey and the WPI

In this situation, the Workplace Value Inventory (WPI) was used because it directly affects the hiring process. The WPI (as discussed in Chapter 1) indicated his high scores as follows:

- High achievement (90%)
- Persistence (90%)
- Initiative (93%)
- Leadership (99%)
- Social orientation (97%)
- Dependability (95%)

His innovation score was low at 7%. However, the community did not want major innovations based on a previous leader who tried too many new ideas which upset people in this conservative community. His low detail score (7%) and relatively low (44%) score on following rules matched the data in the DISC inventory that showed he will likely delegate those compliant type tasks to others on his team. He will be more focused on results at a more global level.

His score of 39% on importance of making a positive impression, while not high, does show that he has some awareness of his limitations, which is a positive sign. He is willing and committed to working on improving his weaknesses. This quality is also helpful in building a team and hiring strong people. He would not be threatened by a strong and intelligent staff.

Therefore, his strengths were the following:

- Financial management
- Strong decision making
- Building a high-performance team
- Communications
- Strong interpersonal skills
- Networking and building external partnerships
- High sense of urgency for short-term, reality-based action
- Driven to results
- Continuous improvement philosophy
- High understanding of limitations

He matched most of the criteria the committee was looking for in a new superintendent. As stated previously, he is self-aware and is open and willing to work on his weaknesses. He needs to work on his conceptual and strategic long-term thinking, patience, empathy, and building a strong educational vision and plan for excellence. The school committee was confident that his strengths would be an asset and his openness to work on his weaknesses would result in a successful leader for the district.

(continued)

Stacey and the Seven Competencies

Stacey matches the seven competencies developed for high-performing leaders.

1. *Challenges the status quo.* Stacey is very willing to challenge the status quo to get results. He tends to determine how to solve a problem or accomplish a goal, then tries to fit it to established protocols. He does not look to the rules or laws to guide his work. Although he does not break the laws and realizes their role, they are guidelines to him rather than absolutes.

2. *Builds trust through clear communications and expectations.* Stacey is a clear communicator. He has established trust with the community through his presentations on the goals for the system and the budget. His high transparency has created additional fiscal support from the community. The trust is also high with his leadership team. He has hired people who he believes match the profile of leadership outlined in this text. He is clear with his expectations and gives them continuous feedback on their performance.

3. *Creates a commonly owned plan for success.* Stacey has developed a strategic plan for the district. The plan has strong ownership from his leadership team. The school committee supports the plan even though it did not have a major role in its creation. The plan was based on Stacey's feedback from parents and the community and the data on student performance and financial management. Although the parents and the community were not directly involved in the plan's formulation, Stacey communicates the goals and strategies of the plan to all constituencies. Stacey also presents a report card to the community on how the district is progressing on the goals.

4. *Focuses on team over self.* Stacey is a team-oriented leader. He has worked hard trying to hire the best people for each key position. He is quick to praise his team for their accomplishments. The team has worked on being an HPT and the results are excellent. Stacey does need to be more consistent in the development of his team. A more consistent approach in his work with the team would be more helpful, especially with new members.

5. *Has a high sense of urgency for change and sustainable results in improving student achievement.* Many people thought a business manager could not lead a good district to be great, and they were wrong. Stacey acts quickly and decisively on needed change. He does not fear criticism and people questioning his approach. He is all about results and believes they speak for themselves.

6. *Commits to continuous improvement for self.* Stacey commits to coaching and learning every day on the job. He has completed his doctorate and attends key state and national conferences. Being slightly unconventional, he will only participate in a training session for superintendents if he believes there will be new concepts or ideas that can increase his learning. He is also very open to learning from leaders in all sectors.

7. *Builds external networks and partnerships.* Stacey is excellent at this competency. He forms partnerships with universities, consulting firms, other school districts, and businesses to help the district succeed. His ability to network outside of the district is exceptional. He delegates leadership to his senior administrators and focuses his time externally and supports other leaders in their jobs. When the fiscal issues became very difficult recently in his state, he was confident that he would regain their funding through his ability to rally the community behind the district's goals.

The Results of a Positive Hiring Process

Stacey immediately hired a coach to work with him, and he has maintained his commitment to improving as a leader and to building a leadership team. This new superintendent has a philosophy consistent with most high-performance leaders. He spends his time leading, not doing everyone's work and micromanaging. He does not attend countless workshops on being an instructional leader, learning all the key legal issues, and understanding all the accountability systems required by the state and the federal government. Instead, he works on hiring the best leaders, building an HPT, developing a strategic plan, and building relationships with key community leaders to achieve results.

He places more emphasis on the external relationships in the community than previous superintendents. He holds focus groups personally with parents, the community, the municipal government, and other leaders to hear their concerns and make the budget transparent. He builds credibility with the community and they trust in his integrity. His belief is that if they believe that their resources are being used properly and that they can trust him, he would gain the community's support. He did not just meet once with external people as part of an entry plan; he maintains ongoing communication with all people.

He knew he had some time to build the external relationships and the trust of his school committee. Because the quality of most of the teachers was excellent in the school system, there would be no immediate decline in results. He knew that building a team that valued the best quality education for the school system—with a belief that the parents, students, and community were the valued customers—would result in a nationally recognized school system. He is highly competitive and wants the best for the school system.

There were people who resisted his approach and believed he was showing his lack of traditional educational background by spending too much time externally. However, because he built so much support with the school committee and the community, he had some time to allow his strategy to work. The results were excellent:

- All test scores have risen in each category of standardized tests.
- A new team of principals and administrators was hired to add to the key successful leaders in the district to form a high-performance team.
- The first override in 10 years was passed and the school system is in good financial shape. This involved the removal of the limit that the town can pay in taxes, which resulted in additional funds for the school system. His is one of the only school systems in the region that is not in dire financial condition.
- He is working on new alternative funding sources to use for investments in new initiatives such as technology for instruction.
- He surveyed parents and has implemented many means of regularly communicating with the public that have received major accolades.
- There is a 3-year strategic plan in place.

He has received a new contract with a raise so he will stay in the community for a long time. He moved his family to the community to show his commitment. He has also answered his critics about his instructional leadership by obtaining a doctorate in education by a prominent university.

This now experienced superintendent has changed the search process for his administrators. He realizes that while the input of stakeholders is important, he must be able to control the process to hire the best people to fit the profile of excellence established in his community.

He uses a recruiter to conduct searches for principals and key administrators. He works on succession planning to build potential candidates from within the system. This has resulted in several key promotions from within that have proved to be excellent choices.

He communicates regularly to a recruiter about his willingness to talk to potential high-performing people who at some point might want to come to his district if an opening occurs. He uses advisory committees to provide input on principal selections; however, he makes it clear that they are advisory only to provide him input for his hiring decisions. They are not doing the search and sending him finalists. He conducts the leadership

(continued)

inventories on all finalists for his administrative positions. His leadership team has completed all the inventories and is aware of his team's strengths and weaknesses. The team uses the inventories to formulate interview questions and to ascertain the issues to check in the reference segment for new hiring. He does not rely on regular references. He uses the recruiter to help with references and his own vast network of colleagues.

He is clear about the type of people he wants for his team. They must have

- A positive "can do" attitude
- Strong communication skills
- A sense of urgency for results without excuses
- A team-oriented attitude
- An understanding of their customers
- The ability to engage positively and openly with the community
- The ability to make tough decisions

He also is always willing and explicit about helping his administrators advance in their careers. One of the best principals he hired, whose school is number one in the state on standardized tests for elementary schools, is a prime focus for his career development assistance. This high-performing principal has a similar leadership inventory profile as Stacey's. The principal has made many contacts who are promoting him for a more senior position. He believes he can become a superintendent now and does not have to wait for more experience. Stacey also provides higher salaries than his neighboring districts for key positions. This gives him an advantage in attracting high performers.

The Final Story

The school committee was in crisis trying to find a new superintendent during a time when the pool was poor for the recruitment of high-performing leaders. Committee members were willing to adjust their process to find the best fit for their community. They placed results over process and are excited about their future. Stacey, the new superintendent, has also adjusted the typical hiring process used in the district to bring in the best performers. This new formula for success has worked and will be sustainable. Even if Stacey leaves and finds a new position for his future, the institutionalization of a high-performance culture will be maintained.

Reflective Questions

1. What would you do to improve your hiring practices?
2. How would you increase the skill level in your school and district on HR and talent management?
3. What biases do you have about who should be hired that need a new perspective?
4. How would you begin to put more effort into hiring and developing?
5. How would you obtain support for changes in the hiring and development process?

7

Building Your Leadership Development Plan

Customized Action Plans That Allow You to Take Charge Now!

As a leader in education you have hopefully learned a great deal about what it takes to be a high-performing leader in today and tomorrow's educational arenas. In this chapter you will have the opportunity to see the leadership development plans (LDP) for several of the leaders mentioned in this text. In addition, you will hopefully be able to find an LDP that matches your leadership style and your position, whether it is as a superintendent, principal, or central office leader.

It is very important to develop a written plan for your growth and development. This plan can be a constant resource throughout your career. You can track your progress and you will be able to review the areas that have been continual challenges for your development. Putting words to paper, or in today's world putting key strokes to your individual plan on your laptop, will be a major step in your professional and personal development.

The key points that need to be explicitly and honestly covered in your LDP are the following:

- What you have learned from your assessments and performance data
- A summary of your strengths to build on for future success
- Your areas that need improvement
- Areas that are causing conflict for you and potentially for other people
- How you can build a team around you
- How you can lead without fear of failure
- How you deal with the challenges in your position such as politics, unions, and stress
- How you can adapt to change effectively
- How you integrate your personal and career goals in your work
- Methods to measure success and progress

PULLING IT ALL TOGETHER: YOUR LEADERSHIP DEVELOPMENT PLAN (LDP)

The goal of this chapter is to provide a simple but comprehensive LDP format and model that you can use as you move through your leadership improvement process and career progression. This format will allow you to use this text to think through your short- and long-term career goals and to assess your strengths and areas for improvement to produce a plan that best serves you. The samples provided include all the components and wording of an LDP. Although this may be repetitive, it is intended to allow you to use any sample as a guide for your own LDP development.

One key idea from this text is to be honest with yourself and use the leadership assessments and other professional development tools and evaluations to directly confront your weaknesses. Being able to confidently face your areas for growth makes you strong and will serve you well through both good and difficult times. As a leader, if you are blind to your weaknesses or are in denial about your leadership style, you will continually become derailed throughout your career. It is important to save the blame for others that have caused you problems and know what you are responsible for in your successes or failures. Although it may be difficult to focus on weaknesses, it is a powerful feeling to know that you control your own success and your career and no matter what barriers confront you, they are yours to remove. You never want to be referred to as the leader who lost his or her job due to being blind to feedback and self-reflection on the areas that need improvement.

The LDP has two sections. The first section is called the Background and Assessment Summary, which records all assessment data on your leadership style, behavior, and performance. The second section is your LDP goals and action plans. This section includes the following:

1. *Name and your title.* This should be easy!

2. *All your assessment data (MBTI, DISC, Values, EQ, etc.).* Your inventory charts and highlights from assessments will be included in this section. Having the actual graph or grid of your style will be an important reference point for you to constantly check to ensure that your plan reflects your unique leadership characteristics. If you have any assessment data on your leadership team, it will be placed in this section as well. This section should be updated every 2 years to keep current.

3. *Summary analysis.* This section includes strengths, areas for leadership growth, potential conflicts and stressors, and how you work in a team. As you know, the leadership profiles can indicate areas that can cause you internal conflict or can be problematic for other people. It is important to be honest with yourself about the areas that can cause you difficulty in dealing with other people. Everyone has his or her stressors, but a high-performing leader who knows and understands his or her problems and can deal with them head on.

4. *Kirtman's Seven Leadership Competencies for School Leadership.* You will assess the competencies that you believe are strengths and the ones that need more attention.

5. *Additional assessment data.* Any other relevant information on your leadership is recorded in your background and assessment summary document. This can include highlights from your 360 degree assessment, your performance evaluation, and any other assessments that you have completed on your leadership style or behavior. The 360 degree process is especially helpful because it provides data from several constituencies that are important to a leader. Input on how you are performing on carefully selected questions helps in the development of strategies for improvement. Direct reports, colleagues, and people higher in the governance structure provide input on what is working in your leadership style and what areas need improvement. This helps you gauge how a specific strategy might improve your relationship with your boss, but might take time away from your direct reports. As a leader, you must choose actions that improve behavior and results but do not have a negative impact on another key constituency. The 720 referred to in Chapter 5 adds a customer component to this effort for leaders that want to expand their feedback mechanisms.

The following are the key components of your new LDP:

1. One-year goals are established with your supervisor, coach, or mentor. These goals are developed based on a review of your assessment data and represent key areas for improvement. Each goal needs to

have at least one indicator of success. This measurement indicates how you will know you are successful. If you do not achieve this measurement, it does not mean failure. However, it does mean that you need to clearly understand the reason you did not achieve this measurement to aid in future planning.

2. The next section is a brief summary about the barriers you believe could directly affect your accomplishment of the 1-year goal. This summary will be used to help develop action plans that are grounded in reality.

3. Action plans are the next component of your LDP. You could put in a timeline for action plan completion, but some of these action plans may be ongoing.

4. Long-term leadership goals should also be included. These 3-year goals can be personal and professional and will prevent you from becoming too myopic. The true leader steps back and maintains perspective and does not get overly focused on short-term problems.

This comprehensive plan will allow you to have one document that summarizes all your leadership development efforts. This plan will be very beneficial for your evaluation process. Evaluations should never surprise you. If you take control of your leadership development, you will be continually working on improving on your weaknesses. You will be seeking feedback regularly and the evaluation session will just be one step of measuring progress. Your supervisor will be a resource, not your evaluator. You are very capable of being your own evaluator.

SAMPLE LDP

MARY (PRINCIPAL) FROM CHAPTER 2

As you may remember, Mary was the model of a leader who did not conform to what she was supposed to do based on the pressure from state, federal, and local rules and regulations for running a high school in a working class urban district. Instead, Mary's leadership profile matched the data cited in this text for a high-performance leader. Her high level of skill in Kirtman's Seven Competencies for School Leadership is a major reason she has been successful. Her leadership assessments indicated her abilities to lead a school to sustainable results. In addition, the data over a 9-year period have confirmed her ability to improve student achievement against all odds in a district that has showed very little progress in other schools.

Why would Mary need an LDP? As noted in earlier chapters, one of the competencies of high-performance leaders is being committed to continuous improvement and receiving critical feedback in a nondefensive manner to improve their skills to get better results for their staff and students. Mary is always open to complete the leadership assessments noted in this text and responds within 24 hours of all requests to assess and learn about her leadership. Although others say they are too busy and tired of tests, Mary always wants to learn. She realizes that there are numerous ways to learn from people no matter whether they are from education or are leaders in other sectors.

Mary's Background and Assessment Summaries

The Myers Briggs Type Indicator (MBTI) is based on the groundbreaking work of psychologist Carl Jung and nearly 70 years of research into personality styles. Based on 16 basic style "types" and the strength of dichotomous traits, we can look at how each individual in the team functions and communicates most comfortably. You can then work with the team to most effectively blend styles and strengths to build a high-performing team. Like all assessments, the MBTI and DISC are simply one small but useful guidepost in the vastly complex assessment of individual personalities and team functioning.

(continued)

Preference Dichotomy	Preference Reported	Strength (1–30)
Extravert (E)/Introvert (I)	E	24
Sensing (S)/Intuitive (N)	N	18
Thinking (T)/Feeling (F)	T	11
Judging (J)/Perceiving (P)	J	18

The ENTJ profile means that Mary

- Is outgoing and engaging
- Is a systemic thinker
- Is often seen as a no-nonsense person
- Will see a job through to the end
- Is responsible and trustworthy
- Is very task oriented, often ignores emotions and feelings around a task

The DISC uses research-based questions to help measure how individuals behave and communicate based on the strength of four basic characteristics: **D**ominance—how you respond to problems or challenges, **I**nfluence—how you influence others to your point of view, **S**teadiness—how you respond to the pace of your environment, and **C**ompliance—how you respond to rules and regulations. The DISC also gives you insight into your natural style and how you are functioning under job and life's current pressures or their "adapted style."

The DISC (see Figure 7.1) indicates that Mary's style can be of value to the team for the following reasons:

- She is motivating and helps others achieve their goals.
- She can prompt and allow other members of the team to take leadership on projects.

FIGURE 7.1 Mary's DISC Bar Charts *Source:* Copyright © 2012 Target Training International, Ltd. Used with permission.

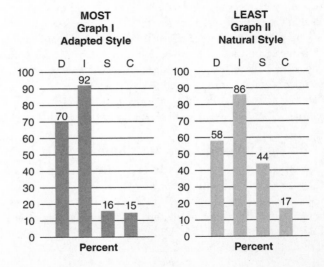

SAMPLE LDP *(continued)*

- She will be a model for taking initiative and being focused on results.
- She can bring people's varying styles and behaviors together to form a well-blended team.
- Her ego will not get in the way of new ideas, but she will want to know how all actions are geared to helping students achieve results.
- She moves quickly and will delegate tasks to others.
- She will not let rules or regulations get in the way of results.
- She is consistent and supportive.

Knowledge of an individual's values help to tell us *why* he or she does things. A review of an individual's experiences, references, education, and training helps to tell us *what* he or she can do. Behavior assessments help to tell us *how* a person behaves and performs in the work environment. The Motivation Insights measures the relative prominence of six basic interests or values (a way of valuing life):

- Theoretical = the drive for knowledge
- Utilitarian = the drive for money
- Aesthetic = the drive for form and harmony
- Social = the drive for helpfulness
- Individualistic = the drive for power
- Traditional = the drive for order

Mary's Values inventory results, shown in Figure 7.2, indicate her high-value areas are individual and social. This means that she wants to have power to influence students' lives. She is slightly below the line in the theoretical value, meaning that data are important but only as a means for actions to help students achieve. Her lowest area is aesthetics, meaning that the need for harmony is low.

360 Degree Review
None completed

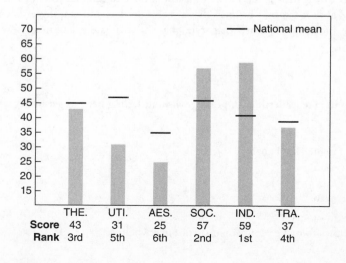

FIGURE 7.2 **Mary's Values Inventory Bar Chart** *Source:* Copyright © 2012 Target Training International, Ltd. Used with permission.

	THE.	UTI.	AES.	SOC.	IND.	TRA.
Score	43	31	25	57	59	37
Rank	3rd	5th	6th	2nd	1st	4th

(continued)

Evaluation Results

Her evaluations have always pointed out great strengths in communications achieving results for her school and public relations. There have been no areas for her improvement noted.

Other Leadership Assessments

Mary's WPI lists the following as high scores (above the norm): persistence, initiative, leadership orientation, independence, stress tolerance, adaptability/flexibility, and innovation. The accompanying notes are areas for improvement: analytical thinking and achievement/effort.

Leadership Competencies

1. Challenges the status quo: Very strong.
2. Builds trust through clear communications and expectations: A strength, but with more deliberate styles she needs more patience and focus on details.
3. Creates a commonly owned plan for success: This is strong, but the plan may need more details for others' styles.
4. Focuses on team over self: She is totally committed to teams, but some think her strong personality means that she is too focused on her own success.
5. Has a high sense of urgency for change and sustainable results in improving student achievement: This is her number one strength.
6. Commitment to continuous improvement for self: She is always learning from others in both education and other fields.
7. Builds external networks and partnerships: She is the model for this work. People come from all over the country to visit and learn about her school.

Summary Analysis

As a school administrator and a member of the administrative team, these inventories can be used to give some preliminary insight into how your style influences your work as a leader, supervisor, and member of a team. The insights, suggestions, and conclusions noted below are just a starting point; it is our intention that they be used for discussion, reflection, and growth with supervisors and teammates. They are not intended as an assessment of your skills or abilities. The author strongly believes that effective leaders and employees have a variety of styles. It is, in the end, how they understand and use their styles that will ultimately determine how well they perform their jobs.

Mary's Strengths

- Task and results driven
- Will allow members of the team to take leadership on projects without letting her ego get in the way
- Good verbal communicator
- Celebrates success and progress
- Is logical and will push others to higher-level goals
- Deals well with constructive criticism

Mary's Areas of Leadership Growth

- Should try to be more patient with others
- Needs to move more slowly at times to make sure people are not overwhelmed

- Needs to explain what she needs in a more patient manner
- Needs to spend more time coaching others
- Needs to make sure that lack of compliance does not cause major problems

Mary's Potential Conflicts and Stressors

- No structure or timetable to follow
- Tasks that need more research
- People who try to intimidate her
- Emotional issues that need a measured response
- Needing to spontaneously present to large groups

Mary's Leadership and Teammate Qualities

- She is steady and consistent.
- She will listen and be strategic.
- She will not intimidate other teammates.

Excerpts from Mary's Goals and Action Plans

One-Year Goals

1. To enhance leadership skills in dealing with people with different styles, values, and behaviors
   Indicator of Success: A teacher in her school or a principal in another school demonstrates new behaviors from her coaching. This would involve the development of new strategies to improve student achievement that show measurable results.
2. To increase her support and participation in the superintendent's leadership team
   Indicator of Success: Members of the leadership team note her positive assistance on school system issues, not just high school goals.
3. To work on developing a high-performance team in her school
   Indicator of Success: There will be an increase in requests for members of her leadership team to speak at community and state-wide events.

General Barriers to Goal Attainment

The major barrier to her achieving her goals is her strong extrovert score and her high thinking score on the MBTI. She is so comfortable expressing her opinions and is so honest and direct with people that introverts and those with feeling styles become intimidated. Although she is very committed to team development, it appears to some people that everything is all about her and the school. Some people think she is more concerned with her success than her school.

Action Plan

1. To use a facilitator to work with her leadership team to document the team development process
2. To work with a coach on her skills in working with people who are not highly motivated
3. Identify another principal to work with to increase his or her success and promotion of his or her results

Long-Term Goals

1. To write a book on leadership development from principal's point of view
2. To work on a program to train future principals

SAMPLE LDP

RON (SUPERINTENDENT) FROM CHAPTER 5

This superintendent is very committed to becoming a high-performance leader. Although he has many of the competencies and characteristics of a high-performing leader, there are a few areas that could derail his success. His LDP clearly shows his strengths and outlines a set of goals and actions to improve his leadership effectiveness.

Ron's Background and Assessment Summaries

The Myers Briggs Type Indicator (MBTI) is based on the groundbreaking work of psychologist Carl Jung and nearly 70 years of research into personality styles. Based on 16 basic style "types" and the strength of dichotomous traits, we can look at how each individual in the team functions and communicates most comfortably. You can then work with the team to most effectively blend styles and strengths to build a high-performing team. Like all assessments, the MBTI and DISC are simply one small but useful guidepost in the vastly complex assessment of individual personalities and team functioning.

Preference Dichotomy	Preference Reported	Strength (1–30)
Extrovert (E)/Introvert (I)	E	18
Sensing (S)/Intuitive (N)	N	19
Thinking (T)/Feeling (F)	F	19
Judging (J)/Perceiving (P)	J	16

The ENFJ profile means that Ron

- Is very engaging
- Is often seen as a no-nonsense person
- Will see a job through to the end
- Is responsible and trustworthy
- Is very task oriented, but attends to the emotions of others
- Is very focused on competence for himself and others

Figures 7.3 and 7.4 are the MBTI grids for Ron's leadership team. The team has a balanced Myers Briggs profile, except in the judging and perceiving area. This raises a concern with lack of flexibility and a team that may not be open and comfortable with change.

The DISC uses research-based questions to help measure how individuals behave and communicate based on the strength of four basic characteristics: **D**ominance—how you respond to problems or challenges, **I**nfluence—how you influence others to your point of view, **S**teadiness—how you respond to the pace of your environment, and **C**ompliance—how you respond to rules and regulations. The DISC also gives you insight into your natural style and how you are functioning under job and life's current pressures or their "adapted style."

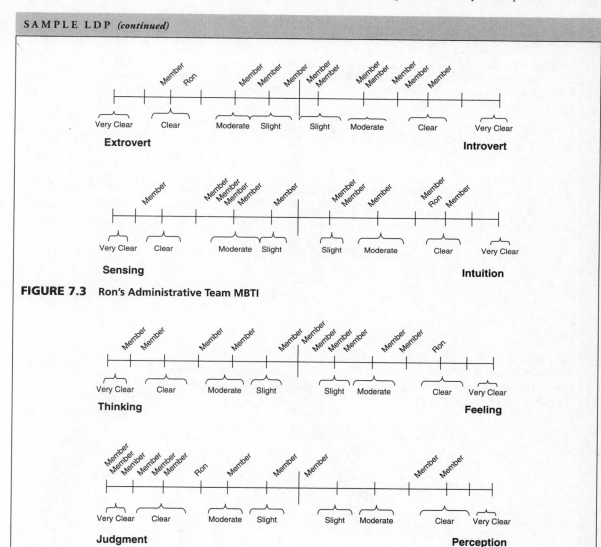

FIGURE 7.3   Ron's Administrative Team MBTI

FIGURE 7.4   Ron's Administrative Team MBTI

Ron's DISC results are shown in Figures 7.5 and 7.6. The DISC indicates that Ron's style can be of value to the team for the following reasons:

- He moves quickly to attain results.
- He can prompt and allow other members of the team to take leadership on projects.
- He can bring people's varying styles and behaviors together to form a well-blended team.
- His ego will not get in the way of new ideas.
- He is consistent and supportive.
- He can be very motivating to staff.

(continued)

FIGURE 7.5 Ron's DISC Bar Charts
Source: Copyright © 2012 Target Training International, Ltd. Used with permission.

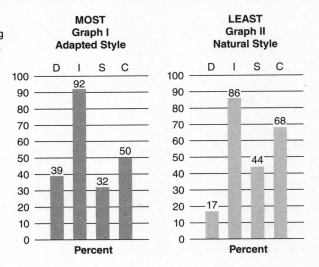

MOST
Graph I
Adapted Style

LEAST
Graph II
Natural Style

FIGURE 7.6 Ron's DISC Wheel
Source: Copyright © 2012 Target Training International, Ltd. Used with permission.

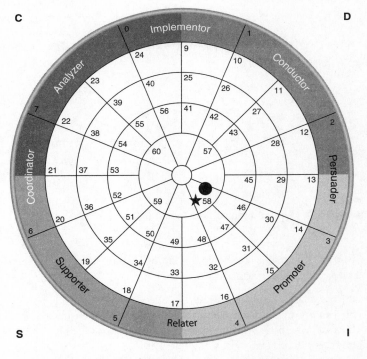

Adapted: ★ (58) Analyzing promoter (across)

Natural: ● (58) Analyzing promoter (across)

- Ron is very focused on building relationships with all groups.
- He is committed to meeting state, federal, and local regulations.
- He tends to move quickly on implementing changes.
- Ron is very focused on building a leadership team and helping members develop their skills.

Knowledge of an individual's values help to tell us *why* he or she does things. A review of an individual's experiences, references, education, and training helps to tell us *what* he or she can do. Behavior assessments help to tell us *how* a person behaves and performs in the work environment. The Motivation Insights measures the relative prominence of six basic interests or values (a way of valuing life):

- Theoretical = the drive for knowledge
- Utilitarian = the drive for money
- Aesthetic = the drive for form and harmony
- Social = the drive for helpfulness
- Individualistic = the drive for power
- Traditional = the drive for order

Ron's Values inventory results, shown in Figure 7.7, indicate a high score on social, individual, and traditional. This translates into a major commitment to improving students' lives, a desire to be in a leadership role, and a strong sense of right and wrong in relationship to family and work values and ethics.

360 Degree Review

Ron has shown that he can overwhelm people. Although people believe in his abilities, he can seem insecure and too worried by what others think of him. His intensity is too strong when he feels he is being evaluated. People admire his knowledge and skills in a range of areas.

Evaluation Results

He has accomplished more in 1 year than previous leaders in the district. He is committed to the district's achievement of high results for all students. His knowledge of curriculum and instruction is exemplary. He needs to be more open to challenges in his ideas or new areas to pursue. He can be defensive.

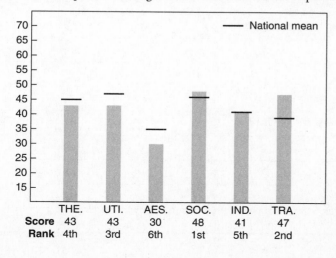

	THE.	UTI.	AES.	SOC.	IND.	TRA.
Score	43	43	30	48	41	47
Rank	4th	3rd	6th	1st	5th	2nd

FIGURE 7.7   Ron's Values Inventory Bar Chart *Source:* Copyright © 2012 Target Training International, Ltd. Used with permission.

(continued)

Key WPI Summary Points

Ron's scores in leadership are significantly higher than those of his principals. He will need to coach and support the principals to increase their leadership capacity. He must be careful in putting too much pressure on the principals so they don't become overwhelmed and too stressed to function effectively.

Leadership Competencies

1. Challenges the status quo: Very strong.
2. Builds trust through clear communications and expectations: A strength, but with more deliberate styles he needs more patience and focus on details.
3. Creates a commonly owned plan for success: This is strong, but the plan may need more details for others' styles.
4. Focuses on team over self: He is totally committed to teams, but some think his strong personality overshadows other people and means that he is too focused on his own success.

TABLE 7.1 Other Leadership Assessments: WPI Principals and Superintendent

WPI Area	Average for Principals	Superintendent Score
Achievement orientation	48	99
Persistence	45	98
Initiative	43	98
Leadership orientation	63	92
Cooperation	56	93
Concern for others	52	81
Social orientation	32	94
Independence	41	19
Self-control	31	65
Stress tolerance	16	30
Adaptability/flexibility	24	55
Dependability	59	95
Attention to detail	61	98
Rule following	35	48
Innovation	45	83
Analytical thinking	37	95
Concern about impressions	57	97

5. Has a high sense of urgency for change and sustainable results in improving student achievement: This is his number one strength.

6. Commitment to continuous improvement for self: He is always learning from others in both education and other fields. He uses his coach and other colleagues to work on his areas for improvement.

7. Builds external networks and partnerships: He attends a variety of conferences and is beginning to connect to education in other countries. He is working on freeing up more time to meet with community leaders.

Summary Analysis

Ron's Strengths

- Engaging and charismatic
- Will allow members of the team to take leadership on projects without letting his ego get in the way
- Good verbal and written communicator
- Is very passionate about his work
- Is open to critical feedback if delivered in a caring manner

Ron's Areas of Leadership Growth

- Should be more patient and slow down
- Needs to listen more and focus on people in a more patient manner
- Needs to prioritize tasks and trust members of the team to gather information and create structure around selected projects
- Needs to delegate tasks to other colleagues and trust them
- Needs to control emotions from getting in the way of results
- Needs to worry less about compliance and coach others for success

Ron's Potential Conflicts and Stressors

- No structure or timetable to follow
- Tasks that need more patience
- People who try to intimidate him
- Emotional issues that require self-control
- Wanting to be open to ideas but feeling the pressure to stick to his plan

Ron's Leadership and Teammate Qualities

- He is motivating and mission driven.
- He can be trusted.
- He will not intentionally intimidate other teammates.
- Teammates must be willing to engage with him or he could overwhelm them.

Excerpts from Ron's Goals and Action Plans

One-Year Goals

1. To increase his impulse control and give more time and support to others on his leadership team to work on goal implementation

   Indicator of Success: A survey of leadership team members cites his control of his extrovert tendencies, fewer interruptions of people when speaking, and an increase in listening skills.

(continued)

2. To reduce his time spent on details and micromanaging and increase his time on coaching
Indicator of Success: The leadership team members and school board note an improvement in communications in the superintendent evaluation document.
3. To decrease his concern for what people think of him (which increases his stress)
Indicator of Success: He will decrease his time worrying about what others think of him.
4. To increase his time on forming external networks
Indicator of Success: He will establish one new formal partnership that will add resources that will help accomplish a school system goal.

General Barriers to Goal Attainment

The major barrier to Ron achieving his goals is his strong extrovert score, concern over what people think of him, high feeling and emotional responses, and the desire for perfection. The combination of his drive for success and his fear of failure put too much pressure on him. This pressure causes him enormous stress and results in him placing inordinate demands on others. This aggressiveness results in behavior that can be distancing and seem overly aggressive to others with different styles. This behavior pattern is even more acute under pressure. He is actually an extremely caring person.

Action Plan

1. Work with a coach on controlling of emotional responses and increasing his listening skills.
2. Increase his self-confidence and his response to critical behavior.
3. Increase his time forming networks and partnerships outside the district and connect them to his key leaders for their development.
4. Continue developing his leadership team into an HPT and working in partnership with the school committee.

Long-Term Goals

1. To apply his skills and abilities to a larger district in a superintendent role
2. To write or co-write a book on his leadership experiences

SAMPLE LDP

KATHY (SUPERINTENDENT) FROM CHAPTER 3

Kathy is the high-performing superintendent studied in Chapter 3. Her background and assessment summary and LDP show her high leadership scores and her challenge in developing a leadership team that can create sustainable change. If Kathy does not develop more leadership capacity in her district, the district will be vulnerable to losing ground if she decides to pursue other career opportunities.

Kathy's Background and Assessment Summaries

The Myers Briggs Type Indicator (MBTI) is based on the groundbreaking work of psychologist Carl Jung and nearly 70 years of research into personality styles. Based on 16 basic style "types" and the strength of dichotomous traits, we can look at how each individual in the team functions and communicates most comfortably. You can then work with the team to most effectively blend styles and strengths to build a high-performing

SAMPLE LDP *(continued)*

team. Like all assessments, the MBTI and DISC are simply one small but useful guidepost in the vastly complex assessment of individual personalities and team functioning.

Preference Dichotomy	Preference Reported	Strength (1–30)
Extrovert (E)/Introvert (I)	E	21
Sensing (S)/Intuitive (N)	N	23
Thinking (T)/Feeling (F)	T	7
Judging (J)/Perceiving (P)	J	6

Kathy's leadership team is operational orientated and needs to be more strategic. The team is very analytical and objective and needs to be more attentive to the people and morale issues of the school systems. The team is very structured and results oriented and needs to be more open to change.

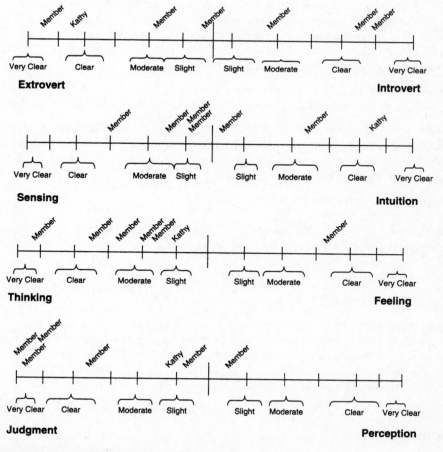

FIGURE 7.8   School District Team MBTI

(continued)

The ENTJ profile means that Kathy

- Is a very strong leader
- Is a strong communicator
- Sets clear expectations
- Is very focused on results
- Believes in developing and executing plans for improvement

The DISC uses research-based questions to help measure how individuals behave and communicate based on the strength of four basic characteristics: **D**ominance—how you respond to problems or challenges, **I**nfluence—how you influence others to your point of view, **S**teadiness—how you respond to the pace of your environment, and **C**ompliance—how you respond to rules and regulations. The DISC also gives you insight into your natural style and how you are functioning under job and life's current pressures or their "adapted style."

The DISC indicates that Kathy's style can be of value to the team for the following reasons:

- She is very direct and result oriented.
- She can prompt and allow other members of the team to take leadership on projects.
- Will move quickly on projects without a lot of process.
- Can bring the varying styles and behaviors together to form a well-blended team.
- Her ego will not get in the way of new ideas, but she will want all members to be driven to results.
- She is extremely engaging with outside groups.

The team's DISC (see Figure 7.9) is oriented toward task completion. The team needs to be more focused on leadership and less on operations. The team is overly dependent on Kathy for strategic and leadership issues.

Knowledge of an individual's values helps to tell us *why* he or she does things. A review of an individual's experiences, references, education, and training helps to tell us *what* he or she can do. Behavior assessments help to tell us *how* a person behaves and performs in the work environment. The Motivation Insights measures the relative prominence of six basic interests or values (a way of valuing life):

- Theoretical = the drive for knowledge
- Utilitarian = the drive for money
- Aesthetic = the drive for form and harmony
- Social = the drive for helpfulness
- Individualistic = the drive for power
- Traditional = the drive for order

Kathy's Values inventory results, shown in Figure 7.10, are as follows:

- Is committed to being a leader in making a difference in student's lives
- Believes it is critical to find root causes of why certain students are not learning and helping them to achieve
- Believes that data and analysis are key to success
- Wants harmony amongst staff
- Is less focused on financial return on investment and more focused on results for students

360 Degree Review

None completed.

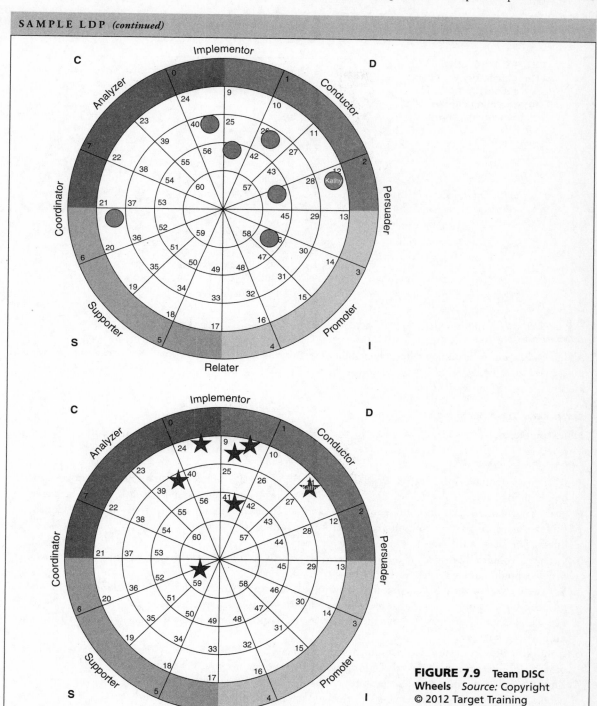

FIGURE 7.9 Team DISC Wheels *Source:* Copyright © 2012 Target Training International, Ltd. Used with permission.

(continued)

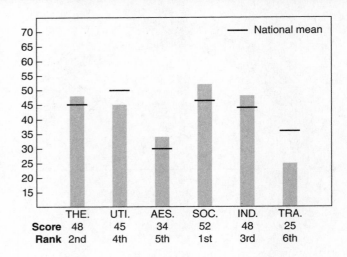

FIGURE 7.10 Kathy's **Values Inventory Bar Chart** *Source:* Copyright © 2012 Target Training International, Ltd. Used with permission.

	THE.	UTI.	AES.	SOC.	IND.	TRA.
Score	48	45	34	52	48	25
Rank	2nd	4th	5th	1st	3rd	6th

Evaluation Results

All her evaluations have been excellent. Her ability to work well with the school board and engage with the community was highlighted in all her evaluations. The results of the system on student achievement and the budget are also models for other districts.

Other Leadership Assessments

None completed.

Leadership Competencies

1. Challenges the status quo: She sets very high standards for herself and her staff. If a rule, regulation, or previous method of action enhances results, she will support the action. If the compliance tasks do not help achieve goals, she will meet the minimum requirements and not spend much of her or her staff's time on them.
2. Builds trust through clear communications and expectations: Her communications are amazingly clear and direct. The trust in the system is very high at all levels.
3. Creates a commonly owned plan for success: This is strong, but the plan may need more details for other people who do not always see the big picture.
4. Focuses on team over self: She is totally committed to teams. However, her team is taking on a lot and is prone to burning out. They must learn how to build teams in each departmental area.
5. Has a high sense of urgency for change and sustainable results in improving student achievement: This is her number one strength.
6. Commitment to continuous improvement for self: She is always learning from others in both education and other fields. She starts each day trying to focus on how she can improve her leadership.
7. Builds external networks and partnerships: She is the model for this work. She has an amazing network of people in her community as well as state-wide and nationally.

Summary Analysis

Kathy's Strengths

- Will take risks
- Will allow members of the team to take leadership on projects without letting her ego get in the way
- Is a good verbal and written communicator
- Is logical and well organized
- Deals well with constructive criticism

Kathy's Areas of Leadership Growth

- May need to slow down on some issues to understand more detail
- Needs to respect the work people are doing before pushing change and improvement
- Needs to commit to team development at next level to relieve her team members' stress
- Needs to look at data more before acting
- Needs to adjust to people with different styles

Kathy's Potential Conflicts and Stressors

- No structure or timetable to follow
- Tasks that need more data and a formal decision-making process before decisions are made
- People who spend too much time on why things can't be done
- Emotional issues that need a measured response
- Needing to spend more time coaching others

Kathy's Leadership and Teammate Qualities

- She is very motivating.
- She will drive results.
- She will not intimidate other teammates.
- Teammates must be willing to work hard for results and then will receive a lot or praise.

Excerpts from Kathy's Goals and Action Plans

One-Year Goals

1. To build a high-performance team at the senior level
   Indicator of Success: The leadership team works on building their team on their own.
2. To provide direct support for each senior team member to develop high-performance teams at his or her level
   Indicator of Success: The scores on compliance have decreased on the DISC for her senior members due to increased delegation.
3. To increase her ability to take on conflict with key senior leaders
   Indicator of Success: Each senior leader has an LDP and is able to review it with the leadership team.

General Barriers to Goal Attainment

The major barrier to Kathy achieving her goals is her success. It is hard for her to stay with the development of her leadership team because there is no obvious problem. The superintendent will need to be able to take a risk and

(continued)

SAMPLE LDP *(continued)*

show her commitment to personal and professional development by motivating each member to work on his or her leadership style and behavior. The team will continually resist this work by stating that they are too busy. Kathy will need to show her commitment to the team development process by staying consistent with the leadership process. She needs to deal with her fear of conflict with senior people and her concern that they will leave if pushed too far.

Action Plan
1. To work with a coach on the team development and conflict resolution process
2. To review other strong districts' work on team development to show as a model for her team

Long-Term Goals
1. To develop a long-term plan for her career
2. To write an article and/or a book on leadership

SAMPLE LDP

LAURA (SUPERINTENDENT)

This case study is an example of an LDP for a superintendent who does not have the natural profile of a high-performing leader but has been able to take an honest, objective look at her style and make adjustments necessary to achieve high-performing results. She has been able to build an HPT that complements her leadership style, which has been very successful in improving student achievement in her district.

Her story is very important for many of our readers because most people in education have similar profiles. Her ability to be open to critical feedback and accept her strengths and weaknesses make her a high-performing leader. She serves as a great model for educators who need to learn new skills for today's world of education. She has shown the ability to learn, adjust, and take advantage of her strengths to model how to create new opportunities to build great leaders from within her school systems.

Because her profile is very different from our profile for a high-performing leader, we must admire her hard work and commitment to her own development and her profession. An added benefit of her profile has been the ability to stay focused and follow through on her goals and commitments. Her detail orientation and commitment to process and following a plan have resulted in a slow and steady path to results. She never gets derailed from her plan, which can be a problem for some of the leaders who may have more natural leadership profiles.

Laura's Background and Assessment Summaries

The Myers Briggs Type Indicator (MBTI) is based on the groundbreaking work of psychologist Carl Jung and nearly 70 years of research into personality styles. Based on 16 basic style "types" and the strength of dichotomous traits, we can look at how each individual in the team functions and communicates most comfortably. You can then work with the team to most effectively blend styles and strengths to build a high-performing team. Like all assessments, the MBTI and DISC are simply one small but useful guidepost in the vastly complex assessment of individual personalities and team functioning.

The ISTJ profile means that Laura

- Is serious and quiet, often seen as aloof
- Is often seen as a no-nonsense person

Preference Dichotomy	Preference Reported	Strength (1–30)
Extrovert (E)/Introvert (I)	I	19
Sensing (S)/Intuitive (N)	S	24
Thinking (T)/Feeling (F)	T	17
Judging (J)/Perceiving (P)	J	18

- Will see a job through to the end
- Is responsible and trustworthy
- Is very task oriented, often ignoring emotions and feelings around a task

The Administrative Council Team has a full balance of MBTI styles (see Figure 7.11). Laura can make sure that all key initiatives have high-performing teams.

The DISC uses research-based questions to help measure how individuals behave and communicate based on the strength of four basic characteristics: **D**ominance—how you respond to problems or challenges, **I**nfluence—how you influence others to your point of view, **S**teadiness—how you respond to the pace of your environment, and **C**ompliance—how you respond to rules and regulations. The DISC also gives you insight into your natural style and how you are functioning under job and life's current pressures or their "adapted style."

The DISC indicates (see Figures 7.12 and 7.13) that Laura's style can be of value to the team for the following reasons:

- She is cautious and pays attention to details.
- She can prompt and allow other members of the team to take leadership on projects.
- She will be a good listener.
- She can bring the varying styles and behaviors together to form a well-blended team.
- Her ego will not get in the way of new ideas, but she will want all the facts and details before moving ahead.
- She is consistent and supportive.

Laura's leadership team (see Figure 7.14) is relatively balanced. There is a lack of people in the conductor and persuader areas, which shows a lack of urgency for results. Laura is in the coordinator area, which is not where a typical high-performing superintendent ideally is placed. Laura is very strong at maximizing the behaviors of her team and putting them in the right position and role to get results. She is not comfortable being out in front as a leader but makes up for that potential weakness by building and fully utilizing the talents of her team.

360 Degree Review

An area noted as needing improvement involved improving regular communications on issues. Her abilities to execute plans and stay focused on priorities were major strengths.

Evaluation Results

She received major accolades for her work in strategic planning and instructional practices. The board did cite a need for more frequent communications on internal issues.

Other Leadership Assessments

On the emotional intelligence (EQ) assessment, Laura's strength was self-awareness and her need for improvement was in the social aspect of the job.

(continued)

SAMPLE LDP *(continued)*

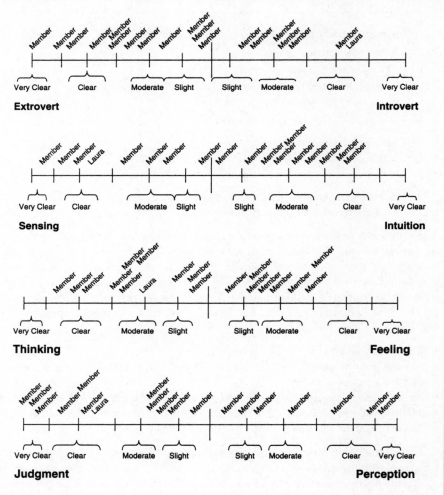

FIGURE 7.11
Administrative Council Team MBTI

Leadership Competencies

1. Challenges the status quo: Laura tends to be reluctant to challenge traditions.
2. Builds trust through clear communications and expectations: Her communications can be confusing to others with different styles.
3. Creates a commonly owned plan for success: This is an area of great strength.
4. Focuses on team over self: She is totally committed to teams and uses all of the talents of her team. Her ego never gets in the way of results.
5. Has a high sense of urgency for change and sustainable results in improving student achievement: She does not have a high sense of urgency. However, she uses her system-wide strategic plan to chart a careful path to success.
6. Commitment to continuous improvement for self: She is a reflective leader and wants to improve her leadership style.
7. Builds external networks and partnerships: This is an area of weakness. She is very hesitant to form new relationships unless they directly relate to a task or a goal.

SAMPLE LDP *(continued)*

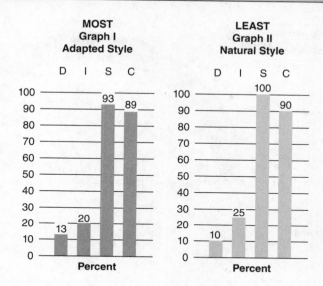

FIGURE 7.12 Laura's DISC Bar Chart *Source:* Copyright © 2012 Target Training International, Ltd. Used with permission.

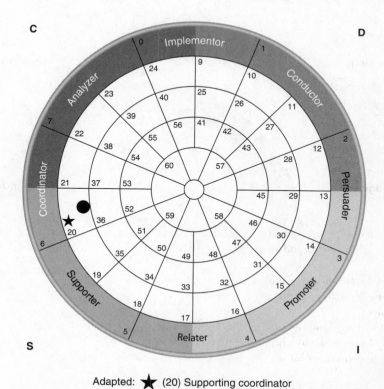

Adapted: ★ (20) Supporting coordinator

Natural: ● (20) Supporting coordinator

FIGURE 7.13 Laura's DISC Wheel *Source:* Copyright © 2012 Target Training International, Ltd. Used with permission.

(continued)

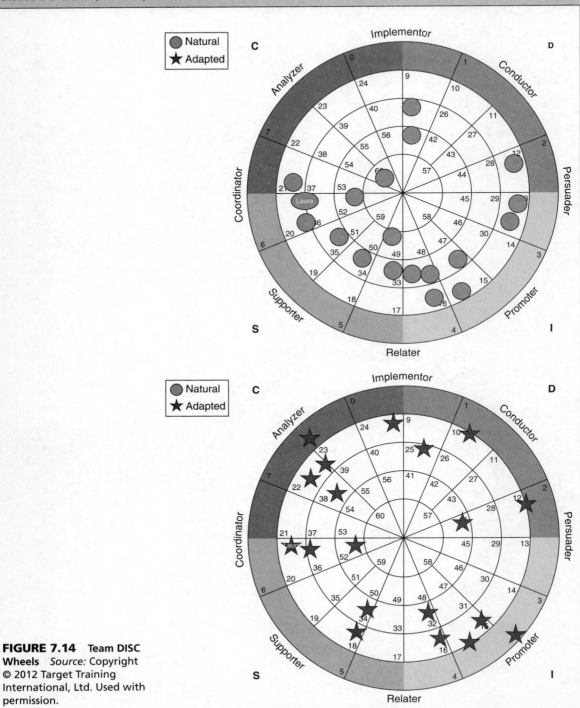

FIGURE 7.14 Team DISC Wheels *Source:* Copyright © 2012 Target Training International, Ltd. Used with permission.

Summary Analysis

Laura's Strengths

- Is cautious and detail oriented
- Will allow members of the team to take leadership on projects without letting her ego get in the way
- Is a good communicator who listens carefully to all sides
- Is logical and realistic

Laura's Areas of Leadership Growth

- Should try to see the "big picture"
- Needs to move more quickly on priority tasks and trust members of the team to gather information and create structure around selected projects
- Needs to delegate tasks to other colleagues
- Needs to rely on intuition/listen to her inner "gut reactions" more often
- Needs to integrate work into big picture rather than deal with separate initiatives

Laura's Potential Conflicts and Stressors

- No structure or timetable to follow
- Tasks that need a quick decision
- People who try to intimidate her
- Emotional issues that need immediate response
- Presenting to large groups spontaneously

Laura's Leadership and Teammate Qualities

- She is steady and consistent.
- She will listen and be thoughtful.
- She will not intimidate other teammates.
- Teammates must allow time for her to look at all alternatives, think of consequences, and question ideas before responding.

Excerpts from Laura's Goals and Action Plans

One-Year Goals

1. To develop a broad-based network of community members to advise her on key district issues
   Indicator of Success: New community members are supporting the district budget at town meetings.
2. To increase communication with the school board and key community leaders
   Indicator of Success: The school board has noted an improvement in communications in the superintendent evaluation document.
3. To improve public speaking skills with large groups both within the school system and with outside groups
   Indicator of Success: There will be an increase in requests for her to speak at community and state-wide events.

General Barriers to Goal Attainment

The major barrier to Laura achieving her goals is her strong introvert score on the MBTI. She is uncomfortable speaking spontaneously with many groups. She would rather have someone else speak and is more comfortable

(continued)

behind the scenes. Her training as a scientist helps her in her goal implementation process, but it has made it difficult for her to change once a process has been developed.

Action Plan

1. To work with a coach on her communication skills, including large group presentations
2. To form a key communicators group in the community to enhance her ability to get her vision and message out to all constituents
3. To form an advisory group of business leaders to provide input on marketing new initiatives
4. To establish two meetings per month with each school board member to improve communications
5. To work with her leadership team on a system-wide communication plan

Long-Term Goals

1. To apply her skills and abilities to a larger district in a superintendent role
2. To write an article and/or a book on strategic planning and implementation for school districts

THE CENTRAL OFFICE: THE FORGOTTEN GROUP

Most articles and books on leadership development or turnaround schools or school systems direct their focus to instruction, teaching and learning, and assessment. These publications are usually focused on the role of superintendents and principals in the change and improvement process. There is very little focus on the central office leaders that play an important role in the success or failure of schools and school districts. The following are examples of positions that serve as an integral part of any district turnaround or success story:

- Special education director or pupil personnel director
- Assistant superintendent for curriculum and instruction
- Information technology manager
- Human resource manager
- Directors of elementary and secondary education
- Chief financial officers or business managers
- Development or grants managers
- Title One director

These positions need high-performing leaders to ensure success in meeting key school and system goals. If the people in these central office positions only focus on their own functions and do not know how to support the goals of the entire school system, these leaders can become a block to progress. If the leaders in the central office become true leaders focused on the system's results, they can become invaluable resources to principals and superintendents.

A technology officer in one urban district has become a system-wide leader whom all constituents call on to learn how technology can make it easier for teachers and administrators to improve student learning. That same technology leader has become a community resource for the municipality as it develops a technology plan for improving police, fire, and transportation services. The parents in the community look to him to learn how to become partners in their children's education.

In another district the IT director stays in his own silo of technology. He does not communicate to other administrators and teachers about trends in technology and how they can help meet district goals. He has become a reactive tech person who fixes computers and buys software. He speaks in meetings in a very technical manner that is not discernible to the majority of people who are not as technically oriented. He is losing his job because he has not developed as a leader in the district. He is seen as too reactive and he does not provide direction for the district. He does not understand what his is doing wrong and has not been given feedback and coaching to develop his leadership skills.

The two preceding examples in IT leadership have very different results. One leader succeeds and will make an enormous impact on his community. The other leader is ineffective and loses his job and does not understand why this has happened to him. We must focus more on the central office and provide coaching and leadership development to prevent situations like the latter.

Curriculum leaders are a key to success for improving student achievement. The successful leaders are proactive on approaches to improving student achievement. They make sure that there is a professional development plan for the district that prepares teachers for the challenges of helping students develop 21st century skills in a world of accountability for improving scores on standardized tests. Principals often engage in strategic discussions with the assistant superintendent or the director of teaching and learning to improve their skills in coaching and supporting teachers.

In one situation, due to a lack of commitment to leadership development, the assistant superintendent for teaching and learning had become a very dictatorial person to the principals, continually pointing out their lack of compliance to state mandates. She is viewed as punitive and focusing on what is not being done and is not seen as helpful to principals in improving their schools' results. Several key leaders in the school system have left other central roles and the principals avoid her as much as possible. The superintendent refuses to deal with this issue of her difficult style and behavior because of the hard work and assistance she provides to handle the work the superintendent prefers to delegate.

In some cases, the ability to hire high-performing leaders in central office roles is much more difficult than finding high-performing principals and superintendents. One of these positions that is hard to find, particularly on the east coast, is a quality special education leader. The right special education leader might be able to improve student achievement and save money, whereas a poor leader might block progress and ignore financial management issues. In the Midwest it might be difficult to find strong business managers. A reactive, controlling business manager that focuses on saying no to new initiatives might be attractive to some districts. However, a real chief financial officer (CFO) with skills to develop financial plans and projections and the ability to be creative on cost savings or new revenue opportunities might be critical to finding the resources needed to implement new instructional strategies.

Central office leaders need more attention in the hiring and leadership development effort. If a superintendent works on building an HPT, the development of the leadership skills of the central office people will be an integral part of the process. If a school system wants its improvement efforts to be sustainable, it needs to be sure that all leaders are high performing. It is important for the school board to understand the importance of the central office roles. Too often these positions are cut or a person is hired for a salary that is not commensurate to attracting a high-performing leader. This strategy can cost districts money and results. In one district, a consultant pointed out that one central office position was posted at a salary that would not attract a strong leader. This short-sighted budget cut would cost the district money because the lack of skills would create problems for the principals in providing quality, cost effective services to students. Once the board understood this issue, they were willing to look for additional funds to attract the right person for the district's needs.

One example of proving feedback and coaching for a central administrator that clearly paid off was in an urban district in the Midwest. The finance director was very effective in managing the budget of this complex school system. However, there were continually clandestine conversations among the female administrators that this leader was sexist and would not take the women's viewpoints seriously. No one had ever brought this issue to the finance director. A consultant working with the team overheard one of these conversations and decided to explore this problem. As this consultant sat in the waiting area of the finance person's office, he watched several women walk up to the open door of the finance director's office. He heard the women say a few words and then walk away. It seemed strange that there were never real conversations that occurred. When it came to the time for the consultant to speak to the finance director, he asked him one key question: Do you have a hearing problem?

The finance director was very surprised by the question, but did answer that he had difficulty hearing women's and small children's voices, especially when he was concentrating on something or when there was background noise. The consultant then asked if he realized that several women just came to the front of his office to speak to him. He said that he did not notice or hear anyone.

Once the finance director heard that women on the staff felt he was disrespecting their viewpoints and that the behavior that the consultant observed may be a factor in this issue, he became very upset. He immediately changed the office setup and established a person who would greet visitors and bring them to his office so this would never occur again. He also spoke to the administrative team about his issue and apologized about his lack of awareness. The team felt terrible that they had assumed his behavior was intentional and became very supportive of his role on the team.

It is important that all central office leaders develop LDPs for their improvement. They must be able to provide support services for the superintendent and the principals for sustained improvement in student achievement. If we do not put the effort to work on central office leadership, these departments can be islands that are not connected to the education delivery process.

The following LDP shows why technology must be integrated into both the instructional and operations areas to support improvement efforts. This IT person would have failed if the focus of the superintendent were not on team development and leadership improvement for all administrators.

 SAMPLE LDP

JOHN (IT DIRECTOR)

The following is the LDP for John, an IT person who was discussed earlier in this chapter. John had a high sense of urgency for change but was steadily becoming less effective in the job. However, through the superintendent's focus on developing a high-performance team, this leader was able to work on a LDP to improve his performance in his IT role and as a contributor to the leadership team.

John's Background and Assessment Summaries

The Myers Briggs Type Indicator (MBTI) is based on the groundbreaking work of psychologist Carl Jung and nearly 70 years of research into personality styles. Based on 16 basic style "types" and the strength of dichotomous traits, we can look at how each individual in the team functions and communicates most comfortably. You can then work with the team to most effectively blend styles and strengths to build a high-performing team. Like all assessments, the MBTI and DISC are simply one small but useful guidepost in the vastly complex assessment of individual personalities and team functioning.

Preference Dichotomy	Preference Reported	Strength (1–30)
Extrovert (E)/Introvert (I)	E	7
Sensing (S)/Intuitive (N)	S	1
Thinking (T)/Feeling (F)	T	5
Judging (J)/Perceiving (P)	J	8

The ESTJ profile means that John

- Is engaging and focused
- Is often seen as a no-nonsense person
- Will see a job through to the end
- Is responsible and trustworthy
- Is very task oriented, often ignoring emotions and feelings around a task

The DISC uses research-based questions to help measure how individuals behave and communicate based on the strength of four basic characteristics: **D**ominance—how you respond to problems or challenges, **I**nfluence—how you influence others to your point of view, **S**teadiness—how you respond to the pace of your environment, and **C**ompliance—how you respond to rules and regulations. The DISC also gives you insight into your natural style and how you are functioning under job and life's current pressures or their "adapted style."

The DISC (see Figures 7.15 and 7.16) indicates that John's style can be of value to the team for the following reasons:

- He pays attention to details.
- He will be a good listener.
- He tends to be more comfortable with people with similar styles.

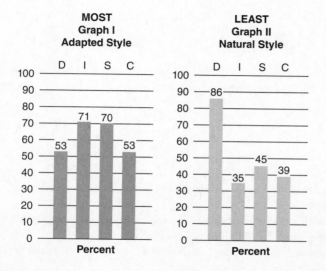

FIGURE 7.15   **John's DISC Bar Chart**   *Source:* Copyright © 2012 Target Training International, Ltd. Used with permission.

(continued)

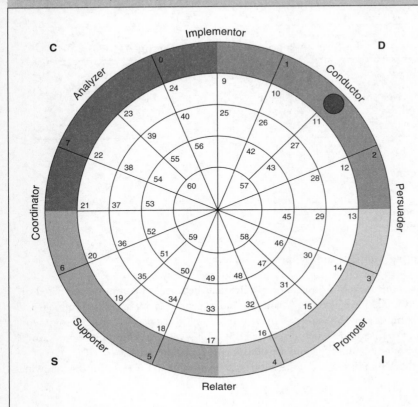

FIGURE 7.16   **John's DISC Wheel**   *Source:* Copyright © 2012 Target Training International, Ltd. Used with permission.

- He could be too direct with some people.
- He is consistent and works hard.

360 Degree Review

None completed.

Evaluation Results

John has been excellent in his technical expertise. It was noted that he needs to enhance his relationships with principals. His dominant behavior around technology goals and expectations needs to be tempered by more training and support for the principals.

Other Leadership Assessments

None completed.

Leadership Competencies

1. **Challenges the status quo:** This leader needs to be more confident to challenge traditions effectively in the district.
2. **Builds trust through clear communications and expectations:** The communications were often clear but lacked a plan that was understood by all groups. Expectations were not as clear to his staff.
3. **Creates a commonly owned plan for success:** This is a strong area, but the plan needed more buy-in.

SAMPLE LDP *(continued)*

4. Focuses on team over self: He is learning how to develop a team.
5. Has a high sense of urgency for change and sustainable results in improving student achievement: This is his number one strength. The urgency is high, but the lack of buy-in by others slows down commitment.
6. Commitment to continuous improvement for self: His commitment to learning is a strength.
7. Builds external networks and partnerships: This is an area that needs work. Being overwhelmed by internal work has prevented the networking that is crucial for this position.

Summary Analysis

John's Strengths

- Is cautious and detail oriented
- Will allow members of the team to take leadership on projects without letting his ego get in the way
- Is a good communicator who listens carefully to all sides
- Is logical and realistic
- Deals well with constructive criticism

John's Areas of Leadership Growth

- Should try to see the "big picture"
- Needs to move more slowly on priority tasks and trust members of the team to gather information and create structure around selected projects
- Needs to delegate tasks to other colleagues
- Needs to develop more written plans and communicate them to others
- Needs to integrate work into big picture rather than deal with separate initiatives

John's Potential Conflicts and Stressors

- No structure or timetable to follow
- Tasks that need more patience and process
- Taking time to coach others
- Emotional issues that need thoughtful responses
- Needing to work in a team with others with different styles

John's Leadership and Teammate Qualities

- He is steady and consistent.
- He works hard.
- He is not afraid to do work himself.
- He is very direct about his concerns with others.

Excerpts from John's Goals and Action Plans

One-Year Goals

1. To develop a high-performance team in his department and increase the leadership capacity of the staff
   Indicator of Success: There will be an increase in requests for his staff to serve on system-wide committees.
2. To increase his contribution to the leadership team by raising key issues outside of his IT functions
   Indicator of Success: The principals will ask for his input on school goals beyond technology.
3. To improve his patience and coaching skills for developing staff and supporting colleagues
   Indicator of Success: His staff is improving their skills and cites his coaching as critical to their development.

(continued)

General Barriers to Goal Attainment

The major barrier to John achieving his goals is his strong dominant DISC score. He can become very autocratic under pressure and demanding of people on his staff and his colleagues. This top-down style prevents him from developing his staff and causes frustration and burnout when he is left as the only one to respond to the myriad of requests from principals.

Action Plan

1. Work with a coach on his patience and ability to coach others.
2. Work with the superintendent on prioritizing issues to keep his workload reasonable so he can find time to develop his staff.
3. Learn more about the curriculum and instruction goals to increase his ability to make a contribution at leadership meetings.

Long-Term Goals

1. To develop a long-term plan for his career
2. To gain more balance in career and personal life

 SAMPLE LDP

REGINA (CENTRAL OFFICE DEPUTY SUPERINTENDENT FOR TEACHING AND LEARNING)

Regina is a deputy superintendent in a large suburban district in the Midwest. She is a very strong leader with an intense passion for helping students achieve at their highest level. She is experiencing some difficulty in her current position, which may not fit her leadership style and values.

Regina's Background and Assessment Summaries

The Myers Briggs Type Indicator (MBTI) is based on the groundbreaking work of psychologist Carl Jung and nearly 70 years of research into personality styles. Based on 16 basic style "types" and the strength of dichotomous traits, we can look at how each individual in the team functions and communicates most comfortably. You can then work with the team to most effectively blend styles and strengths to build a high-performing team. Like all assessments, the MBTI and DISC are simply one small but useful guidepost in the vastly complex assessment of individual personalities and team functioning.

Preference Dichotomy	Preference Reported	Strength (1–30)
Extrovert (E)/Introvert (I)	E	42
Sensing (S)/Intuitive (N)	N	47
Thinking (T)/Feeling (F)	T	25
Judging (J)/Perceiving (P)	J	50

The ENTJ profile means that Regina

- Is engaging and focused
- Will see a job through to the end
- Is responsible and trustworthy
- Is very task oriented, often ignoring emotions and feelings around a task
- Develops and executes plans to perfection

The DISC uses research-based questions to help measure how individuals behave and communicate based on the strength of four basic characteristics: **D**ominance—how you respond to problems or challenges, **I**nfluence—how you influence others to your point of view, **S**teadiness—how you respond to the pace of your environment, and **C**ompliance—how you respond to rules and regulations. The DISC also gives you insight into your natural style and how you are functioning under job and life's current pressures or their "adapted style."

The DISC (see Figures 7.17 and 7.18) indicates that Regina's style can be of value to the team for the following reasons:

- She is focused on results
- She has a high sense of urgency
- Tends to meet all requirements of regulators
- She can be very motivating of others
- Can be very directive

Behavior Hierarchy

- Very high in versatility, urgency, and frequency of interaction with others
- Low organized workplace and analysis of data

Regina's Values inventory, shown in Figure 7.20, indicates that she is very value driven to helping students achieve. She has a real passion for underserved students that have not had the opportunities to succeed. She has

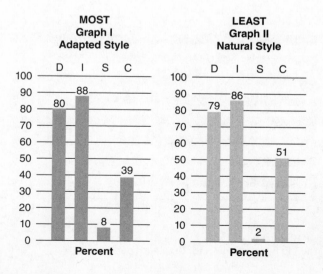

FIGURE 7.17   Regina's DISC Bar Charts *Source:* Copyright © 2012 Target Training International, Ltd. Used with permission.

(continued)

FIGURE 7.18   Regina's DISC Wheel   *Source:* Copyright © 2012 Target Training International, Ltd. Used with permission.

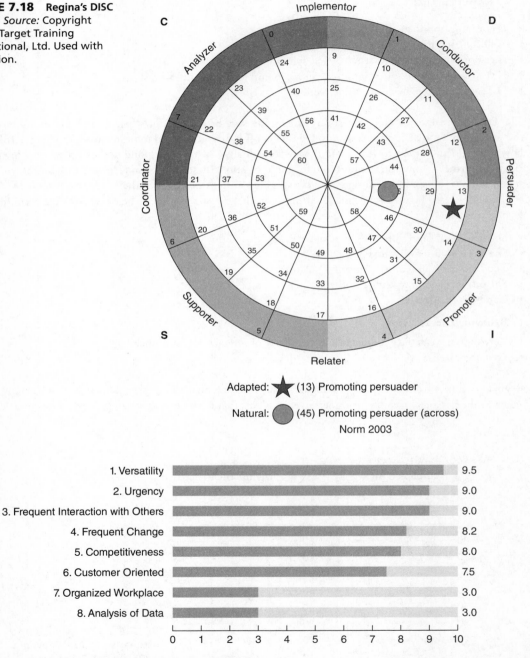

Adapted: ★ (13) Promoting persuader

Natural: ● (45) Promoting persuader (across)

Norm 2003

1. Versatility		9.5
2. Urgency		9.0
3. Frequent Interaction with Others		9.0
4. Frequent Change		8.2
5. Competitiveness		8.0
6. Customer Oriented		7.5
7. Organized Workplace		3.0
8. Analysis of Data		3.0

0 1 2 3 4 5 6 7 8 9 10

FIGURE 7.19   Regina's Behavioral Hierarchy
Source: Copyright © 2012 Target Training International, Ltd. Used with permission.

SAMPLE LDP *(continued)*

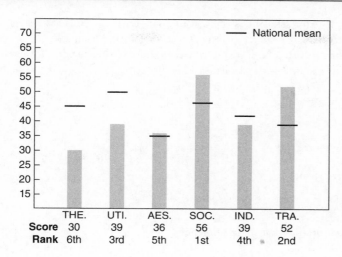

FIGURE 7.20 Regina's Values Inventory Bar Chart
Source: Copyright © 2012 Target Training International, Ltd. Used with permission.

	THE.	UTI.	AES.	SOC.	IND.	TRA.
Score	30	39	36	56	39	52
Rank	6th	3rd	5th	1st	4th	2nd

strong traditional values which are both religious and work ethic oriented. She has trouble dealing with people who are not dedicated to their work of serving students in education.

360 Degree Review

The 360 degree feedback has noted that she is too challenging to her colleagues. They believe she is judgmental and tends to point out problems regarding what she believes they are not doing for students. They would like to see more encouragement and fewer challenging statements and actions.

Evaluation Results

Her evaluations by the superintendent have been positive about her great abilities to improve the teaching and learning in the district. However, the superintendent believes her difficult work style creates too many problems for her colleagues.

Other Leadership Assessments

The WPI notes that she is very innovative and independent. All her leadership scores are very high. She is strong at detail and handles critical feedback very well.

Leadership Competencies

1. Challenges the status quo: Very strong if she believes it will help students.
2. Builds trust through clear communications and expectations: This is a strength in relation to tasks and plans. However, the trust is weak with some colleagues who feel her style is too direct about performance issues.
3. Creates a commonly owned plan for success: This is strong, but the plan may need more details for others' styles and more patience for some that need more time to complete the work.
4. Focuses on team over self: She is very team oriented. However, she expects people to speak their mind and be able to handle critical feedback. Because many people are reticent to be able to receive and provide feedback to others, she is not able to develop a team.
5. Has a high sense of urgency for change and sustainable results in improving student achievement: This is her number one strength. Her high sense of urgency is not shared by her colleagues.

(continued)

6. Commitment to continuous improvement for self: She is the consummate learner. She is always learning from others in both education and other fields. She is very strong at receiving critical feedback.
7. Builds external networks and partnerships: She has been strong at networking over her career. However, she has fallen back on this issue as she has had to deal with problems in her district.

Summary Analysis

Regina's Strengths

- Has a very strong leadership style
- Is very results oriented
- Is able to develop relationships and drive results
- Gets results quickly

Regina's Areas for Leadership Growth

- May have difficulty adapting to different profiles that see less urgency
- Could intimidate people
- Can be too quick in integrating ideas and can become impatient with people

Regina's Potential Conflicts and Stressors

- May switch to being direct, which could confuse people
- May avoid conflict or be so direct it can cause conflict
- Tension between getting quick results and building relationships
- Can move too fast and fear that things won't be done right

Excerpts from Regina's Goals and Action Plans

One-Year Goals

1. To develop a high-performance team in her department and increase the leadership capacity of the staff.
   Indicator of Success: There will be an increase in requests from her staff for coaching and support that they are anxious for her to provide.
2. To enhance her relationships with colleagues and people with different styles.
   Indicator of Success: Her colleagues will provide feedback to the superintendent about how their relationships with her have improved. People will request that she join committees for her support.
3. To improve her patience and coaching skills for developing staff and supporting colleagues.
   Indicator of Success: Her staff is improving their skills and cites her coaching as critical to their development.

General Barriers to Goal Attainment

The major barrier that is interfering with Regina achieving her goals is her intensity and drive to achieve results quickly. She appears impatient and judgmental with people who have lower drive and leadership profiles. She needs to learn how to ask more questions and engage and support people from their current state. They currently feel threatened and do not want her support. The high performers enjoy and look for her support. Her speed at processing information is intimidating to people who are less secure. Based on excessive critical comments on her behaviors, and the belief that she should be a role model for African American students in the district, there is concern that she is being judged differently and held to a higher standard because she is an African American female.

Action Plan

1. To work with a coach on her patience, ability to build relationships, and skills in coaching and supporting others
2. To work with the superintendent on how she is progressing and how she can use his mentoring skills to help her adjust to the culture of the district
3. To develop skills to work with people with different skills, styles, and value systems

Long-Term Goals

1. To develop a long-term plan for her career that will involve a district with a style that matches her values
2. To gain more balance in career and personal life to allow her to manage her intensity in her work

HOW TO USE YOUR LDP

Hopefully, you have now developed your own LDP with the help of the examples provided in this chapter. Now it is time to discuss how to use the LDP plan for your professional development. Although it may not be practical to carry your LDP with you as you move through the challenges of your day, there are ways to use your LDP to stay focused on your progress.

The first step is to communicate the results of your assessment data to the people you work with on a regular basis. The act of talking about your strengths and weaknesses with colleagues, staff, and your boss or school board is very important. Although most leaders believe that admitting weaknesses to others will decrease their support, this rarely occurs. In fact, people who are confident and secure enough to admit they have areas for improvement gain respect from most people. The ability to be open and explicit about wanting to be a better leader usually inspires others to look at themselves with a more critical eye. It is important to realize that most people already know your strengths and weaknesses. If you do not believe that, you are probably in denial. If you think your staff does not talk about these weaknesses when you are not in the room, you are mistaken. The act of openly talking about improvements often stops secretive discussions about your performance. Have you ever walked into a room, notice that people stop talking, and wonder what they were talking about before you arrived? Don't be surprised, because they are usually talking about you due to their own reticence to say things directly to you. These side conversations occur with respect to most leaders and are unproductive.

An approach to talking about your assessment results is to call a meeting of your staff and discuss with them why you are working on your leadership development. It is important to tell your staff that you want to hear honest feedback to the data you have gathered about your leadership to help you set goals and plans for improvement. It is important to encourage your staff to speak openly without fear of repercussions, and remind them that the process of looking at your own profile is helpful and beneficial. Once you speak with them about your development, it is easier to encourage them to engage in a similar process with their staff.

Do not be surprised that they will be shocked that you are willing to engage in this self-development effort. You will find that after you are open about your improvements the staff will often express their admiration for the courage that this work shows and indicate that it serves as inspiration for them to do the same. Some people will not be as willing to work on their own development. Realize that it takes time for some people to feel safe enough to engage in a real self-improvement process.

Showing people the charts and graphs of your style or other evaluation results or a 360 review will be helpful for people to understand your style and will help you become more knowledgeable and comfortable with your own data. Ask people for their reaction and feedback on what makes sense to them or areas that they may not agree with in your presentation. It is helpful to use real examples of where you believe your strengths were helpful or your weaknesses presented a problem. This openness will help others bring up similar examples. The participation of your staff in this effort will go a long way toward making you more comfortable with the process and help them see that this effort might be beneficial to them.

To many people this process seems daunting. Although this may be scary to many of you, it will bring you and your staff closer together as a team and will help you when the issues in your school or district become difficult.

The same discussion should happen with your boss or supervisor. This may seem risky to you. However, once again, most supervisors will admire your strength and courage and they will be more comfortable raising issues with you that they may now hold secret. Although this practice may result in your supervisor raising concerns to you that you have not heard, it is better for you to know the concerns so you can work on improvement and make needed changes to succeed. It is also more likely that your supervisor will be more open to acknowledging his or her own role in helping you and may look at how his or her style might be contributing to your performance. Too often, the real issues of concern are never discussed and people are judged without ever knowing what is behind an evaluation.

An example of this occurred with two central office leaders in a west coast suburban district. The two leaders had a great deal of difficulty working together. The differences seemed, on the surface, to be philosophical on the topic of freedom that teachers should have to structure their own professional development. Therefore, everyone in the district just determined that this disagreement would not change. When the two people really looked at their leadership styles openly and honestly, they were able to have a much more honest conversation. Although there were some philosophical differences, the real problem was that each person's style was very problematic for the other. One leader tended to make judgmental statements and did not seem to be listening to the other's point of view. The other leader believed that the colleague was too surface oriented and did not respect the depth of the work that was done by others before his arrival in the district. They were able to use their leadership assessments to help each other understand why these judgments were occurring. In reality, both people were right in some of their points of view. However, since they were afraid that an honest discussion of their true feelings would hurt their relationship, they never had a framework for compromise. The leader who was new realized that some of the past practices were consistent with many of his beliefs. The leader who was in the district for a long period of time realized that the tone of voice she used and her judgmental behavior were driving the other person away.

Sharing your assessments allows others to understand you and helps you understand the other person. This information enables real conversations to occur that solve problems. Once the people on your staff understand your style and can give you open feedback, you can discuss your goals for improvement. You will need others to help you achieve these goals.

In an environment in which organizational and professional goals are shared openly everyone can help each other succeed. The secrecy and indirect discussions tend to allow people to stay in their silos. If you hold your concerns and opinions to yourself you tend to focus on what you believe you can control. This insular point of view prevents people from expressing points of view on others' goals that may be critical to the person's success.

High-performing leaders are usually very open to sharing their LDPs. They often hand their staff and their boss the plans as written without fear. This openness pays off for them as they admit their need for the help of others to succeed. Although these people are very capable of operating independently, their ability to be vulnerable only improves their chances of success.

TRACKING, MONITORING, AND REVISING YOUR LDP

Now that you have communicated your plan to others, it is important to find an approach to staying focused on implementing the plan. As you try to improve you will find that just saying you are committed to improvement does not change some behaviors. The areas you need to change have been developed over a long period of time. You are trying to change fundamental aspects of your style or behavior and integrate them into your day-to-day activities.

It is important to realize that you may show signs of improvement and then slide back in your progress when you become stressed. It is important to tell people that you are committed to change and want their feedback on success. However, your team and supervisor need to understand that true behavioral change takes time and setbacks are opportunities to learn, not reasons to give up. An example of making progress and dealing with setbacks occurred with one superintendent who worked on not responding to his e-mails during meetings. His behavior was seen as a lack of respect for others in the meeting. The superintendent was having a time management problem and lacked a process to keep track of items he thought about during meetings. Therefore, he needed a process to write down items during the meeting to act on after the meeting was complete. The discipline to change a lifelong behavior is very difficult. He explained to his team that he would try to change and did not give any excuses. The team members started to think about how they would change a behavior that may be presenting a problem to others and how difficult the change would be for them.

Real change requires discipline, focus, and new systems and techniques for improvement. It is important for any leader to work toward 100% success, not just try to improve. For example, a leader of a major educational organization was told by her team that her being late to meetings was seen as disrespectful. Although she was not trying to be disrespectful of her team, she had had a time management problem for as long as she could remember. She had set goals for improving her time management over the years and never achieved her goals. She had tried to be on time for more meetings and set a goal of decreasing being late by 10%.

She tried to read books on time management, she allowed more time between meetings to make sure she arrived on time, and she purchased a GPS device to prevent her from getting lost. All her methods were positive, but none worked. Finally, her coach told her one statement that changed her life in relation to being on time. He told her that you cannot improve time management. You either must live your life as a person who is on time or not. He proposed that she change her plan to improve her time management. Instead of trying to track her improvement in being on time for meetings, her goal was to be 100% on time.

He told her to go home and write down how she would live a life of being on time. He suggested that she talk to people who were on time and ask them what they did to be so punctual. Her MBTI style of ENFP is a profile that generally has difficulty being on time. The extrovert style resulted in her taking on many projects at one time and spending a lot of time talking to people during the day. Her highly intuitive style resulted in her thinking about big picture long-term goals with little focus on details. Her feeling style was also contributing to her time management problems. After a conversation or a meeting in which she believed she said something that could have offended a person, she would stay after to make sure the person was not upset. This extra time often made her late to her next appointment. Finally, her perception style presented several issues. Seeing boundaries on agendas as restrictive made her meetings go late, and her last minute work to get a document in by a deadline caused other projects to become neglected.

As she began her process of writing down what a life of being on time would be like, she needed to look at her assessment data and incorporate her MBTI results into the action plan. Following are some of her ideas of what being on time would look like:

- Being early for every meeting
- Adding extra time to her travel plans in anticipation of problems
- Planning projects months in advance
- Telling people at the beginning of calls about how much time she had for the call
- Bringing reading or paperwork with her that she could work on when she arrived early to meetings
- Making sure that she left on time for her next appointment and if she wanted to call someone, the call would be from the car
- Leaving plenty of time between meetings
- Feeling less stressed

She began to feel more in control as she wrote down her plan for 100% success. It felt calming and less stressful to be confident that she could control her time. She began to think about her old internalized thoughts about time management that caused her problems. She would think that she was trying hard to improve her time management and could afford to be late for some meetings as a reward. She thought people would understand if she was late sometimes if she said she was improving. She also thought that some meetings were important and that going over the time limit would be appreciated and that her ability to make the next meeting would be understood. As she made her new plan for being 100% on time, these thoughts seemed absurd and completely irrational for a person who was committed to being on time. She would no longer be making excuses about traffic or last-second crises that caused her to be late.

Her new plan for time management was working even before she put it in place. She was changing her attitude and her behaviors followed. Her assessment data and feedback from staff were critical to her improvement process. Her commitment to working with a coach and being able to hear honest feedback were instrumental in revising her plan and finding new measurements for success.

One more important point of information that she received from a person who had conquered his time management problem involved stress and health. Being late, rushing from meeting to meeting, and always trying to catch up with projects that were about to be late were causing this person so much stress that his doctor said his blood pressure and heart were at risk. The feeling of running around, the rush of doing too many things at once, and completing projects at the last second were causing him physical health problems. This last piece of information provided the impetus for real change for this leader. Her plan was revised and now would be a key part of her success as a leader.

The process of writing a plan, reviewing the progress, and determining the root cause of why change needs to occur is a lifelong endeavor. Having a mentor or a coach to help you look at yourself with objective eyes will help you make meaningful change that will result in achieving your goals.

BUILDING PERSONAL AND CAREER GOALS INTO YOUR ACTION PLAN

Why is it important to build in your career goals into your LDP? In the corporate world, people are usually very ambitious and always looking for the next job with more money. It is normal to build career goals into all actions plans. A person who left education and found a job in a corporation was very surprised when his boss asked him on his first day what job he wanted next.

The culture in education is quite different. The drive for mission and commitment to making a difference in children's lives often overtake self-serving goals of career advancement. Some people feel that they should not talk about their career goals when they are employed in a position. It is almost like cheating on your employer. It is common that many leaders hold back their career goals to be sure their current district is meeting its goals before they would consider their own career advancement. School boards can often become critical of a leader when they find out he or she is a finalist for another position. These same board members, who might be in the corporate world, would take care of themselves first before caring about their organization. However, something happens when they join a school board that makes them believe educators need to always serve others and not take care of themselves.

It is the author's experience in leading many searches for leaders in education that women care more than men about staying with their current districts to be sure they are okay before considering moving on to a new opportunities. The men seem to be more interested in their careers and the extra money they can obtain with a career move. Although it is admirable that many women care about their staff and making sure that their school or district is in a good position, they often turn down opportunities for advancement that might be beneficial to them and provide new districts the opportunity to experience their skills and abilities.

In the corporate world, it is accepted that one must constantly manage his or her career. Educators need to feel comfortable managing their careers as part of their development. In addition, it is also important for educational leaders to understand and accept that their personal goals are relevant to the LDP. Executives in the corporate world often plan for their lifestyle and personal situations as a part of their professional development. Although some of the lifestyle issues in corporate America have become negative and newsworthy, the concept of an executive considering his or her personal goals in relation to career is actually beneficial.

If leaders have plans for looking at options for their career and feel that they could move to a new opportunity, it can help them manage the stress of their current positions. When leaders feel trapped they will often make poor judgments and not take a key stand on an issue or may keep someone in a role that they know is underperforming. The fear of being criticized by a supervisor or the school board should not affect key decisions. The frustration of feeling trapped in a job can show in anger, erratic behavior, and irrational actions. If a leader is confident that he or she is doing a great job and has options to find new opportunities, he or she can be free to lead without fear. This is why some people who are interim leaders or are transitional in their role can make key changes in a school. They do not fear the consequences because they will be leaving in 6 months to one year.

Leaders need to help their staff manage their careers too. Some of the most successful superintendents are always trying to help their high-performing staff find new opportunities. This commitment to the growth of others pays these leaders back in significant ways. Because education is a small and close-knit world, certain superintendents have reputations of developing future leaders. This attracts the best people to want to join their administrations for the learning and support for their careers.

One of the key characteristics and competencies noted in Kirtman's Seven Competencies for School Leadership is to develop external networks and partnerships. With all the pressure to focus internally on the school and the classroom, educators are often discouraged from looking for outside networks of colleagues for support and contacts. There is a fear that they will be outside their school too much and not be able to lead effectively. However, the most effective leaders in education have developed significant networks of educators nationally that can provide them feedback on key issues and resources to solve problems. The high-performing leaders in education actually pursue networks outside education in the nonprofit, government, health care, and corporate arenas. These relationships become invaluable to their work and provide unlimited contacts for their careers.

It seems interesting that the world of social and business networking has exploded in every sector across the world at the same time education is promoting an internal focus and becoming more insular. The young people today in our schools will live in a world in which social and business networking will be how they find jobs and do their work without leaving their home and office. How can we in education help them work in today's society when we are reticent to engage in their world?

Many educators are engaged in social networking but are slow to engage in business networking. Joining LinkedIn is starting to grow in education, but it is not developing in the same way as other sectors. One superintendent that is very successful not only belongs to a national superintendent network but also joins leadership groups with nonprofit and corporate leaders. He realizes his colleagues are not interested and comfortable in these arenas outside education. He is concerned that their internal focus will limit their opportunities to learn new practices that could help them solve problems that need new perspectives.

Unfortunately, most educators do not know very much about the private sector and what leaders do in other public sector arenas. This prevents them from forming partnerships with other organizations that could benefit their district or school. This reluctance to spend time learning about leadership in a broad-based arena decreases their career options.

Although many superintendents believe they could lead effectively in other sectors, they would have a much more difficult time than they realize. The pressure on attaining financial goals and results would cause many educators great stress. High-performing leaders are very open and curious about what they can learn from other leaders. They tend to see leadership as universal and not isolated to one's technical background. These leaders find interesting new possibilities for their schools and for their future.

One superintendent might pursue a partnership with China on professional development using technology. This partnership allows teachers to see what their colleagues in another country do and how they handle challenges. This openness to learn from others often improves teachers' practice and allows them to form a new network of contacts.

Another superintendent worked with a local nonprofit on a new grant opportunity for after-school programs for students. Her district was awarded the grant and learned how she could bring social workers into their school system. Typically superintendents also join the Rotary or other organizations to show their connection to the community. This is an excellent practice for networking. However, this is a safe practice that should only be a small part of the networking process. There are many other opportunities for networking that can be pursued.

If principals or superintendents embraced networking and partnership work as a key to their success in their job and to their future, the possibilities would be endless. Very few educators are on nonprofit boards and almost none are on corporate boards. People would be surprised that their skills and perspectives in education could be very attractive to both private and public sector organizations.

Most educators are probably thinking that they do not have any time now, so how could they become involved in other organizations? If you are really a leader and building a high-performance team, you can afford to become more involved outside your immediate job. In addition, the investment will pay off for your school and for you.

Mary, discussed in Chapter 2, has a broad network of contacts in education and outside her field. She speaks nationally on leadership and change and spends significant time outside her school. Her students' test scores keep improving because of her commitment to building a team and her focus on results. Because of her success and extensive networking, her school receives national attention that attracts people and financial resources of grants and gifts.

This principal stays dedicated to her school and is not looking to retire. However, her opportunities for consulting, speaking, and writing are endless. She could leave at any time and obtain more financial benefits than she receives in her current role. This knowledge keeps her committed and satisfied in staying where she is now to help the students and staff she loves.

The educational leaders who engage in networking often are criticized by their colleagues or people in their communities. This jealousy is understood by these high-performing leaders. However, they are secure in themselves and confident in their abilities to succeed and do not let the criticisms hold them back.

To begin to build your career goals into your LDP try the following steps.

1. Make a list of your strengths, interests, and the opportunities that you believe are open to you. Once you have built your network, the people in your contact list can help you with this exercise. If you have strength but there is no opportunity to act on it, it is not a strength from a career perspective. If you have a strength and you are no longer interested in using it, that talent will not be a career motivator.

2. Now begin to develop your network. Start this by making three lists. List A will be family and friends. List B will be people you know who have a great network of contacts but do not have the power to hire you. List C will be people who can hire you or have a major influence on others who may want your services. This list needs to be at least 75 people to start your process. Most people are shocked and say they cannot come up with 75 people. You can do this! Family and friends do not seem to be helpful to people's careers unless they have highly influential relatives. This is not true. You will be surprised when you make your list and think about and talk to people on your A list about who they know. The networking process is not about looking for a direct job; it is about sharing your goals with others to gain new insights, advice, and more contacts.

3. Building your network will open new doors for you. A dancer in a small nonprofit organization once stated that this exercise was ridiculous because she was poor and did not know anyone. When she made her list, she forgot that she used to babysit for a person who was a famous CEO and philanthropist. She sent a letter to this person to catch up and tell him what she was doing and her future goals to run a dance studio. The CEO sent her back a letter with a $10,000 check and wished her good luck.

4. Now that you have your list, begin to increase your comfort in building a network by starting with your A list. It is easy to speak to family and friends without fear of looking foolish or making mistakes. Introverts and low influencing people struggle with this process. This is why the social networking sites have grown—because you can avoid personal contact. However, personal contact still makes a difference. Call someone on your A list and ask him or her to have a cup of coffee with you or a 15 to 30 minute call. Tell the person you are thinking about your career goals and you want to discuss your strengths and interests and ask him or her for feedback. Ask whether you are missing anything. Does he or she know someone else you could talk to who might be helpful to explore possibilities and share common goals? Do not ask for a job contact. The person who asks for the job contact cuts off opportunities because that puts pressure on the other person. In addition, it requires a yes or no answer and eliminates the building of a network. You will also ask your contact for advice on your career goals.

5. Once you have spoken to a few A-list contacts, move to the B-list contacts and have a similar conversation. Your network list should now be well over 100 people. You are probably thinking that you hope you do not have to stay in contact with all these people. One of the major criticisms of social networking is that it seems to require so much time to get back to people. Try to stay in contact with quick notes and be selective about whom you pursue. Most people understand that it is difficult to stay in contact with everyone.

6. Be careful about how you use your C list. These are national treasures who are only used once when you want a new job or need influence on a major decision. Because many educators are retiring early and usually want to pursue work in education or other sectors after they retire, starting this networking process well before you retire is very important. You will end up with a series of options once you retire. Most retirees wait until they retire to start this process. That is a mistake and limits their options.

7. An educational leader should spend about 5 hours per week on networking. The high-performing leaders spend much more and get great results in their schools and districts.

Once you have spoken to 5 to 10 people on your A and B lists, begin to write one or two career goals. One principal called the author and said she wanted to be a commissioner after only one year as a principal. Although the conversation was filled with some of the challenges that the principal would have in order to reach that goal, the principal should be admired for her ambition. That same principal had the highest results on standardized tests in her state for elementary schools.

Another superintendent pursued consulting opportunities in the publishing field while he was in his position. His contacts did not have any immediate opportunities, but spent time looking for possibilities to use his skills on new product offerings.

The personal aspect of this plan involves looking at your interests and lifestyle goals. One leader loved travel and wanted to build her work life after retiring with a travel aspect. She began to pursue this while in her current job by looking for partnerships for her district and becoming part of accreditation teams in other countries. This provided new ideas that helped her district and a new set of contacts for her future goal of traveling with her family.

Another superintendent who built a network of contacts while in the position and pursued his goals after retirement created a new job out of nothing. He had a background in teaching reading and a love of teaching reading skills. He developed a broad network in industry and other fields and was able to create two contracts after retirement in banking and health care that used his reading skills and interest in the field. This provides significant resources and opportunities for him to work with exciting people and participate in research to help the field he loves.

CONCLUSION

This chapter provides a practical way to begin your journey as a leader who engages in constant reflection and continuous improvement. Whether you use leadership inventories or other means to obtain data on your style and performance as a leader, the LDP is a helpful format to pull all the information together to formulate your personal and professional plan for improvement. In education today, using student data is critical for improving the teaching and learning process. This new LDP format provides a vehicle for you to use data on your leadership in a plan to improve your practice. Your ability to be honest with yourself and be explicit with your staff, your superintendent, or your school board will be perceived as a strength and a model for others to look at their self-improvement. The highest-performing leaders realize they are works in progress and can never master the leadership process.

It is also important for you to realize and become comfortable with the fact that your personal life and goals and your career development are part of your leadership development process.

Educators tend to feel guilty dealing with their personal and career goals as part of their work life. Perhaps it is because educators dedicate themselves to others and feel that they should not focus on themselves. It is the hope of this author that the reader understands that if you focus on yourself and all parts of your development, it will increase your effectiveness in leading your school or school system. As your effectiveness increases, the climate in your school becomes more motivating and the students benefit from you and your staff's best efforts.

As the pressures on urgency and accountability keep increasing in education, each leader must find a new way to lead based on his or her values and beliefs and not let the outside pressures derail the work. Accountability and urgency can be positive if they are part of an environment of motivation and excitement. Each leader must find a way to love coming to work each day. Unfortunately, too many educators are not enjoying their work as much as in the past. The author hopes that the concepts and approaches provided in this text will bring a more positive energy and outlook for our educational leaders. The profession and the students need each and every one of you.

Self-Evaluation Resources

ASSESSMENT TEMPLATE:
KIRTMAN'S SEVEN COMPETENCIES FOR SCHOOL LEADERSHIP

Name of Person Self-Assessing _____ Date _____

Self-Reflection

1. CHALLENGES THE STATUS QUO

Competency	Self-Rating (Circle One)					Score
	Target for Improvement				Strength	
Maintain focus on a vision for success	1	2	3	4	5	
Prioritize getting results over following traditions	1	2	3	4	5	
Question or challenge current practices	1	2	3	4	5	
Take risks to achieve results	1	2	3	4	5	

COMPETENCY SUMMARY FOR "CHALLENGES THE STATUS QUO"

Ratings	Vision for Success	Results over Traditions	Challenges Current Practices	Take Risks to Achieve Results
1 = Target for Improvement				
2 = Needs Improvement				
3 = Low Improvement Priority				
4 = Strength Most of the Time				
5 = Strength to Build On				

2. BUILDS TRUST THROUGH CLEAR COMMUNICATIONS AND EXPECTATIONS

Competency	Self-Rating (Circle One)					Score
	Target for Improvement				Strength	
Is direct and honest about performance expectations	1	2	3	4	5	
Follows through with actions and on all commitments	1	2	3	4	5	
Ensures a clear understanding of written and verbal communications	1	2	3	4	5	
Is comfortable dealing with conflict	1	2	3	4	5	

COMPETENCY SUMMARY FOR "BUILDS TRUST THROUGH CLEAR COMMUNICATIONS AND EXPECTATIONS"

Ratings	Direct about Expectations	Follows Through	Ensures Clear Understanding of Communications	Comfortable Dealing with Conflict
1 = Target for Improvement				
2 = Needs Improvement				
3 = Low Improvement Priority				
4= Strength Most of the Time				
5= Strength to Build On				

3. CREATES A COMMONLY OWNED PLAN FOR SUCCESS

Competency	Self-Rating (Circle One)					Score
	Target for Improvement				Strength	
Creates written plans with input of stakeholders	1	2	3	4	5	
Ensures that people buy into the plan	1	2	3	4	5	
Monitors implementation of the plan	1	2	3	4	5	
Adjusts the plan based on new data and clearly communicates changes	1	2	3	4	5	
Develops clear measurements for each goal in the plan	1	2	3	4	5	
Creates short- and long-term plans	1	2	3	4	5	

COMPETENCY SUMMARY FOR "CREATES A COMMONLY OWNED PLAN FOR SUCCESS"

Ratings	Creates Written Plans with Stakeholders	Ensures That People Buy In	Monitors Implementation	Adjusts the Plan Based on New Data	Develops Clear Measurements for Each Goal	Creates Short- and Long-Term Plans
1 = Target for Improvement						
2 = Needs Improvement						
3 = Low Improvement Priority						
4 = Strength Most of the Time						
5 = Strength to Build On						

4. FOCUSES ON TEAM OVER SELF

Competency	Self-Rating (Circle One)					Score
	Target for Improvement				Strength	
Hires the best people for the team	1	2	3	4	5	
Commits to the ongoing development of a high-performance leadership team	1	2	3	4	5	
Builds a team environment	1	2	3	4	5	
Seeks critical feedback	1	2	3	4	5	
Empowers staff to make decisions and get results	1	2	3	4	5	
Supports the professional development of staff	1	2	3	4	5	

COMPETENCY SUMMARY FOR "FOCUSES ON TEAM OVER SELF"

Ratings	Hires the Best People for the Team	Commits to Ongoing Team Development	Builds a Team Environment	Seeks Critical Feedback	Empowers Staff to Make Decisions	Supports Professional Development
1 = Target for Improvement						
2 = Needs Improvement						
3 = Low Improvement Priority						
4 = Strength Most of the Time						
5 = Strength to Build On						

5. HAS A HIGH SENSE OF URGENCY FOR CHANGE AND SUSTAINABLE RESULTS IN IMPROVING ACHIEVEMENT

Competency	Self-Rating (Circle One)					Score
	Target for Improvement				Strength	
Is able to quickly move initiatives ahead	1	2	3	4	5	
Can be very decisive	1	2	3	4	5	
Uses instructional data to support needed change	1	2	3	4	5	
Builds systemic strategies to ensure sustainability of change	1	2	3	4	5	
Sets a clear direction for the organization	1	2	3	4	5	
Is able to effectively deal with and manage change	1	2	3	4	5	

COMPETENCY SUMMARY FOR "HAS A HIGH SENSE OF URGENCY FOR CHANGE AND SUSTAINABLE RESULTS IN IMPROVING ACHIEVEMENT"

Ratings	Move Initiatives Quickly	Can Be Very Decisive	Uses Instructional Data to Support Change	Builds Systemic Strategies	Sets Clear Direction	Able to Deal with and Manage Change
1 = Target for Improvement						
2 = Needs Improvement						
3 = Low Improvement Priority						
4 = Strength Most of the Time						
5 = Strength to Build On						

6. COMMITS TO CONTINUOUS IMPROVEMENT FOR SELF

Competency	Self-Rating (Circle One)					Score
	Target for Improvement				Strength	
Has a high sense of curiosity for new ways to get results	1	2	3	4	5	
Possesses a willingness to change current practices for themselves and others	1	2	3	4	5	
Listens to all team members to change practices to obtain results	1	2	3	4	5	
Takes responsibility for their own actions—no excuses	1	2	3	4	5	
Has strong self–management and self–reflection skills	1	2	3	4	5	

COMPETENCY SUMMARY FOR "COMMITS TO CONTINUOUS IMPROVEMENT FOR SELF"

Ratings	High Sense of Curiosity	Willingness to Change Current Practices	Listens to All Team Members	Takes Responsibility for Actions	Strong Self-Management and Self-Reflection Skills
1 = Target for Improvement					
2 = Needs Improvement					
3 = Low Improvement Priority					
4 = Strength Most of the Time					
5 = Strength to Build On					

7. BUILDS EXTERNAL NETWORKS AND PARTNERSHIPS

Competency	Self-Rating (Circle One)					Score
	Target for Improvement				Strength	
Sees his or her role as a leader in a broad-based manner outside the work environment and community walls	1	2	3	4	5	
Understands his or her role as being a part of a variety of external networks for change and improvement	1	2	3	4	5	
Has a strong ability to engage people inside and outside in two-way partnerships	1	2	3	4	5	
Uses technology to expand and manage a network of resource people	1	2	3	4	5	

COMPETENCY SUMMARY FOR "BUILDS EXTERNAL NETWORKS AND PARTNERSHIPS"

Ratings	Sees Role as Leader on a Broad Base	Understands Role for Change and Improvement	Strong Ability to Engage People	Uses Technology to Expand and Manage Network
1 = Target for Improvement				
2 = Needs Improvement				
3 = Low Improvement Priority				
4 = Strength Most of the Time				
5 = Strength to Build On				

Leadership Competency Summary

HOW COMPETENT A LEADER ARE YOU?

Competency	Total Possible Score	Your Item Score
1. Challenges the status quo	20	
2. Builds trust through clear communications and expectations	20	
3. Creates a commonly owned plan for success	30	
4. Focuses on team over self	30	
5. Has a high sense of urgency for change and sustainable results in improving student achievement	30	
6. Commits to continuous improvement for self	25	
7. Builds external networks and partnerships	20	
TOTAL	**175**	

What Your Scores Indicate

A score of	Indicates that you are . . .
175–120 points	A strong and competent leader
119–80 points	A capable principal-leader who needs development in selected targeted areas
79 points or below	A principal with potential who needs development in multiple targeted competencies

Summary of Targeted Areas for Improvement

For scores of two or less on self or peer assessment

Prioritized Areas for Improvement/Strategies		
Competency	Self Score	Peer Score

SAMPLE ASSESSMENT:
KIRTMAN'S SEVEN COMPETENCIES FOR SCHOOL LEADERSHIP

Name of Person Self-Assessing _____ *Alex Sanchez* _____ Date _3/30/13_

Self-Reflection

1. CHALLENGES THE STATUS QUO

Competency	Self-Rating (Circle One)					Score
	Target for Improvement				Strength	
Maintain focus on a vision for success	1	2	3	4	5	3
Prioritize getting results over following traditions	1	2	3	4	5	3
Question or challenge current practices	1	2	3	4	5	4
Take risks to achieve results	1	2	3	4	5	2
						12

COMPETENCY SUMMARY FOR "CHALLENGES THE STATUS QUO"

Ratings	Vision for Success	Results over Traditions	Challenges Current Practices	Take Risks to Achieve Results
1 = Target for Improvement				
2 = Needs Improvement				x
3 = Low Improvement Priority	x	x		
4 = Strength Most of the Time			x	
5 = Strength to Build On				

2. BUILDS TRUST THROUGH CLEAR COMMUNICATIONS AND EXPECTATIONS

Competency	Self-Rating (Circle One)					Score
	Target for Improvement				Strength	
Is direct and honest about performance expectations	1	2	3	4	5	3
Follows through with actions and on all commitments	1	2	3	4	5	3
Ensures a clear understanding of written and verbal communications	1	2	3	4	5	4
Is comfortable dealing with conflict	1	2	3	4	5	2
						12

COMPETENCY SUMMARY FOR "BUILDS TRUST THROUGH CLEAR COMMUNICATIONS AND EXPECTATIONS"

Ratings	Direct about Expectations	Follows Through	Ensures Clear Understanding of Communications	Comfortable Dealing with Conflict
1 = Target for Improvement				
2 = Needs Improvement				x
3 = Low Improvement Priority	x	x		
4 = Strength Most of the Time			x	
5 = Strength to Build On				

3. CREATES A COMMONLY OWNED PLAN FOR SUCCESS

| Competency | Self-Rating (Circle One) | | | | | Score |
	Target for Improvement				Strength	
Creates written plans with input of stakeholders	1	2	3	4	5	3
Ensures that people buy into the plan	1	2	3	4	5	3
Monitors implementation of the plan	1	2	3	4	5	4
Adjusts the plan based on new data and clearly communicates changes	1	2	3	4	5	2
Develops clear measurements for each goal in the plan	1	2	3	4	5	2
Creates short- and long-term plans	1	2	3	4	5	4
						18

COMPETENCY SUMMARY FOR "CREATES A COMMONLY OWNED PLAN FOR SUCCESS"

Ratings	Creates Written Plans with Stake-holders	Ensures That People Buy In	Monitors Implemen-tation	Adjusts the Plan Based on New Data	Develops Clear Mea-surements for Each Goal	Creates Short- and Long-Term Plans
1 = Target for Improvement						
2 = Needs Improvement				✗		
3 = Low Improvement Priority	✗	✗				
4 = Strength Most of the Time			✗			
5 = Strength to Build On						

4. FOCUSES ON TEAM OVER SELF

Competency	Self-Rating (Circle One)					Score
	Target for Improvement				Strength	
Hires the best people for the team	1	2	3	4	5	3
Commits to the ongoing development of a high-performance leadership team	1	2	3	4	5	3
Builds a team environment	1	2	3	4	5	4
Seeks critical feedback	1	2	3	4	5	2
Empowers staff to make decisions and get results	1	2	3	4	5	4
Supports the professional development of staff	1	2	3	4	5	4
						20

COMPETENCY SUMMARY FOR "FOCUSES ON TEAM OVER SELF"

Ratings	Hires the Best People for the Team	Commits to Ongoing Team Development	Builds a Team Environment	Seeks Critical Feedback	Empowers Staff to Make Decisions	Supports Professional Development
1 = Target for Improvement						
2 = Needs Improvement				x		
3 = Low Improvement Priority	x	x				
4 = Strength Most of the Time			x			
5 = Strength to Build On						

5. HAS A HIGH SENSE OF URGENCY FOR CHANGE AND SUSTAINABLE RESULTS IN IMPROVING ACHIEVEMENT

Competency	Self-Rating (Circle One)					Score
	Target for Improvement				Strength	
Is able to quickly move initiatives ahead	1	2	3	4	5	3
Can be very decisive	1	2	3	4	5	3
Uses instructional data to support needed change	1	2	3	4	5	4
Builds systemic strategies to ensure sustainability of change	1	2	3	4	5	2
Sets a clear direction for the organization	1	2	3	4	5	4
Is able to effectively deal with and manage change	1	2	3	4	5	4
						20

COMPETENCY SUMMARY FOR "HAS A HIGH SENSE OF URGENCY FOR CHANGE AND SUSTAINABLE RESULTS IN IMPROVING ACHIEVEMENT"

Ratings	Move Initiatives Quickly	Can Be Very Decisive	Uses Instructional Data to Support Change	Builds Systemic Strategies	Sets Clear Direction	Able to Deal with and Manage Change
1 = Target for Improvement						
2 = Needs Improvement				x		
3 = Low Improvement Priority	x	x				
4 = Strength Most of the Time			x			
5 = Strength to Build On						

6. COMMITS TO CONTINUOUS IMPROVEMENT FOR SELF

Competency	Self-Rating (Circle One)					Score
	Target for Improvement				Strength	
Has a high sense of curiosity for new ways to get results	1	2	3	4	5	3
Possesses a willingness to change current practices for themselves and others	1	2	3	4	5	3
Listens to all team members to change practices to obtain results	1	2	3	4	5	4
Takes responsibility for their own actions—no excuses	1	2	3	4	5	4
Has strong self–management and self–reflection skills	1	2	3	4	5	5
						19

COMPETENCY SUMMARY FOR "COMMITS TO CONTINUOUS IMPROVEMENT FOR SELF"

Ratings	High Sense of Curiosity	Willingness to Change Current Practices	Listens to All Team Members	Takes Responsibility for Actions	Strong Self-Management and Self-Reflection Skills
1 = Target for Improvement					
2 = Needs Improvement					
3 = Low Improvement Priority	x	x			
4 = Strength Most of the Time			x	x	
5 = Strength to Build On					x

7. BUILDS EXTERNAL NETWORKS AND PARTNERSHIPS

Competency	Self-Rating (Circle One)					Score
	Target for Improvement				Strength	
Sees his or her role as a leader in a broad-based manner outside the work environment and community walls	1	2	3	4	5	3
Understands his or her role as being a part of a variety of external networks for change and improvement	1	2	3	4	5	3
Has a strong ability to engage people inside and outside in two-way partnerships	1	2	3	4	5	4
Uses technology to expand and manage a network of resource people	1	2	3	4	5	2
						12

COMPETENCY SUMMARY FOR "BUILDS EXTERNAL NETWORKS AND PARTNERSHIPS"

Ratings	Sees Role as Leader on a Broad Base	Understands Role for Change and Improvement	Strong Ability to Engage People	Uses Technology to Expand and Manage Network
1 = Target for Improvement				
2 = Needs Improvement				x
3 = Low Improvement Priority	x	x		
4 = Strength Most of the Time			x	
5 = Strength to Build On				

Leadership Competency Summary

HOW COMPETENT A LEADER ARE YOU?

Competency	Total Possible Score	Your Item Score
1. Challenges the status quo	20	12
2. Builds trust through clear communications and expectations	20	12
3. Creates a commonly owned plan for success	30	18
4. Focuses on team over self	30	20
5. Has a high sense of urgency for change and sustainable results in improving student achievement	30	20
6. Commits to continuous improvement for self	25	19
7. Builds external networks and partnerships	20	12
TOTAL	**175**	113

What Your Scores Indicate

A score of	Indicates that you are . . .
175–120 points	A strong and competent leader
119–80 points	A capable principal-leader who needs development in selected targeted areas
79 points or below	A principal with potential who needs development in multiple targeted competencies

Summary of Targeted Areas for Improvement

For scores of two or less on self or peer assessment

Prioritized Areas for Improvement/Strategies		
Competency	Self Score	Peer Score
Take risks to achieve results	2	3
Communicate expectations	3	1

Bennis, W. (1985). *Leaders: The strategies for taking charge.* New York, NY: Harper & Row.

Bennis, W., Parikh, J., & Lessem, R. (1994). *Beyond leadership: Balancing economics, ethics and ecology.* Cambridge, MA: Blackwell.

Berens, L. V., & Isachsen, O. (1988). *Working together: A personality centered approach to management.* Coronado, CA: Neworld Management Press.

Blake, R. (2006). Employee retention, what employee turnover costs your company. Retrieved from www.webpronews.com/employee-retention-what-employee-turnover-really-costs-your-company-2006-07

Blanchard, K. (2006). *Leading at a higher level.* Upper Saddle River, NJ: FT Press.

Bonnstetter, B., & Suiter, J. (Eds.). (2004). *The universal language DISC.* Scottsdale, AZ: Target Training International.

Boss, S. (2008). *Digital storytelling: Helping students find their voice.* Retrieved March 4, 2008, from www.edutopia.org/digital-storytelling-resources

Bridges, W. (2009). *Managing transitions: Making the most of change.* Philadelphia, PA: Da Capa Press.

Center for Applications of Psychological Type. (n.d.). The story of Isabel Briggs Myers. Retrieved from www.capt.org/mbti-assessment/isabel-myers.htm

Center for Creative Leadership. (2010). Addressing the leadership gap in health care: What's needed when it comes to leader talent. Retrieved from www.ccl.org/leadership/index.aspx

Collins, J. (2001). *Good to great: Why some companies make the leap . . . and others don't.* New York, NY: Harpers Business.

Coutu, D., & Kauffman, C. (2009). *The realities of executive coaching.* Cambridge, MA: Harvard Business Review Research Report.

Cromwell, S. (1997, Oct. 27). Inclusion in the classroom: Has it gone too far? Retrieved from www.educationworld.com

Dinan, S. (2009, March 10). Obama wants teacher "accountability." *Washington Times.* Retrieved from www.washingtontimes.com/news/2009/mar/10/obama-calls-accountability-education

Edmondson, A. (2011). Strategies for learning from failure. *Harvard Business Review, 89*(4).

Garfield, C. (1987). *Peak performance.* New York, NY: Harper Paperbacks.

Garvin, D., & Roberto, M. (2001). What you don't know about making decisions. *Harvard Business Review, 79*(8).

Glass, T., & Franceschini, L. (2006). *State of the American school superintendency: A mid-decade study.* Blue Ridge Summit, PA: Rowman and Littlefield Education.

Goleman, D. (1996). *Emotional intelligence.* New York, NY: Bantam Books.

Guggenheim, D. (2010). *Waiting for Superman* [film].

Heifetz, R. A., & Linsky, M. (2002). *Leadership on the line*. Boston, MA: Harvard Business School Press.

Jentz, B. (1982). *Entry: The hiring, start-up and supervision of administrators*. Desoto, TX: McGraw-Hill.

Johansen, R. (2009). *Leaders make the future: Ten new leadership skills for an uncertain world*. San Francisco, CA: Berrett-Koehler.

Kowalski, T. J. (2006). *The school superintendent: Theory, practice, and cases*. Thousand Oaks, CA: Sage Publications.

Lencioni, P. (2005). *Overcoming the five dysfunctions of a team: A field guide for leaders, managers, and facilitators*. San Francisco, CA: Jossey-Bass.

Lunnenburg, F., & Ornstein, A. (2012). *Educational administration: Concepts and practices*. Belmont, CA: Wadsworth.

Marzano, R., Waters, T., & McNulty, B. A. (2005). *School leadership that works: From research to results*. Alexandria, VA: Association for Supervision and Curriculum.

Menn, J., & Silverstein, S. (2002). IBM CEO to step down: He led Big Blues' turnaround. *Los Angeles Times*. Retrieved from http://articles.latimes.com/2002/jan/30/business /fi-ibm30

Myers, M. B., Griffith, D. A., Daugherty, P. J., & Lusch, R. F. (2004). Maximizing the human capital equation in logistics: Education, experience, and skills. *Journal of Business Logistics, 25*(1), 211–232.

Obama, B. (2009a, Nov. 4). *Education Reform Package* speech.

Obama, B. (2009b, Nov. 23). *Education to Innovate* speech.

Obama, B. (2009c, Mar. 10). *Remarks on Education* speech.

Rath, T. (2007). *Strengthfinders 2.0*. New York, NY: Gallup Press.

Reeves, D. (2007a). *The daily disciplines of leadership: How to improve student achievement, staff motivation, and personal organization*. San Francisco, CA: Jossey-Bass.

Reeves, D. (2007b). Leading to change: Coaching myths and realities. *Educational Leadership, 65*(2), 89–90.

Reeves, D. (2011, August). Making lasting change in schools. *American School Board Journal*.

Schultze, C. L. (1989). Of wolves, termites and pussycats: Or why we should worry about the budget deficit. *The Brookings Review, 7*, 26–33.

Sergiovanni, T. (1995, Fall/Winter). The politics of virtue: A new compact for leadership in schools. *School Community Journal, 5*(2). Retrieved from www.adi.org/journal

Siccone, F. (2012). *Essential skills for effective school leadership*. Upper Saddle River, NJ: Pearson.

Smith-Conway, K., & Houtenville, A. (2008). Parent involvement strongly impacts student acheivement. *Science Daily*.

Strauss, V. (2011, February 10). Missing the point on Rhee. *The Washington Post*. Retrieved from http://voices.washingtonpost.com/answer-sheet/michelle-rhee/missing-the-point-on-rhee.html

Taylor, B. (2011, Feb. 1). Hire for attitude, train for skill. *Harvard Business Review*. Retrieved from http://blogs.hbr.org/taylor/2011/02/hire_for_attitude_train_for_sk.html

Toch, T. (2010, July/August). Small is still beautiful. *Washington Monthly*. Retrieved from www.washingtonmonthly.com/features/2010/1007.toch.html

Ury, W., & Fisher, R. (1991). *Getting to yes: Negotiating agreement without giving in*. New York, NY: Penguin Books.

The Wallace Foundation. (2010). School improvement: Learning from leadership. Retrieved from www.wallacefoundation.org/Pages/2_1-school-improvement-learning-from-leadership.aspx